PROGRAMMING & RESEARCH

Skills and Techniques for Interior Designers

PROGRAMMING & RESEARCH

Skills and Techniques for Interior Designers

Rose Mary Botti-Salitsky

MOUNT IDA COLLEGE

Fairchild Books
New York

Executive Editor: Olga T. Kontzias
Acquisitions Editor: Olga T. Kontzias
Editorial Development Director: Jennifer Crane
Development Editor: Rob Phelps
Associate Art Director: Erin Fitzsimmons
Production Director: Ginger Hillman
Production Editor: Jessica Rozler
Cover Art: Getty Images
Text Design: Renato Stanisic Design
Page Composition: Dutton & Sherman Design
Copyright © 2009 Fairchild Books, A Division of Condé Nast Publications, Inc.

Library of Congress Catalog Card Number: 2008934261
ISBN: 978-1-56367-637-6
GST R 133004424

Printed in the United States of America
TP09

Dedication

This book is dedicated to my husband Joe, my love and soul mate. I'm eternally grateful for his constant support in my endeavors and for always believing in me. Somehow he always knows exactly when I require solitude and when I need to be rescued from my computer to rejuvenate my mind, body, and spirit. I also dedicate this book to our two precious daughters, Ava and Madisyn. To Ava, who supported me more than she knows, for helping with her little sister and for her gentle words of encouragement, which were invaluable. Her wisdom far surpasses her years. And to my little "pocket of sunshine" Madisyn, who sometimes patiently and sometimes not so patiently supported her mom in her own special way. I am forever thankful and grateful to experience our life journey together.

Contents

Extended Contents

Preface

Eighteen years of programming instruction inspired this book. Throughout that experience, I found that most of the programming textbooks fell in the realm of architecture, which is a parallel profession to interior design. With work, much in these texts could be adapted for the interior design profession, but I became increasingly moved to create a textbook that focused specifically on interior design and the unique programming and research skills needed to enter this profession.

Having taught programming as an independent course and as part of studio classes, I have learned a great deal over the years about the benefits of programming and the skills needed to do it well. The end results are considerably stronger when the appropriate amount of time is committed on the front end of the design process. Clients are keenly aware of the benefits of programming and research skills; the knowledge that these skills bring to their businesses increases their capacities for strategic planning and decision making.

Interior designers are participating more regularly in programming and research studies. As the results are published, everyone benefits from the findings. The specialty of training that interior designers bring to the table can benefit a multitude of spaces that all sectors of our society occupy. Think, for instance, of the health-care worker in a hospital setting, the student in a classroom, or the elderly couple adapting their residence in order to age in place.

Interior designers, in my opinion, are the most potent type of artist, as we design spaces in the fourth dimension. We envelope and encompass our occupants in what we have designed. Think of the ramifications of your decision making. The information gleaned from the research and programming phase should aid both the designer and client in creating a successful environment. People occupy what has been created, and in some cases they have no choice in the matter. It might be their work location, school, hospital, or a public building, but in any case it is where they will spend the majority of their time. This power is not to be taken lightly. You must be keenly sensitive to these end users' needs. This book will help you create the best environments for everyone.

Acknowledgments

The author would like to express sincere appreciation to all the interior designers that took the time to share with me their unique approaches and diverse expertise with programming. Specifically to: Dianne A. Dunnell, IIDA, NCIDQ, associate with MPA | Margulies Perruzzi Architects; Associate Principal Director of Interiors Kate Wendt, IIDA, NCIDQ, Tsoi/Kobus & Associates; Director of Interiors Howard L. Thompson, AIA, IIDA, LEED, AP Spagnolo/Gisness & Associates; Jeanne Kopacz, IIDA, ASID, NCIDQ, Allegro Interior Architecture; Cris Cavataio, IDEC, NCIDQ, professor, Newbury College; Jean Verbridge, ASID, IIDA, NCIDQ, principal, Siemasko + Verbridge; Christine Shanahan, ASID, NCIDQ, principal, Studio East Design; David D. Stone, IIDA, LEED AP, NCIDQ, senior associate; Lynne Bryan Phipps, IIDA, LEED AP, NCIDQ, Design One Consortium; and Senior Interior Designer Gable Clarke, IIDA, LEED AP. NCIDQ, Spagnolo/Gisness & Associates.

I would also like to thank my past, present, and future students for inspiring me every day and keeping me motivated with their inspirational ideas and approaches to programming, research, and design. A special thanks to all of my past students who allowed me to include their work in this book. Specifically, to Jessica Breton, LEEDTM AP, IIDA, Cannon Design, Boston, Massachusetts; Monica Mattingly, interior designer, Allegro Interior Architecture; Colleen Anderson, interior designer, Nelson Group; Jennifer Cilano, interior designer, Cubellis; Nicole M. Stewart; interior designer, HVS Compass Interior Design; Marcia A. Gouveia, allied ASID; associate designer, Barrtlett Design; Jeana Richard, interior designer, SMRT Inc.; Kristen Patten, interior designer, MCM USA; Samantha E, Roblee; Lindsey Dinsmore; Elizabeth Carter, interior designer, Cannon Design, Washington DC; Ashley Johnson; Nicole Heerdt; Ashley Benander; Michelle (Haven) Beattie; Erin Anthony; and Ana Karen Angulo-Gutierrez.

A special thank you to Samantha E. Roblee, Annie Wocken, Colleen Anderson, Corey Chung, and Monica Mattingly for taking the time to read, comment, and help with everything. Heartfelt thanks to family, friends, and colleagues whose support and encouragement enabled this journey. Specifically, to my colleagues at the Chamberlayne School of Design at Mount

Ida College for their unwavering support and encouragement. Particular thanks to my parents, who have always provided me with inspiration.

Much thanks to Fairchild Books' Executive Director Olga Kontzias and Editorial Development Director Jennifer Crane. Special appreciation to Development Editor Rob Phelps, for his ongoing support, words of encouragement, and the editorial magic that he performed. Thanks to the talented production team of Art Director Adam Bohannon, Production Editor Jessica Rozler, and Associate Art Director Erin Fitzsimmons. And thanks to the development reviewers: Linda Davisson, Art Institute of Washington; Nancy E. Hackett, The New England School of Art and Design; and Bridget May, Marymount University. The Fairchild team made this book a reality; from the inception of the idea, you helped me take a conceptual notion and made something tangible.

CHAPTER 1

What Is Programming?

After reading this chapter, you should be able to:

- Define programming.
- Understand how and why programming is used in the profession.
- Understand conceptually how the research process parallels the programming process of design.

Programming is the first step in the process of design. It is the time for designers to research, explore, and investigate numerous facets of a project in order to gain insight into the work to come. During the preliminary phases of a design project, design professionals consider programming critical to the entire design process. Many professionals use programming as a tool; those in the fields of architecture, facilities management, and engineering all implement programmatic skills. This textbook focuses on how the study of programming for interior design prepares students for and advances them into the professional realm.

Often in haste, students jump right into a project, trying to solve the problem and generate the best design solution. This is not the most advantageous approach. The programming phase, when the steps are followed properly, gives students and professional designers alike time to research the topic, explore precedent studies, and develop a comprehensive program. This valuable commitment at the front end of a project is time well spent. An in-depth programming phase allows students to become more knowledgeable on their topics, engage in more thorough research, and gain a greater insight into their design options.

Programming, when committed to existing or original research, can help make informed and intelligent decisions. Dedication to the programming of a project may amount to "front-loading" one's work. But this time spent up front results in a road map that will guide everyone involved through the process of design and, more importantly, provide a clear and shared vision of common goals that will lead smoothly toward the final design.

Interior designers offer a great skill set to businesses and consumers; these programming skills are certainly ones that are on the forefront of economic decision making. Employing an interior designer to complete the programming phase of a project can lend great insight into the proposed project for everyone involved, many of whom do not possess these skills. If the programming phase is well executed, it can help with key decisions during all phases of a project.

Often interior designers are pulled in to help evaluate **demographics** of the proposed site, efficiency of the proposed space, and location. Interior designers are trained to evaluate space occupancy and anticipate projected growth or shrinkage. They are trained to look at **energy efficiency, life cycle cost**, and **space-planning adjacencies** to evaluate individual, group, and **location productivity**.

HOW AND WHY PROGRAMMING IS USED IN THE PROFESSION

Two predominate organizations within the field of interior design identify programming as an essential core of knowledge for interior designers: the **National Council for Interior Design Qualification** (NCIDQ) and the **Council for Interior Design Accreditation** (CIDA). NCIDQ offers the following definition of programming:

> Programming is the process of setting forth, in written form, clients' and users' requirements for a given project. Specifically, the designer identifies and analyzes client and user needs and goals, evaluates existing premises, assesses project resources and limitations, identifies applicable life safety, accessibility and **building code requirements**, considers site issues, prepares the **project schedule**, develops a budget, and analyzes design objectives and spatial requirements. The need for, and coordination of, consultants also is determined, as well as an investigation made of requirements for regulatory approval. The data developed usually culminates in a formal programming document. (2008)

CIDA states within the guidelines of Standard 4, that:

> Students understand and apply the knowledge, skills, and theories of interior design. Student work MUST demonstrate programming *skills*, including:

- problem identification.
- problem solving.
- identification of client and/or user needs.
- information gathering research and analysis (functional requirements, code research, etc.). (CIDA 2006, Section II)

It is imperative that you, as interior design students, gain knowledge of programming within your academic setting. This is essential not only for preparation to enter the field of design but also in preparation to take the NCIDQ exam. NCIDQ has determined that six performance domains characterize the work of interior design:

- Programming
- Schematic Design
- Design Development
- Contract Documents
- Contract Administration
- Professional Practice

Programming is an important domain that warrants in-depth inquiry. The other five domains are adequately covered in interior design curriculums; programming, however, is an area academia has not yet adequately explored or developed to its fullest potential. This book aims to help fill that gap.

A significant part of the NCIDQ exam test is committed to programming. As shown in Table 1.1, the NCIDQ exam identifies that programming skills are needed in 33.23 percent of Section I and 24.61 percent of Section III. This is important because many U.S. states require interior designers

TABLE 1.1 DOMAIN MATRIX FOR THE NCIDQ EXAMINATION

	PROGRAMMING	SCHEMATIC DESIGN	DESIGN DEVELOPMENT	CONTRACT DOCUMENTS	CONTRACT ADMINISTRATION	PROFESSIONAL PRACTICE
Section I (multiple choice)	33.23%	31.78% 40 Questions	34.99% 44 Questions			
Section II (multiple choice)				35.03% 35 Questions	31.50% 32 Questions	33.47% 33 Questions
Section III (practicum)	24.61%	23.54%	25.91%	25.94%		

Source: National Council for Interior Design Qualification (NCIDQ). 2008. *Certification & Licensure*, Regulatory Agencies, Definition of Interior Design, Exam Eligibility Requirements. Retrieved, April 2008, from http://www.ncidq.org.

to pass the NCIDQ exam as part of their state certification or registration to use the title "interior designer" or practice "interior design" as a profession.

Programming knowledge is also required by CIDA. Students are expected to identify problems, demonstrate problem-solving skills, and identify client and/or the user needs. Students should also know how to gather information and apply research and analysis skill to their findings.

The interior design field is vast and covers abundant and diverse applications in which one can work. Residential, corporate, institutional, retail, and hospitality are some options in the field where designers work. Each type of design comes with its own set of requirements and unique features. Because it is virtually impossible to become an expert in all areas, many designers choose to work within a specific application, and that may become their specialty. Some designers have a multidiscipline approach and choose to work in more than one area.

FIRMS THAT PRACTICE SUCCESSFUL PROGRAMMING

For this chapter, both Allegro Interior Architecture and Spagnolo/Gisness & Associates were interviewed to show how practitioners in the real world implement

programming through their firms. Both firms implement similar techniques, but they have different styles.

Throughout the book, design firm interviews have been included to give you a broader perspective on how professionals implement programming in their practice. Allegro Interior Architecture, for example, was selected because it specializes in **interior architecture** and design for corporate and academic clients. The diversity of its work includes offices for consultants in the fields of law, accounting, and technology; conferencing and training facilities; and headquarters space for companies who provide goods and services such as pharmaceuticals, retail products, health care, **venture capital**, and **asset management**. Allegro's team effort and approach to each project distinguishes itself in its attention to programming. Results of this approach meet the needs of clients in the spaces they create.

Interview with Allegro Interior Architecture

Representing Allegro is Jeanne Kopacz, IIDA, ASID. Kopacz is a NCIDQ-certified interior designer who serves as managing partner for the firm. Her expertise includes **strategic planning**, alternative workspace analysis, and color/form integration. She

FIGURE 1.1
**Jeanne Kopacz,
IIDA, ASID, NCIDQ
Certificate 005539.**

frequently speaks at industry events on topics related to **color theory** and practice. Kopacz is most known for her book *Color in Three-Dimensional Design.*

Allegro's Approach to Programming

For the Allegro team, programming is the key to getting diverse results. The project begins with a series of interviews with key people on the client side. No questionnaires are used, since the presence of a questionnaire tempts clients to fill them out on their own. Through direct conversation, the designers often find the answer to one question generates another—something that a questionnaire may not address. Through direct probing, individual natures are uncovered. Diagrams are sketched during the interview to more precisely ascertain what is being shared.

Questions usually include those about specific space needs, such as the quantity and size of the workstations, as well as inquiries as to what works and what doesn't work within the space currently occupied. Ms. Kopacz finds the interview is best done in the client's space so designers can observe what is meant by the words chosen. When the users describe something they envision, they are asked if they have seen anything similar. For example, one client desired a formal boardroom entrance. When asked if

he'd ever seen one, he said, "like the one in the conference room on Boston Legal."

Word descriptions are relative to one's individual experience. What is sophisticated to one may be overly fussy or alternatively gutsy to another. Real examples are better communicators. Realizing this, the Allegro team often follows interviews with an initial schematic design meeting, at which time images of spaces or products are shown for confirmation or clarity as appropriate.

According to Kopacz, a key program topic is what drives the clients' business. It often takes some conversation for a team to get at the essence of this. If they do, they enable their designers to develop something beyond what they could ever envision for themselves. For some, visual access to something can expedite communications, which means the designer needs to know those limits, and their associated acoustic implications. For others, paper management is critical, in which case it may be worth spending 30 minutes just to follow a piece of paper through its logical process. Some companies need specific sensations such as the presence of earth materials or informal forms to establish the right environment. Others need to position critical cogs-in-the-wheel so that everyone has a right to use. The designer's job during programming is to pry through the question-and-answer time to uncover what specifically gives the client entity its advantage over competitors, or its individual character. The designer's goal is to uncover opportunities to enhance that advantage or uniqueness through the design of the space.

At the end of the interview process, the designer produces a program summary that includes space needs calculated as a sum of the parts, plus appropriate markups for circulation, rentable factors, and so on. (See Figure 1.2.) If the space is already selected, an Allegro designer uses the program to de-

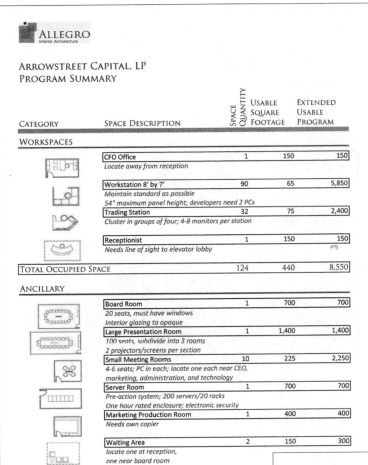

ALLEGRO
Interior Architecture

ARROWSTREET CAPITAL, LP
PROGRAM SUMMARY

CATEGORY	SPACE DESCRIPTION	SPACE QUANTITY	USABLE SQUARE FOOTAGE	EXTENDED USABLE PROGRAM
WORKSPACES				
	CFO Office	1	150	150
	Locate away from reception			
	Workstation 8' by 7'	90	65	5,850
	Maintain standard as possible			
	54" maximum panel height; developers need 2 PCs			
	Trading Station	32	75	2,400
	Cluster in groups of four; 4-8 monitors per station			
	Receptionist	1	150	150
	Needs line of sight to elevator lobby			
TOTAL OCCUPIED SPACE		124	440	8,550
ANCILLARY				
	Board Room	1	700	700
	20 seats, must have windows			
	Interior glazing to opaque			
	Large Presentation Room	1	1,400	1,400
	100 seats, subdivide into 3 rooms			
	2 projectors/screens per section			
	Small Meeting Rooms	10	225	2,250
	4-6 seats; PC in each; locate one each near CEO,			
	marketing, administration, and technology			
	Server Room	1	700	700
	Pre-action system; 200 servers/20 racks			
	One hour rated enclosure; electronic security			
	Marketing Production Room	1	400	400
	Needs own copier			
	Waiting Area	2	150	300
	locate one at reception,			
	one near board room			

FIGURE 1.2 Program summary for Arrowstreet capital project.

CATEGORY	SPACE DESCRIPTION	SPACE QUANTITY	USABLE SQUARE FOOTAGE	EXTENDED USABLE PROGRAM
ANCILLARY (CONTINUED)				
	Lunch Room	1	350	350
	2 full refrigerator, 2 microwave, 2 coffee maker			
	sink, 2 trash, recycle bin, cabinets, beverage cooler			
	Kitchenette	1	100	100
	1/2 refrigerator, sink, microwave			
	Quality Control/Quality Assurance	1	400	400
	Include 2 racks for test equipment			
	Seat 5 people for training			
	Records Storage Room	1	300	300
	Rolling file system; locking			
	Operations File Room	1	120	120
	Lateral files; locking			
	Pre-action Room	1	100	100
	Adjacent to Server Room			
	Service Area	2	13	26
	Include copier, printers, supplies			
	AV Equipment/PC Closet	2	13	26
	Locate adjacent to Presentation Room			
	Shower Room	1	100	100
	Locate away from Reception			
	Client Powder Room	1	75	75
	Locate near Reception Area			
	Meditation Room	1	75	75
	Locate near Reception Area			
	Coat Closets	2	35	70
	One adjacent to Server Room, one opposite end of floor			
	IDF Room	2	13	26
	One adjacent to Server Room, one opposite end of floor			
	Storage Cabinets	6	13	78
	Compliance binders, locate near marketing			
	Files, Lateral	10	13	130
	Locate in common area			
TOTAL ANCILLARY SPACE				7,726
TOTAL PROGRAMMABLE SPACE (OCCUPIED + ANCILLARY)				16,276
	Circulation factor at 35% of total usable			8,789
TOTAL USABLE SQUARE FOOTAGE				25,065
	Average Rentable Factor of 18%			4,512
TOTAL RENTABLE SQUARE FOOTAGE				29,577

termine what adjustments are needed based on the size and condition of the available space. For example, if the program is a wish list that calculates out to 20,000 usable square feet, but the space available is only 18,000 square feet, there would be a conversation about whether fewer workspaces would meet business goals. Or the designer might also suggest items that could go off-site such as a very large presentation room that is used once a month, or a large amount of file storage that is accessed infrequently.

For more complex projects, diagrams are used at Allegro to articulate conclusions about new work processes. Like the program summary, diagrammatic information becomes a baseline for evaluating design recommendations (see Figure 1.3). **Sketches** are also prepared to communicate the key solutions that will make the project more effective. These need to be loose and apparently incomplete so that clients will

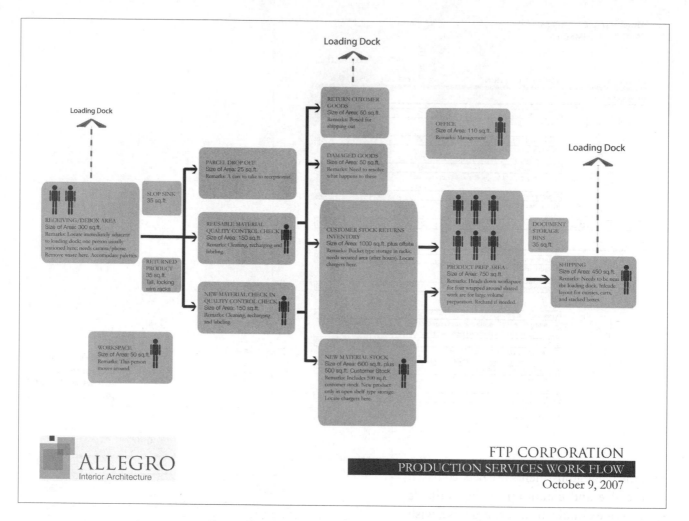

FIGURE 1.3 Workflow diagram for Arrowstreet capital project flowchart.

feel comfortable participating in their resolution. If the sketches are too polished, the idea may be accepted or rejected as a finished solution. In a loose collaboration, the client can "try it on" and is more likely to comment on what is or is not effective about it. The example here is for Arrowstreet Capital, LP, an asset management company focused on global markets. Arrowstreet is organized to work more collaboratively and in a less hierarchical manner than its competitors. It is located on the 30th floor of the John Hancock Tower in Boston.

The bubble diagram tells what functions go where and gives the client an overall idea of where each space is designated (see Figure 1.4). This is very different than a **concept diagram**. A designer uses the concept diagram to begin organizing the physi-

cal space so that it makes sense as a whole (see Figure 1.5).

The concept diagram in Figure 1.5 is a simple illustration of how the designers at Allegro organized the form within a very rectilinear building to be anything but rectilinear. Kopaz states that the circles show how they intended on imposing onto the rectilinear form in the space. The concept is one of the first images, but in the final design it shows where the designers dropped the ceiling and changed materials and floor color to emphasize their vision of the space. The black lines show circulation. By imposing the circles, the designers were able to shift the perspective so that the view along the main circulation did not look long and straight. At the ends of the floor, the circulation was fanned out in a radial movement

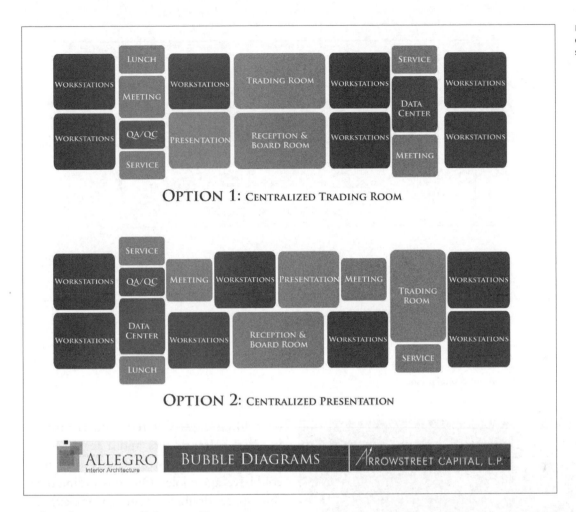

OPTION 1: CENTRALIZED TRADING ROOM

OPTION 2: CENTRALIZED PRESENTATION

FIGURE 1.4 **Bubble diagram for Arrowstreet capital project.**

rather than in parallel rows. Kopacz states that this planning diagram was in the study they did in-house in response to the clients request for "no rows of Dilbert cubes."

Figure 1.6 is the furniture plan. This is the final layout for the space, including workstations and freestanding furniture. You can see how the curves break up what could be long corridors, and how the workstations fan out at each end of the floor. You can also see how the large meeting room is split into three analysis rooms for their global teams to compare data during non-meeting days.

Figure 1.7 shows the final design of the reception space. This is the main reception area, with the boardroom to the left and the elevator lobby in the background. It shows the curved elements winding through the lobby and slamming through the wall into

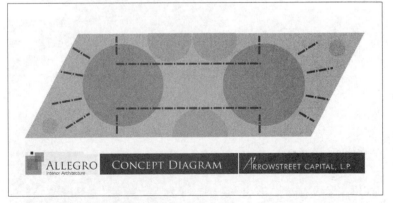

the boardroom. The dropped sections of ceiling have LED lights along the face. Even though this section of workstations is square with the building, it doesn't look square at all because of the well-conceived design.

Figure 1.8 shows how the curve continues through the workspace area. You

FIGURE 1.5 **Concept diagram for Arrowstreet capital project.**

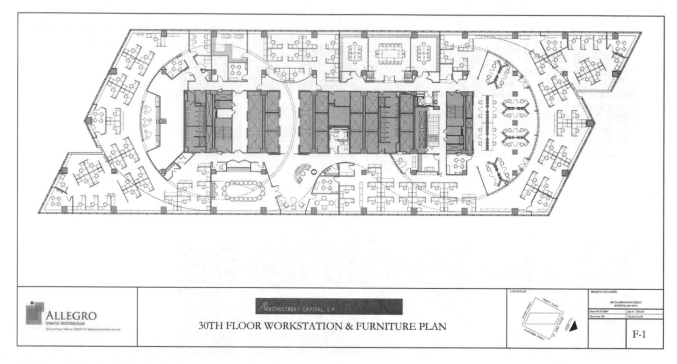

30TH FLOOR WORKSTATION & FURNITURE PLAN

FIGURE 1.6 Furniture plans for Arrowstreet capital project.

LUCY CHEN PHOTOGRAPHY

FIGURE 1.7 Reception area designed by Allegro Interior Architecture. Photo © Lucy Chen.

can see where the glass wall separates the work area from the public walkway, and the curve continues through the glass wall. The workstations are by Knoll. All the lighting is direct/indirect pendants (there is no recessed lighting). Figure 1.9 shows where the clients set up lunch for their team

on trading days. Catered food is brought in. Two coffeemakers and a teapot stand ready, along with two refrigerators and a cold beverage cooler. On non-trading days, this space doubles as an eat-in kitchen. Stools and tables are high enough to offer views through the windows of the harbor and beyond.

Kopacz and her team listened closely to their clients' needs, requirements, and desires at the beginning—the programming phase of design. This early effort is reflected in their final design, which dovetails programmatic needs with a beautifully designed work environment.

Interview with Spagnolo/Gisness & Associates

Architects Al Spagnolo and Bill Gisness together with interior designer Jeff Tompkins founded Spagnolo Gisness & Associates, Inc. (SG&A) in 1991. Their goal was to create a full-service architectural, interior design and planning firm built around a strong, client-inclusive design culture. Located on the historic Boston waterfront, SG&A offers comprehensive design services for office buildings, mixed-use, corporate interiors, multifamily housing, and higher-education projects throughout the Northeast and beyond.

Providing an overview of the firm are Senior Associate and Director of Interiors Howard L. Thompson, AIA, IIDA, **LEED AP**, and Associate and Senior Interior Designers Gable Clarke, IIDA, LEED AP.

Thompson is a registered architect who discovered early in his career that he enjoyed the interiors aspect of the profession more than the traditional role of an architect. He has worked in all phases of interiors projects for more than 20 years.

With more than 10 years of experience in the industry, Clarke has worked in a variety of market sectors and currently specializes in corporate interiors. Along with her work at SG&A, she teaches at the Boston Architectural College and is heavily involved in the New England chapter of the International Interior Design Association (IIDA).

SG&A's Approach to Programming

Thompson prefers to start with a conversation first as a way to get to know the clients and their style. Programming gathers the likes and dislikes of the current space in addition to giving insight into the personalities of the space and the people who work within it.

Similarly, the initial programming interviews and observations are conducted to document the details of the use and purpose of the space; this lays the foundation for the questions "Who are you and who do you want to be?"

For SG&A it's important to include the personal element in programmatic research because the designer gets the specifics and actual feel of the space instead of just collecting an "inventory" of formal data (e.g., number of conference rooms and cubicles.)

Clarke points out that a significant result from the interviewing process is that a knowledgeable programmer makes note of any unrealistic wish on the client's list. It is here where the programmer re-creates an applicable programming strategy for the client to consider. Typically during the programming phase, the designers have an initial meeting with the senior staff of the client, followed by an extensive interview process, and concluded by another meeting with client leaders. After the initial interview process, another important key is to touch base with the decision-makers as a checkpoint and summarize findings.

FIGURE 1.8 Workstations designed by Allegro Interior Architecture. Photo © Lucy Chen.

FIGURE 1.9 **Lunch area designed by Allegro Interior Architecture. Photo © Lucy Chen.**

At SG&A the information gathered is tested conceptually as a "test fit" for the programming of the space. This helps address issues that might surface very early in the process and lays the foundation for schematic design.

During the interview process, the programmer works as a mediator on all levels, working with all client members involved as well as the countless industry standards and further analytical research and requirements. Tangible and nontangible issues are addressed and documented. An example of a nontangible issue might be the need to promote collaboration, while a tangible issue would be more specific, such as the need for a 50-person training room.

The programmer needs to experience the existing space and setting by having a walk-through or reference precedent studies to understand and plan for feasible design options. The efficiency of this knowledge is proven in the program produced. At SG&A it is vital to get to know the clients and understand what is truly required; otherwise, the information gathered is just numbers and data.

According to both Thompson and Clarke, the hardest thing is to understand and plan for growth. In the corporate field, many company executives plan on growth, but it is important for the designer to design for it. Take the sizes of an office or conference room, for example. A conference room that is equivalent to the space of two offices can be reconfigured if the firm grows and more office space is required (see Figure 1.12).

At times, planning for growth may very well be a guessing game based on information and data collected, but anticipation is the key to a program that allows change. If and when growth deviates from expected patterns, having a flexible workspace can be very beneficial to a client.

For SG&A, "the programming document is now a tool for design, again, test-

FIGURE 1.10 Howard L. Thompson, AIA, IIDA, LEED AP.

FIGURE 1.11 Gable Clarke, IIDA, LEED AP NCIDQ certificate 015528.

fitting the interpreted data and designing with imagination to fit the needs."

With much of the programming, the client will often dictate the specific details and requirements. It is then the programmer's job to "design and teach." Education is the key to all varying styles of programming. It is the programmer/designer's job to acknowledge the necessities (i.e., the wants and needs) of the client, in addition to demonstrating all applicable codes to the client. For example, this may be seen as a "push-and-pull" function in areas such as **net-to-gross ratios**. It is essential for the client to understand the functional usage of any space.

Clarke notes that a successful program relies on the ability to "listen . . . truly

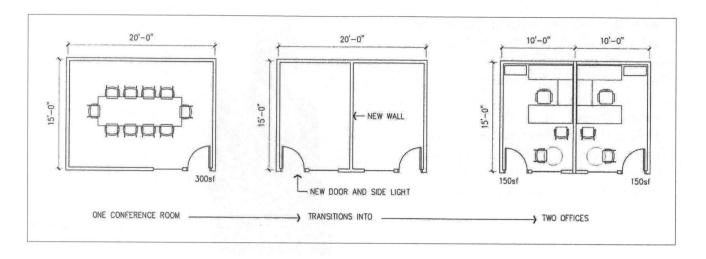

FIGURE 1.12 This drawing for a conference room demonstrates potential growth options.

listen." By hearing what the clients say, the programmer/designer absorbs and understands what is truly needed. The programmer then comprehends the client's "philosophy and culture" by following the client-driven hierarchy. This status not only moves the process along and keeps it up-to-date but also works as data to program and plan out the space. The technical process essentially depends on the ease of programming, but many designers find interviews and spreadsheets convenient programming tools.

The idea is to work **"macro-to-micro."** It is best to start on the large scale, initially noting all the key concepts and necessities. Obviously it is easier to move large groupings during the exploratory phases than to revisit the space at a later point. Once all that information has been gathered, the programmer analyzes the facts and sorts the responses, creating the fundamental information for the Schematic Design phase of the design process.

One example is an online supplier of high-quality graphic design services and customized printing products headquartered in Lexington, Massachusetts. After interviewing this client, the designer created a series of blocking plans (see Figures

1.13a and b). These plans explore department placement within the building. Plans like these can be created quickly for the client's approval before more detailed space planning begins. Again, the idea is to move from macro to micro with regard to detail.

The first three plans shown in Figure 1.13 are schematic block plans for the human resources department. They were created in order to help the client understand how the offices and workstations could be oriented. These plans allow the client to visualize traffic flow, adjacencies, and access to natural light. The fourth plan in Figure 1.14 is a key plan that shows the orientation of the human resources department location in the context of the building.

While meeting the programmatic needs for layout and floor plan, the designers were also gathering information about the client. Sketches or renderings of the space can bring about new ideas and concepts that then become part of the three-dimensional design. High-quality graphic design and customized printing generate sketches and explore how these ideas would then translate into interior three dimensionally. Figures 1.15a to c show the progression of a concept from sketch phase, through rendering, to the final photographed space.

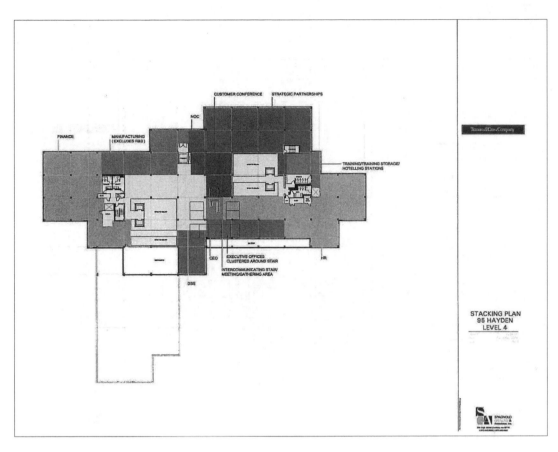

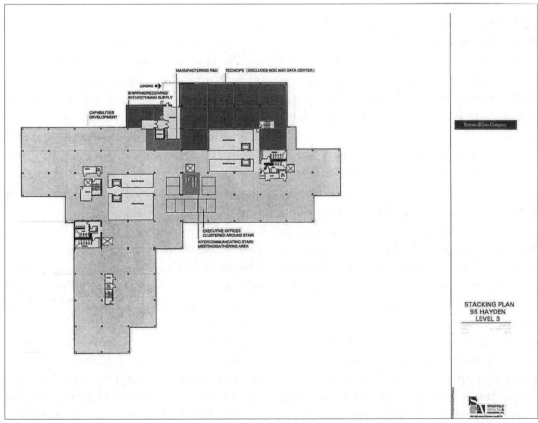

FIGURE 1.13 Blocking plans to help visualize the space and options.

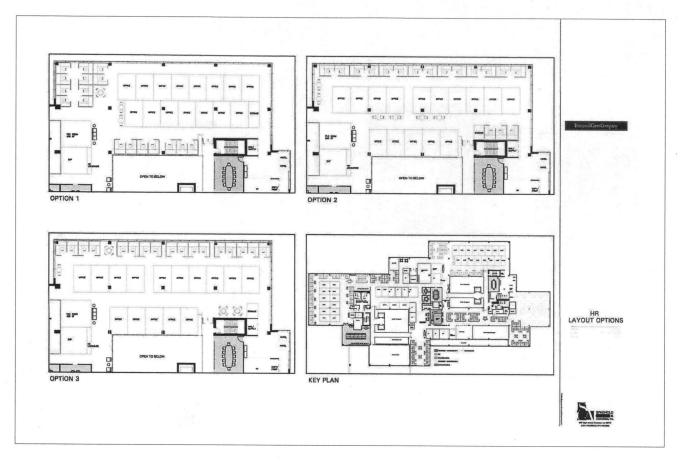

OPTION 1

OPTION 2

OPTION 3

KEY PLAN

HR
LAYOUT OPTIONS

FIGURE 1.14
Key plan for a human resources department to conceptualize— how it fits into the building in relation to all other departments.

TAKING PROGRAMMING TO AN ACADEMIC SETTING

Within the academic setting students train their research, programming, and design skills, tightly weaving these skills into a single set that is critical to employing great design.

Programming or predesign is executed in varied applications when a design project is started, as noted within the professional design interviews throughout the text. The approach of this book will guide you to become a holistic thinker with analytical skills that help in programming and design decision making. The programming process should start as an inclusive fact-finding mission followed by an analysis of the data collected, which will result in intelligent design decision making. In many ways the process of programming parallels standard research methods. This text aims to bridge the research process with the programming process that an interior designer employs.

When research is conducted, many research models follow a cyclical process. This can be a parallel process for a comprehensive programmatic research model to implement as well.

A visual model can help identify the parallels of the research and programming process (see Figure 1.17). This book, aligned with the steps depicted here, proposes that you follow this model.

Taking the Next Steps

Chapter 2, "The Process of Design," provides an overview of the design process. It represents a holistic interpretation of the process and varied approaches. It will also help you place programming in the context of the design process. Chapter 3, "Defining a Topic and Structuring Your Program Document," is where one begins to identify the problem and generate a problem statement and questions. Chapter 4, "Defining Research Methods," outlines selected research methods that are most applicable to the design fields. Chapter 5, "Historical, Observational, and Interactive Research," discusses research as it applies to the selected design topic. Chapter 6, "Building and Site Analysis," outlines how to document and analyze the site location of the design project—specifically with regard to interiors and how decision making can affect location and site. Chapter 7, "Precedent Studies," covers precedent studies and how to analyze the data collected in order to help the designer make informed decisions about the programmatic requirements within the space. Chapter 8, "Generating the Program," identifies the programming requirements and space adjacencies. Chapter 9, "Written and Visual Analysis," is an analysis of the solutions presented and addresses the visual language used in programming. Chapter 10, "Conclusion," draws together all that is covered in the previous chapters, emphasizing the advantages to programming as well as careers in programming.

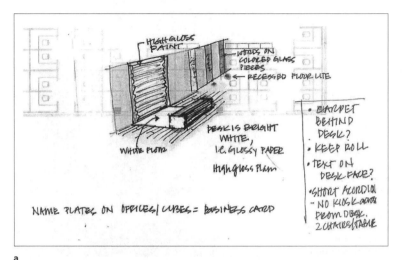

a

b

c

FIGURE 1.15 (a) Conceptual sketches help the client explore ideas during interviews, (b) drawings help develop the ideas, and (c) photos document the finished product, in this case a space developed by SG&A.

The programming process is a natural fusion of exploratory design to pragmatic research. It is important for designers to "seek out the problems, not the solutions" (Pena, 2001). The goal of programming and research is to help generate a plan of action that all can follow that is not unlike a business plan; this, then, becomes the model for implementation of design.

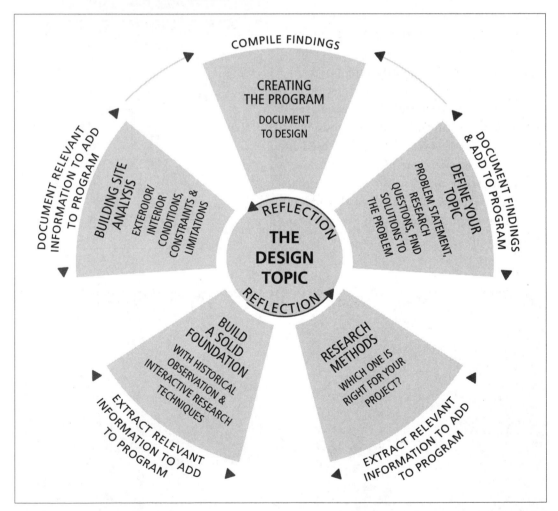

FIGURE 1.17 A diagram depicting a circular model of programming and research. This model was developed by Rose Mary Botti-Salitsky.

KEY TERMS

- Asset management
- Bubble diagram
- Building code requirements
- Color theory
- Concept diagram
- Contract administration
- Contract documents
- Council for Interior Design Accreditation (CIDA; www.accredit-id.org)
- Demographics
- Design development
- Diagrammatic information
- Energy efficiency
- Interior architecture
- International Interior Design Association (IIDA; www.iida.org)
- LEED AP (www.usgbc.org)
- Life cycle cost
- Location productivity
- Macro-to-micro
- Mediator
- National Council for Interior Design Qualification (NCIDQ; www.ncidq.org)
- Net-to-gross ratios
- Precedent studies
- Professional practice
- Program summary
- Programming
- Project schedule
- Registered architect

The Process of Design

After reading this chapter, you should be able to:

- Understand the process of design.
- Understand what is expected in each step in the process of design.
- Understand how the process of design in academia differs from that in the professional setting.
- Identify where programming fits into the process of design.

In the interior design curriculum, the process of design typically mimics that of the profession. Identifying the steps that a professional designer might take from the inception to completion of a project is therefore very important. Figure 2.1 depicts this process. In many ways, what happens in the classroom is very similar to what goes on out in the field. In some cases, there are slight variations. For example, note how this diagram shows that the client is a participant throughout the professional process; in the studio setting, the educator often assumes the role of the client.

WHERE DOES PROGRAMMING FIT INTO THE DESIGN PROCESS?

Descriptions of the design process have evolved over the years as researchers struggle to capture the essence of what people do when they invent new and interesting ways of doing things (Duerk, 1993). "There are three-step, seven-step, ten-step processes, and numerous other processes with various numbers and names for the steps" (Koberg & Bagnall, 1991, p. 27). Professor and author Donna P. Duerk points out that all of these descriptions of the design process have three activities in common: analysis, synthesis, and evaluation. This can be a cyclical process, adding the cumulative information as one gleans greater insight during the design process.

According to interior designer, author, and professor John F. Pile, "Every interior design project must be taken through a number of working steps in a logical order, the steps can be followed through within individual phases in a linear path or combined phases for smaller projects" (Pile, 1995, p. 129). Pile identifies the following steps to facilitate the process of design:

1. Project Begins—Establish contact with client.
2. Programming—Obtain or prepare a survey of spaces.
3. Preliminary Steps—Develop preliminary design.
4. Design Development—Develop detailed design.
5. Working Drawings and Bidding—Prepare constructions documents.
6. Supervision—Supervise construction.
7. Post-Completion—Make needed adjustments and evaluations.

The design process is complex and collaborative. It has necessitated modification to be adapted to an academic curriculum. For the purpose of common ground and to create common terminology, we can identify the process in five phases:

1. Programming
2. Schematic design
3. Design development
4. Construction documentation
5. Final critique

The goal of the academic program is to educate students with the knowledge and understanding of the phases of design. Figure 2.2 depicts each step in an interior design studio, where specific tasks

FIGURE 2.1 Process of design within the interior design profession

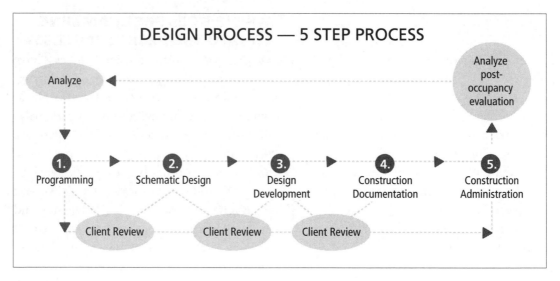

FIGURE 2.2 Process of design within an interior design studio class.

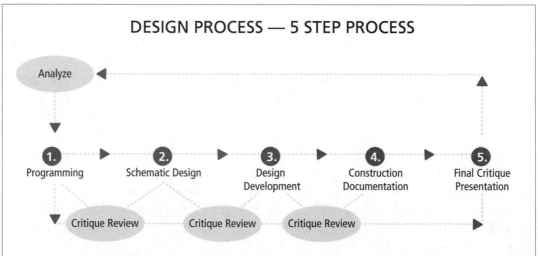

are to be completed while ongoing critique and analysis take place simultaneously. Here, the process of design has been adapted from a professional setting to an academic one. This adaptation is evident, as Figures 2.1 and 2.2 share many of the same developmental phases of the design process.

Some aspects of the two models, however, differ somewhat. Note, for example, how, within the professional model depicted in Figure 2.1, the last phase of design is construction administration. This phase can, of course, only be studied in theory and through limited observation within an academic setting. In the academic model, the last phase focuses on the final presentation and critique. Both Figures 2.1 and 2.2 share ongoing analysis, but critique and review are performed by different parties. Another important distinction is that within the profession, the client controls the passage from one phase to the next. Within academia, the professor and external critics typically give students the approval to move on to the next phase of design. In academia, the course calendar also limits the number of revisions that can be made, whereas other influences, such as time and money, can restrict professional revisions.

Expected Outcomes for Each Phase of Design

Within each phase of design during a studio course, you, the student, are expected to perform the following tasks.

Phase 1: Programming

Within the programming phase of design, you are expected to research the topic and space under investigation (Allen, Jones, & Stimpson, 2004; Neilson & Taylor, 2002). Typically, the instructor outlines a fictitious client with a list of requirements (Tate, 1987). On occasion, the instructor might have a client for you to interview and inter-

act with, simulating the process as it would be within the profession. "Historical, observational, and interactive literature reviews are often produced" (Neilson & Taylor, p. 10). You are required to generate a problem statement that includes the basic nature of the project as well as the concept (Neilson & Taylor, 2002; Tate, 1987). Interviews, adjacency space studies, and space requirements are also included within this preliminary phase. Often, images of the site and building orientation on the site are included to help students understand how the interior would be affected by exterior conditions and site placement (Duerk, 1993; Pena, 1987).

NCIDQ offers the following summary of what might be included and expected from a professional interior designer within the preliminary phases of design:

> Identify and analyze the needs and goals. Evaluate existing documentation and conditions. Assess project resources and limitations. Identify life, safety, and code requirements. Develop project schedules; work with their experience and knowledge of interior design. Determine the need, make recommendations, and coordinate with consultants and other specialists when required by professional practice or regulatory approval. (NCIDQ, 2008, Definition Section, ¶5)

At the completion of the programming phase, you are expected to have a solid understanding of the project and documented research. The program is specific, including square footage requirements, space needs, and the preliminary development of a concept (Allen et al., 2004). Typically, you have ongoing dialogue and critique with the instructor, a peer review, and a self-evaluation. Some instructors have mini-group critiques at the end of each phase of design, designating benchmarks for your transition to the next phase. Within the profession, common practice is to have client approval, signature, and payment upon completion of each phase of design.

Phase 2: Schematic Design

Within the schematic phase of design, you are expected to begin the allocation of space by generating bubble or blocking diagrams through which you'll be able to explore numerous potential options. Pile (1995) refers to this phase as preliminary steps, stating: "This is the most crucial point in the design process, creativity comes into play in the effort to find approaches that will be original, aesthetically satisfying, and valid solutions to the problems defined through programming" (p. 133).

In developing the idea, the concept or theme of the project begins to infuse itself into the design. Once a concept is developed, it begins to influence every decision that you, the student, makes, from sculpting the interior surfaces, to selecting fabric and furnishings, to impacting the physiological human interaction within the environment. Tate (1987) believes that a concept or theme "in interiors therefore, means some dominant characteristic; and this characteristic may be thought of as a theme; in every complex work of art, there is a dominating characteristic" (p. 98).

While developing a concept, you are also expected to begin visualizing the space not only two dimensionally but also three-dimensionally. Freehand sketches and schematic models help you visually articulate your ideas (Crowe & Laseau, 1986; Mitton, 2004).

NCIDQ offers the following definition of what might be included and expected from a professional interior designer in the schematic phase of design: "Formulate for client discussion and approval preliminary plans and design concepts that are appropriate and describe the character, function, and aesthetic of a project" (NCIDQ, 2008, Definition Section, ¶6).

Phase 3: Design Development

Within the design development phase, students are expected to begin generating hard-line drawings. The design is now in transition from sketches to more defined drawings using dimensions, color, fabric, and finishes (Pile, 1995). You begin to generate hard-lined perspectives, elevations, sections, and details to explore the development of the spaces. This is also the point in the process when you begin to select a color scheme, materials, equipment, accessories, and lighting that will be integrated within the space. Hard-line documentation of the design can be done by hand or by using CAD software (Allen et al., 2004; Mitton, 2004; Pile, 1995).

The NCIDQ definition of what might be included and expected from a professional interior designer working in the design development phase actually encompasses two phases, as outlined in Figure 2.1. It fuses both design development and construction documentation. In the profession, it would be more economical to approach this phase as one step, but within an academic setting, this part of the process must be completed in two steps. Marking the completion of design development, it would be common within the studio setting to have a group, an individual, or even a guest critic evaluate the design up to this point.

Phase 4: Construction Documentation

Within the construction documentation phase of design, you are expected to generate a complete set of working drawings, specifications, and schedules of interior construction (Allen et al., 2004). The working drawings consist of a title sheet, index, perspective drawings, site plans, floor plans, electrical plans, reflected ceiling plans, elevations, details, interior elements, cabinetwork, fixtures, moldings, and schedules (Neilson & Taylor, 2002). Specifications are also generated for furnishings, equipment, materials, accessories, and lighting. These can be separate from the working drawings or be included within the packet. Often you will be asked to generate a projected estimated cost or a budget based on the specifications.

While you work on the execution of your designs, you produce a set of working drawings, specifications, and presentation boards. The presentation boards usually are visually pleasing and rendered, and include fabric and finishes (Tate, 1986). Students will often include a model to accompany the presentation. A virtual walk-through or animation might be included. Typically, the boards document the phases of design with the concept emphasized throughout. The documentation of all phases of design is a preparation for the final critique of the studio project.

Phase 5: Final Critique

As identified in Figure 2.2, the last phase of design within an academic setting is the final critique. "A critique is unique in the dominant position it holds within the framework of studio design education; it is the central experience of design schools" (Dozois, 2001, p. 1). While in the studio, you, a student of the applied arts, are exposed to the process of critique. The design studio critique, or "crit" for short, is a unique educational event that has strong historical patterns (Anthony, 1991; Eisner, 1985, 2002). These traditional architectural design experiences continue to be embed-

ded in the design studio practice as well as in general applied arts education (Anthony, 1991; Dozois, 2001; Dutton, 1991).

The critique experience is unique in that it brings together undergraduate students "engaging them in dialogic relationships with instructors similar to a graduate student's experience with their advisor" (Dozois, 2001, p. 1). It is not uncommon for programs in the applied arts to have budgetary funds set aside to compensate or even provide transportation and accommodation for guest critics. The goal is to entice prestigious design professionals to participate and critique your final work (Anthony, 1991; Tate, 1987).

Lastly, the critique is unique because it is an essential tool in the evaluation and assessment process of your work within the art and design curriculums. Both CIDA and the National Architectural Accrediting Board (NAAB) include in their accreditation standards and guidelines a section where all visiting critics are to be listed. You spend long hours in the studio classroom to complete the bulk of your design work, and you depend highly on your professors' critiques throughout the process of design (Anthony, 1991; Tate, 1987). The critique is often an ongoing process in the studio community, shared between classmates and the professor. It is this experience that helps prepare you for a formal final design critique or jury.

In a studio classroom, instructors determine readiness for criticism in several ways. In some cases, you can approach the teacher or raise your hand (Tate, 1987 p. 74). Some instructors post a list, and you can sign up for a time block reserved exclusively for a private critique with the professor (Tate). In some cases, the instructor might float from student to student, critiquing each one and committing varying amounts of time to each depending on the level of work completed. "Some instructors will insist on doing some drawing themselves while talking through a critique; some instructors cannot really explain unless they draw, other instructors will give a critique with words alone" (Tate, p. 74).

The history of the critique stretches far back into the seventeenth century. The **École des Beaux Arts**, for instance, was founded in 1648 by Cardinal Mazarin. Disciplines studied at the school focused on architecture, drawing, painting, sculpture, engraving, modeling, and gem cutting. The school was originally created for the purpose of having artists available to decorate the palaces and paint the royalty portraits in France. Now it is a destination for those studying studio arts.

During the École des Beaux Arts era, the final critiques were held behind closed doors, and students only received their work back with a letter grade and perhaps a few comments (Anthony, 1991; Bosworth & Jones, 1932). In 1919, the German architect Walter Gropius founded the Bauhaus School in Weimar Germany. The school and philosophy promoted individual creative expression and collaboration among the art and design disciplines to create environments. With the transition to a **Bauhaus philosophy** in schools of design, the critique has become an inclusive experience. Often, the critique is treated like an event, with the date announced in the format of an invitation. It may be sent to students of design as well as to the faculty and the local design community. In both the École des Beaux Arts and the Bauhaus School, "it was common for faculty to compete informally with each other to see who could invite the most prestigious practitioners to serve as a critic—a practice that remains to this day" (Anthony, p. 11). In many cases, a brief biography of the critic, along with the dates he or she will be visiting the school, is posted internally and externally for all to see.

WORKING WITH THE DESIGN PROCESS

Within the academic setting you have the opportunity to experience most of the phases of design as a hands-on experience. This repetitive experience as you approach each design problem helps you build your skills and knowledge as a designer. This text is focused on strengthening your skills in programming, the first phase of design. Your goal as the reader is to grasp the full realm of programming. Once you've achieved that, the attributes of programming will become a natural part of your approach as you begin designing your next projects in academia and in your future professions.

KEY TERMS

- Bauhaus School
- Concept
- Constructions documents
- Critique
- École des Beaux Arts
- Hard-line documentation
- National Architectural Accrediting Board (NAAB; www.naab.org)
- Physiological human interaction
- Presentation boards
- Schedules
- Specifications
- Square footage
- Working drawings

Defining a Topic and Structuring Your Program Document

After reading this chapter, you should be able to:

- Select a topic.
- Generate a problem statement.
- Understand conceptually what is included in programming based on a program document template.
- Create the first chapter of your program.

Typically, within the academic setting the instructor assigns a design topic to the student. Many students within their senior year or graduate studies, however, may select a topic of their own. Selecting your own topic is a wonderful opportunity to focus on an area of design that you feel passionate about. Your choice may represent cumulative knowledge from your academic experience. Nevertheless, defining the parameters of a programming topic can be an overwhelming task. This chapter will help you achieve that task.

The selection of your topic should not be taken lightly. Your topic can build on existing research within the field of interior design and explore original ideas that will add to the body of knowledge within this profession. Best results often come when you pursue an area of design that you find both enjoyable and challenging. Thus, topics tend to vary from student to student.

WHAT IS A PROGRAMMING TOPIC?

When talking about a "topic" for the programming phase of design, we mean a type of subject, study, or theme that you are planning to research. It can encompass commercial or residential design applications or another subject that you find interesting. The term *topic* in the programming phase of design is not unlike a "topic" of a research paper. It is the subject area that you will be exploring and researching.

SELECTING YOUR TOPIC

Many students find it hard to select and then commit to a topic. In most situations, your professor assigns you one. The selection of a topic in the professional world falls in the realm of the type of design you work on and directly from the clients you work for and their requirements for a particular job. This could be a new restaurant for a local chef or examination rooms for a health-care client. It is highly desirable for you to take time and investigate your topic as it relates to the profession. As noted, it is wise to select a topic that you find particularly interesting. Choose something that you discovered through previous studies and that you'd like to study further. Programming of a topic can take a semester, a year, or even multiple years of study. This will be time well spent, however, because if you choose well, you will gain greater insight into a topic that truly matters to you. Moreover, your efforts will contribute to the advancement of the greater body of knowledge and research within interior design.

Topics that would contribute to this advancement of the profession include the following:

- Aging in place
- Anthropometry/anthropometrics
- Barrier-free design
- Business of design
- Corporate design
- Environmental behavior
- Ergonomics
- Facilities planning
- Green/sustainable design
- Health-care design
- Historic preservation and restoration
- Hospitality design
- Human factors
- Institutional design
- Lighting design
- Museum and exhibit design
- Residential design
- Retail design
- Set design
- Universal design
- Way-finding methods

It is worthwhile to spend some time at this point in your research investigating current and emerging trends within the realm of interior design.

When conducting your investigative research on a topic that you think you would like to pursue, you should always include a few global examples. The world of design functions within a global market, and issues may surface when you include an international perspective and diverse global cultures. Be sure to conduct a preliminary search of your topic, as sometimes too much information surfaces, indicating you may need to consider refining or narrowing your topic. If too little information emerges, you might consider expanding your topic to include related issues.

The interior design profession truly encompasses all facets of our society. The profession touches all aspects of design, encompassing the health, safety, and welfare of the spaces where individuals live, work, learn, heal, worship, and play.

The programming topic could also be a social issue or a special interest you have. Or you could focus on an area of design that you might be interested in pursuing as a career upon graduation.

STRUCTURING YOUR PROGRAM DOCUMENT

After you've arrived at your topic, you need to begin structuring your program through the creation of a **programming document**. A programming document is a comprehensive report detailing the programmatic requirements for the structure. This document addresses an abundance of issues in an attempt to identify and outline the needs for the potential users of the space.

Following is a suggested template for a comprehensive programming document. You can follow this template each time you begin working on a design problem. Sections of the template will vary based on the studio problem, scope of the project, and time constraints. We will follow this template throughout the text. Each of the parts of the following template will be discussed in ensuing chapters of this book.

Your Programming Document Template

Each document should contain but not be limited to the following:

Title page:
- Student's name and the date
- Course name; in addition, faculty advisors sometimes have a sign-off sheet that might appear on the title page.
- Note at the bottom of your title page: This document has been prepared for educational purpose only. Limited edition: (add how ever many you plan on reproducing 1 or 2) printed. No further copies shall be made.

Table of Contents, including page numbers
Acknowledgements
List of Tables
List of Figures and Illustrations

Chapter 1: Introduction
- Introduction to the Study
- Problem statement
- User Client needs
- Rationale for the Study
- Organization of the Project

Chapter 2: Historical, Observational, Interactive Research
- Introduction: Research Topic
- Part 1: Historical documentation
  - Type of research completed and docu¬mented
- Part 2: Observational research
  - Type of research completed and docu¬mented
- Part 3: Interactive research
  - Type of research completed and docu¬mented

- Part 4: Conclusion
  - Synthesize the data documented in the chapter. What was gleaned from this research?

Chapter 3: The Building and Site Study
- Introduction
- Part 1: Overview of the state
  - Introduction (text)
  - Maps (images)
  - Major forms of transportation (Air, train, highway)
- Part 2: Overview of town
  - Introduction (text)
  - About the community (text and images)
  - Places of particular interest (text and images)
  - Demographics
- Part 3: Overview of the building inte¬rior and exterior
  - Introduction to the structure
  - Location and street (text and images)
  - Document the following
  - Surrounding structures
  - The exterior of the building
  - Interior of the building
- Part 4: Conclusion
  - Synthesize the data documented in the chapter that validate the appropriate application of design usage.

Chapter 4: Precedent Study
- Part 1: Introduction to the sample selected sites that will be studied
  - General guidelines: Pick five to eight examples to study.
  - Select examples that represent a global perspective of your topic (e.g., photos that you have taken or from a book or the Internet, assuming you have permission to use, of course)
- Part 2: Study the same information from each one, employing qualitative and quantitative research techniques.

BOX 3.1 STUDENT EXAMPLE: JESSICA BRETON, 2006

Interior design student Jessica Breton selected a specialized topic in the health care field as her programming topic, specifically an assisted-living Alzheimer's unit. (Her first job out of school as an interior designer was with a multidiscipline firm known for their outstanding commitment to health care.)

In her own words, Breton selected this area of design for the following reasons:

1. "My grandmother recently passed away from Alzheimer's."
2. "The exposure to the various types of facilities when my parents and I were looking for the right location for her to live in."
3. "During this experience I realized this is an area of design that not only could benefit from interior design but one that I'm passionate about."

"I gained such insight during my programmatic research phase," Breton said. "One example was the use of color and lighting to help Alzheimer's patients recall the time of day and recall various locations."

The following are excerpts from her programming thesis:

Designed by Nathaniel Bradlee, the Danvers State Lunatic Hospital was designed based on the Kirkbridge Plan. During the research phase I discovered that there are many features that he used in his design that related to aging. Based on the layout, I tried to encompass all the stages that one would go through in the later years of life. Designing for the users of the space to live a happy and comfortable lifestyle, I focused specifically on the Alzheimer's unit.

BOX FIGURE 3.1B Interior Design student Jessica Breton's rendering of a piano room for an Alzheimer's care facility.

Figure Box 3.1b is a perspective I designed of the interior space with a piano. This space allows the residents to have outside entertainment come and perform for them. Through my programmatic research I discovered that music brings memories and familiar feelings to all populations, including the elderly. Keeping this in mind, I wanted to create a space that would help unlock a little bit of what many Alzheimer patients aren't able to remember on their own. Also music can be very soothing and allow the residents' minds to be at ease. I took advantage of the existing large windows in the space, allowing the residents to see the exterior and let some natural light come in. In this case, the windows are facing the north side and so there is hardly any direct sunlight coming in. But this does allow the residents to see the outside as much as possible. This was an important fact I learned during the research, as it helped the Alzheimer patient be aware of time by having visual connection to the outside.

BOX FIGURE 3.1A Interior Design student Jessica Breton's rendering of Hawthorne Village Retirement Center, converted from the Danvers State Lunatic Hospital.

Figure Box 3.1c is a perspective I designed of the interior space including a fireplace. In this perspective view, one can see the openness of the community space. There are two stories. The second story is for residents who are still slightly independent. They have a half wall with glass above to allow for them to see into the community space. In the community space there are a series of half walls. This allows for a more open plan. The colors in each area help define the space. Through my research I also discovered the use of blocking of colors for different functions. Without restricting with high walls, there is a TV and fireplace area, a reading/library area, and a game and computer area. No matter what stage of Alzheimer's the resident is experiencing, this facility aimed to be accommodating. The fabrics and flooring that were used are very durable products that are antimicrobial, nonabsorbent, and have an ease of maintenance.

BOX FIGURE 3.1C Interior design student Jessica Breton's rendering of a TV room for an Alzheimer's care facility.

Figure Box 3.1d is the waiting room. A water element was used to add a sense of relaxation, and a large clock was strategically placed to help patients with time.

BOX FIGURE 3.1D Interior design student Jessica Breton's rendering of a reception room for an Alzheimer's care facility.

BOX 3.2 STUDENT EXAMPLE: MICHELLE HAVEN, 2006

Interior design student Michelle Haven explored the topic of a music center. She was required to select her own topic, location, and building site for her thesis. The following are her comments about the topic she selected and how the historical, observational, and interactive research impacted her design decisions.

Idea for Thesis

For my thesis I designed the Music Center of Lowell, it includes a music school and store. The idea came from my brother and sister-in-law. They both are interested in starting a nonprofit organization where children from lower income families can take music lessons. The profits from the music store would help towards the expenses of the building along with the organization itself. The space would be located in downtown Lowell, at 92 Merrimack Street.

Problem Statement

There is currently no organization like this in Lowell Massachusetts. The city of Lowell has developed a master plan to revitalize its city, Lowell has gone through some economic struggles, and one way they are looking to revitalize their city is by occupying downtown storefront properties with businesses. This is one of the reasons why 92 Merrimack Street was chosen. Lowell has also put a strong focus on the visual arts, and the Music Center of Lowell would be a way they could now put a focus on the performing arts. In doing so, they would enhance a vibrant and diverse community, which is one of the city's goals. The site was also chosen because it is in walking distance from the high school; this close proximity would attract students to the school and store and also make it accessible for them.

The design of the space will be creative, playful, and inspirational for the students and patrons. This will be executed through the use of color and light and through the forms of music. Sustainable design will be incorporated wherever it is possible. The Music Center of Lowell will provide new and exciting opportunities for the people in the community.

Description of the Space

Figure Box 3.2a is an image of the performing arts and function room. During the programming phase of design, it was found that because of the diversity of needs in a music studio the space had to be multifunctional. All the chairs and seating are stackable and movable. Color also played an important roll in the design. The color purple has been shown to calm, relax, and stimulate creative thinking. This is important because performing for a young child can cause anxiety, so purple was used to help calm nerves. Also, purple is associated with the right side of the brain, which is the creative side.

BOX FIGURE 3.2A Interior design student Michelle Haven's rendering of a performance space inside a nonprofit music center

BOX FIGURE 3.2B **Interior design student Michelle Haven's rendering of a proposed waiting area inside a nonprofit music center.**

Figure Box 3.2b shows the waiting area on the second floor. This is where students wait for their lessons. The design of the space was intended to be very creative and playful—the piano key design on the floor, and the mobile-like chandelier, for instance. Blues were used because it is a color associated with the right side of the brain and connected with artistic and musical impulses. This research was discovered during the programming phase, and then implemented during the design phases of the project. The design was meant to inspire and encourage students to express themselves creatively through music.

Figure Box 3.2c shows the music store. In programming studies, it was found that most music stores are very dark and can be intimidating to enter. In order to create a more positive and creative environment, especially for children to be comfortable, the colors were intentionally bold, bright, and cheerful. The front desk was designed in the shape of a guitar, which can be recognized not only from above but creates a fluid feel that helps carry the customers through the space upon entering.

BOX FIGURE 3.2C **Interior design student Michelle Haven's rendering of a proposed music store inside a nonprofit music center.**

- Part 3: Analyze the information
  - Introductory statement: What have you discovered?
  - Matrix or chart outlining the information in a visual format
- Part 4: The Conclusion
  - Reflect on the five to eight you se¬lected to study and the findings of your matrix. Summarize your findings.
  - Predict what you will include in for your programmatic requirements based on the findings of the precedent study

Chapter 5: The Program
- Address Significant Findings
- Part 1: Space square footages
  - Existing square footages
  - Space utilization
  - Space adjacencies
  - Issues related to building permits/ac¬tivities
- Part 2: Proposed Program
  - The Program Exterior
    - Space requirements
    - Space square footages
    - Space adjacencies
  - The Program Interior
    - Space requirements
    - Space square footages
    - Space adjacencies bubble/blocking plans
    - Space diagrams
- Part 3: Conclusion

Chapter 6: Analysis of the solution
- Include analysis of the best solution and proposal for the problem stated in Chapter 1.
- Limitations and Recommendations
  - Include visuals with your written word.

References
Appendix

Programming Document Tips

When you are preparing a comprehensive programming document, it is hard not to try and solve the problems. Within the last section of the document, you can begin to address and position some ideas about how the problems and sub-problems will be addressed.

You should start the first chapter of your programmatic research with a clear and concise statement, often referred to as a **problem statement**. Along with the problem statement, the first chapter should include the following, each of which is further discussed below:

- Problem statement, including research questions/sub-problems
- Mission statement
- Concept statement
- Introduction to the project

Generating Your Problem Statement

When generating a problem statement, you need to provide a background for the research study and typically identify questions that the research hopes to answer. It is important to create a few problem statements during the beginning exploratory phases of your topic. You need to take the time to think about the issues surrounding the problem. Try to envision all scenarios when looking at the proposed problem. The problem should have some questions within it. These questions would then become focus areas and be defined by a research question. Examples of problem statements and questions are included later in the chapter in Boxes 3.1 and 3.2.

What, How, Where, When, Why, and Who?

It is important to ask yourself the following about the problem: what, how, where, when, why, and who? Specifically, address the following:

- What is the problem?
- Why is it worth pursuing?
- Are there many areas of opportunity within the problem?
- Are there sub-problems to the problem?
- Have others tried to solve the problem or a similar one?
- What are the scope and limitations of the problem?

Finding the answers to these questions can be a tad tricky. As you are exploring your proposed problem, you also need to remember to keep it very focused when writing the final problem statement. As mentioned, it must be focused and concise, not only for you to keep on track but also for the scope to be defined and achievable in the given time frame. Successful researchers and practitioners need to pause and ask themselves throughout the process, "What am I doing and for what purpose am I doing it?" (Leedy, 1989).

Composing Your Mission Statement

Often within the profession, the designer will interview the client and ask if he or she has a "specific goal to be accomplished." The designer then transcribes this into the mission statement for the project. Many clients already have a very specific mission statement with accompanying goals (Duerk, 1993; Pena, 1987). Clients might defer to their mission statement, to assist in the programming process.

Composing mission statements is slightly different than creating problem statements. Mission statements are very specific to the company's image or goals and may have nothing to do with space and how the employees interact. A mission statement is often posted for all internal and external components of the company to see. Sometimes a firm will have an internal mission statement regarding corporate goals but an external motto or brand identity such

as Nike's "Just do it." Problem statements describe the problem to be solved. Ideally, problem statements should be one sentence followed by supportive sentences that describe the problem and identify a range of sub-problems. It is in these supportive sentences where you include the client's mission statement. Your client's mission statement and goals are extremely valuable in backing up your stated problem.

Keeping Your Statements Straight

Students often confuse the terms **problem statement, thesis statement,** and **mission statement.** Most students have generated a thesis statement for writing assignments. A thesis statement often summarizes the main point of a paper in a nutshell; it contains a clear position of the research or the essay. Often a thesis statement is expressed in a sentence or two. It is sometimes limited and does not encompass solving a problem but merely addresses issues and ideas of a problem.

Each academic institution and practitioner's office will employ standardized terminology. For the purpose of this text and focus on programming, the term that will be used is problem statement. That said, you should be aware that some academic institutions and practitioner's offices might use these terms interchangeably.

Creating Your Concept Statement

Typically students are asked to create a **concept statement** in all of their studio courses. A concept statement is often confused with a problem statement, but the two terms are not synonymous. When one is creating a concept statement at the beginning of a project, much is unknown because most of the ideas are yet to be explored; therefore, a concept statement usually describes the anticipated outcome of the design. The exploration of these ideas lies in the preliminary phases of thinking. Hence, it is vital to revisit the original concept statement at the end of the design project. This allows the designer the opportunity to reflect on the design, the process, and the element of discovery, which can then be documented. The transformation of the design can then be articulated in greater detail.

The process of moving forward and then revisiting your work is important for all elements of your work here. In generating your problem statement, for example, your first attempt is simply to state the facts of the problem. Then, after you've completed all of the introductory elements of the program, revisit that first attempt at the problem statement and see if it could be better stated. And then, after all of the precedent studies have been identified and researched, do it again. (Precedent studies will be covered in Chapter 7.) At each point, as you develop your research, you'll find that you have a greater understanding of what exists relative to your topic and you can revisit your problem statement and reevaluate your design ideas and solutions. In Chapter 2, the process of design was laid out in a linear fashion; you can also employ programming, however, as a cyclical process (refer back to

Figure 1.17). As you complete each step of research on your topic, turn back and re-evaluate your initial statements with a new perspective and sharpened perspective.

INTRODUCING YOUR PROGRAM

Once you have embarked on the topic of your choice, embrace it. Engross yourself in the subject. Discuss it with your professor, other faculty members, and classmates. Seek input from everyone, everywhere. Take the opportunity to conduct preliminary investigative research to evaluate the viability of your topic. This will provide vital information to help you outline your problem statement and its sub-problems. Remember to keep documenting the client and the user's preliminary needs of the space as you identify each one over the course of your research.

The student example in Box 3.3 documents the facts about the site and why they are important. The student then begins to tell us about the design problem as well as some of the design ideas.

When generating your own problem statement, consider the following:

BOX 3.3 STUDENT EXAMPLE: ANA KAREN ANGULO-GUTIERREZ

Interior design student Anna Karen Angulo-Guitierrez comments on her hospitality project:

One of the most important issues when starting a project in hospitality design is to be sure that the location of the hotel will provide its guests the opportunity to learn history or participate in other activities. Besides history, there should be many other activities in close proximity where guests can relax and learn more about the area or the city that they are visiting.

The location of the hotel is close to the center of Guadalajara, the second largest city in Mexico. This site has been selected to create guest interest to learn and have fun while enjoying the city of Jalisco, Mexico. The city's historic district is downtown and there are several

museums and amazing streets where guests can view Mexican art and spend some time shopping.

The building to be renovated has been successfully in use for more than 25 years by commercial store owners and residents, and there are a variety of beneficial options to create an economical investment if the building is used in a different way. Considering that the population in Guadalajara is increasing year by year and the popularity of Guadalajara City promoted by the Government of Jalisco, Mexico has been successful, there is a need to increase hospitality spaces in the city. This hotel can create the appropriate space needed for new residents to the area and guests expecting to see what the city can offer.

- What am I aiming to accomplish?
- What is the location of the site?
- Who will be its users?
- What are my anticipated outcomes?

The introduction to your project should include the scope of the project and anticipated users of the space. It should also mention the actual space interior and exterior of its site location as well as the site location's size and conditions. One might also include the fiscal impact of the project and a historical perspective and the current and future impacts of the project.

KEY TERMS
- Aging in place
- Anthropometry/anthropometrics
- Barrier-free design
- Concept statement
- Environmental behavior
- Ergonomics
- Facilities planning
- Green/sustainable design
- Health-care design
- Historic preservation and restoration
- Human factors
- Lighting design
- Museum and exhibit design
- Problem statement
- Programming document
- Stacking diagrams
- Thesis statement
- Topic
- Universal design
- Way-finding methods

CHAPTER 4

Research Methods

CHAPTER OBJECTIVES

After reading this chapter, you should be able to:

- Understand different research methods.
- Understand the varying degrees of reliability and validity of different research methods and how different methods are more appropriate for different projects.
- Begin to determine which method would work best for your design project.

As designers, most of us are visual thinkers. How we analyze data is personal, reflecting our level of interest in what we see and how and where we intend to apply our observations. There are at least as many different approaches to a project as there are designers; however, a few basic modes of research can serve every designer equally.

This chapter provides an overview of research methods, encompassing both quantitative and qualitative methods as well as the two combined, which is referred to as a **mixed method approach**. As a researcher, you may choose to employ any of these modes. The intent of this chapter is to show how you can easily apply them in your own work. This chapter gives an overview of

research methodologies that may seem quite daunting, but most of these practices become easy with experience. Then, in Chapter 5, "Historical, Observational, and Interactive Research," we will see how the research methods directly apply to interior design.

As you read this chapter, you need to think as a student, as a designer, as a researcher, and as a programmer—all at the same time. As a professional designer, you'll need to take basically the same multipurpose approach. This chapter shows how all of these roles fit neatly—and, with practice, easily—into the job requirements of one person.

There is a fine line where researcher becomes programmer, and then programmer becomes designer. As a student, you need to engage in each activity mindful that you are also going to facilitate the program and design. Taking on this additional role may or may not be required when you enter the profession; that will depend on the type and structure of design firm that employs you.

Lastly, the intent of this chapter is to serve as a foundation to help you to grasp a firm understanding of research methodology as it relates to data collecting, and to analyzing and documenting your find-

FIGURE 4.1 Researcher, programmer, designer—all three roles fit neatly into your job as interior designer.

ings. As you take up these tools and begin to practice using them, choose the research method or methods that meet your own level of comfort or are best suited for the information available. In this way, you'll build expertise and eventually find yourself easily engaging the methodology that best suits any given project.

INTRODUCTION TO RESEARCH

Qualitative? Quantitative? Mixed method?

How do you choose the one that's right for you? How do you even begin to understand what they mean and how to apply them to interior design? The term "research methods" alone can certainly make one nervous. But the truth is that many of the methods that are described below run parallel to the activities that have traditionally

been documented within the programming phase of design and may well be familiar to you; often, it's only the terminology that varies.

For this chapter (and the book as a whole), numerous sources supplied insight into the research methods discussed. You might consider adding them to your personal reference list. One book you might consider purchasing, for example, is *An Introduction to Educational Research*, by Meredith D. Gall, Walter R. Borg, and Joyce P. Gall. Also, there are numerous texts written by John W. Creswell, Ph.D., who is the Clifton Institute Professor of Educational Psychology at the University of Nebraska-Lincoln. Creswell specializes in research methods, and he writes, teaches, and conducts research about mixed method research, **qualitative research**, and research designs. At Nebraska, he co-directs the Office of Qualitative and Mixed Methods Research, a service/research unit providing methodological support for proposal development and funded projects. Included in the references for this chapter are not only text citations but also some very helpful Web sites. Be sure to also browse through the Resources appendix at the back of this book.

Qualitative Research

Qualitative research methods were developed in the social sciences for researchers to study social and cultural experiences. Borg and Gall offer the following definition:

Qualitative research or postpositivist research [is] the inquiry that is grounded in the assumption that individuals construct social reality in the form of meaning and interpretations, and that these constructs tend to be transitory and situational. The dominant methodology is to discover these meanings and interpretations by studying case intensively in natural settings and by subjecting the resulting data to analytic induction. (p. 767)

Following are some examples of qualitative methods that can be easily applied to the interior design discipline:

- **Action research** is a focused effort to find a solution to improve the quality of an organization or group and its performance in its particular setting. In many cases, educators or practitioners who analyze the data to improve the outcomes carry out action research.
- **Case study research** is an in-depth study of an instance, event, or situation; in short, a case. When one looks at more than one instance to document and compare the findings, it's called comparative case study research. When looking at the case studies, one may begin to identify emerging themes.
- **Ethnography** is observation in the field of a group in its natural setting. It is important to record as much as possible in the setting being studied. This can be extremely helpful when researching the layout of classroom and educational facilities to understand, for example, how students and teachers interact.

Qualitative Data

Qualitative data sources include observation and participant observation, interviews and questionnaires, documents and texts, and the researcher's impressions and reactions (Creswell, 1998 p.15).

Quantitative Research

Quantitative research methods were originally developed in the natural sciences to study natural observable facts. Following are some examples of quantitative methods accepted in the social sciences:

- **Survey methods** are commonly used in business, educational, health-care, and government settings. Surveys are implemented to retain an abundance of information based on the research topic.
- **Laboratory experiments** can include observation that employs statistical techniques. The selection of a sample group can vary from specific to random.
- **Formal and numerical methods** is the testing of a specific group using statistical methods to analyze the data.

Borg and Gall offer the following definition:

Quantitative research or positivist research [is] the inquiry that is grounded in the assumption that features of the social environment constitute an objective reality that is relatively constant across time and settings. The dominant methodology is to describe and explain features of this reality by collecting numerical data on observational behaviors of samples and by subjecting these data to statistical analysis. (p. 768)

Mixed Method Research

To summarize, qualitative data is the descriptive, personal data observed and gathered by the researcher of impressions and reactions. Quantitative data, on the other hand, is the numerical information that the researcher charts and/or graphs to represent the **statistics** of that research.

Combining qualitative and quantitative techniques within a single research design represents a methodological union between two different research traditions. A mixed method research process is defined by Creswell:

A mixed method approach is one in which the researcher tends to base knowledge claims on pragmatic grounds (e.g., consequence-oriented, problem-centered, and pluralistic). It employs strategies of inquiry that involve collecting data either simultaneously or sequentially to best understand research problems. The data collection also involves gathering numeric information (e.g., on instruments) as well as text information (e.g., on interviews) so that the final database represents both quantitative and qualitative information. (p. 20)

For the mixed method researcher, Creswell suggests that "pragmatism opens the door to multiple methods, different worldviews, and different assumptions, as well as to different forms of data collection and analysis in the mixed methods study" (Creswell, 2003, p. 12). Table 4.1, developed by Creswell, outlines strategies of inquiry.

To help validate findings within a mixed method approach, Borg and Gall refer to a triangulation process of using multiple data collection methods. They state that it helps to eliminate biases that might result from relying exclusively on any one data collection method, source, analyst, or theory (p. 575). Simply put, you, the student/researcher/designer, should select a professional array of sources from both sides of

any argument. This way, you can formulate your own opinion based on and supported by cited information.

Your Method-Choosing Goal

Our goal in defining various research methods is to ensure that the methods selected are sound and demonstrate **reliability** and **validity**. Reliability is an important concept that is defined in terms of its application to a wide range of activities. In identifying key methods and creating a project outline, the hope is that the experiments and tests would yield the same result on repeated trials. According to William Trochims (2006) of The Research Methods Knowledge Base, there are four key types of reliability estimates, each of which estimates reliability in a different way:

- **Inter-Rater or Inter-Observer Reliability**—Used to assess the degree to which different raters/observers give consistent estimates of the same phenomenon
- **Test-Retest Reliability**—Used to assess the consistency of a measure from one time to another
- **Parallel-Forms Reliability**— Used to assess the consistency of the results of two tests constructed in the same way from the same content domain

TABLE 4.1 ALTERNATIVE STRATEGIES OF INQUIRY

INQUIRY METHOD	APPLICATIONS
Quantitative	• Experimental designs • Nonexperimental designs, such as surveys
Qualitative	• Phenomenologies • Ethnographies • Grounded theory • Case studies
Mixed Methods	• Sequential • Concurrent • Transformative

Adapted from *Research Design Quantitative, Qualitative and Mixed Methods* by J. Creswell, 2003, p. 13.

- **Internal Consistency Reliability**— Used to assess the consistency of results across items within a test

Validity refers to the degree to which a study accurately reflects or assesses the specific concept that the researcher is attempting to measure (C. S. University, 2002, Writing guide, Reliability and Validity, ¶5). When research is valid, it accurately reflects and assesses the specific concept being measured. Reliability is concerned with the accuracy of the actual measuring instrument or procedure, whereas validity is concerned with the study's success at measuring what it set out to measure. For example, a student designer plans to create a functional office space. Through extensive research, the student finds various reliable sources supporting the concept that ergonomic considerations are key to a successful office design. It is at this point that the student can personalize the research by citing specific information supporting and validating that concept.

APPLYING QUALITATIVE RESEARCH

There are numerous research methods you might choose to employ a qualitative study. However, we will focus here on case study and **observational research** because of their natural application to the field of interior design.

Qualitative Case Study Research

Case studies are not a new form of research, and they include multiple methods and approaches. Case studies typically examine all facets of an experience in order to provide a complete understanding of what is being studied. Often the term "precedent study" will replace "case study" within the design field; however, the two are different. A case study is a qualitative form of re-

search that aims to provide in-depth documentation of one experience, situation, or condition. These are usually formal studies used in the medical profession and business schools. Harvard University is famous for its business case studies. A **precedent study**, on the other hand, focuses on one specific type of design and compares a group of similar examples. These examples can be in the form of individual case studies. As it relates to interior design, a precedent study could include similar retail, educational, or health-care spaces in different locations. The researcher compiles a list of attributes to compare from each example in order to determine which of these would best contribute to a successful design. As a student in the field, you are often asked to analyze precedent studies prior to starting a design project. Chapter 7, "Precedent Studies," discusses these studies further.

Categories of Case Studies

There are many categories of case studies. The researcher needs to carefully select the appropriate one depending upon the goals and/or objectives of the project (Clandinin, 1994). Types of case study include the following:

- **Cumulative case studies** combine information from different locations collected at different times that bring together findings from many case studies. The goal is to answer an evaluation question, whether descriptive, normative, or cause-and-effect.
- **Critical instance case studies** examine one or more sites for either the purpose of examining a situation of unique interest with little to no interest in generalization-ability, or to call into question or challenge a highly generalized or universal assertion. This method is useful for answering cause-and-effect questions.

- **Exploratory case studies** are descriptive and condensed. Sometimes referred to as pilot studies, researchers perform them before implementing large-scale studies.
- **Illustrative case studies** are descriptive in character and intended to add realism and in-depth examples to other information about a program or policy.
- **Program implementation** investigates operations, often at several sites and normatively.
- **Program effects** use the case study to examine causality and usually involve multi-site, multi-method assessments.

(C.S. University, 2002, Writing Guide, Reliability and Validity, ¶5)

Thick Description and Thin Description

When one is writing case studies, two modes of description are commonly used: thick description and thin description. Thick description is a process used to give an in-depth account of the study being evaluated (Guba, 1985, p. 363). A thick description outlines the characteristics of the people involved and the nature of the community and/or setting where the case is being conducted (p. 363). In the field of design, case studies are frequently discussed within the context of qualitative research and naturalistic inquiry.

Thin descriptions, in contrast, outline the facts with limited storytelling experience of inquiry (Guba & Lincoln, 1985, p.363). This could be where just the facts are stated with no elaboration.

Pilot Studies

Pilot studies, by definition, are condensed case studies performed before implementing a large-scale investigation. Many researchers perform pilot studies first in order to help them fine-tune and define the scope of their research problem. Valerie J. Janesick points out, "[B]efore devoting oneself to the arduous and significant time commitment of a qualitative study, it is a good idea to do a pilot study . . . [T]he pilot study allows the researcher to focus on particular areas that may have been unclear previously" (1994, p. 213).

Before a pilot study is launched, exploratory or field test studies should first be conducted. You might think of this as the *pre-pilot* study. Such smaller exploratory studies allow the researcher to develop relationships to pursue a larger study in the same way that the pilot study prepares for the full study. In doing this, researchers may uncover some insight into the shape of the study that previously was not apparent (Janesick, 1994).

Qualitative Observational Research

Qualitative observational research consists of many different approaches that often overlap and possess subtle distinctions. The type of approach used depends on the research question and area of discipline. The observer's role is to record group interactions and behaviors as objectively as possible using various qualitative inquiry tools (e.g., interviews, questionnaires, impressions, and reactions). It is the observer's responsibility to record his or her participation as the observer during the research and identify his or her point of view as the observer. The researcher is in essence "telling the story" (Stake, 1994, p.239). A qualitative observational research is naturalistic because it studies a group in its natural setting. Yvonne S. Lincoln and Eagon G. Guba state that nowhere in their text, *Naturalistic Inquiry*, will the term "naturism" be defined; instead, one needs to gain an overall understanding of the concept (1985, p. vi).

Qualitative observational research is another approach used by designers researching within the built environment. As an example, imagine that you were planning to design an educational facility. You could observe educational facilities and classroom layouts as they relate to student participation and productivity. You could select four elementary classrooms with different layouts and observe the environment and the student's interaction within the space.

In the design fields, this might be called observational research. The designer photographs or even videotapes a specific space over time—almost like a video diary that documents the users in the space. This form of analysis is extremely helpful, as it gives you an outside snapshot peering into the day and life of the users and how they interact with their space. Also, it can allow you to document long periods of time and look for repeating themes that might begin to emerge. These themes or key elements may be repeated within recurring phrases culled from the responses. Authors Anselm Straus and Juliet Corbin, (1998) refer to this step "as axial coding in axial coding, which is to say that categories are related to their subcategories to form more precise and complete explanations about the phenomena" (p. 124). This cross-analysis of identified phrases from the data collected and analyzed can then be categorized into main themes. Straus and Corbin (1998) refer to this process as **selective coding**. This is a useful tool when analyzing thick or thin descriptions of space or interviews. The concept of identifying repeating themes will be explored in detail in Chapter 7, "Precedent Studies," where examples of analyzing such studies are addressed.

Shaping Your Study to Reach the Goal
The goal of qualitative observational research is to define and answer a specific research problem or question. The problem or question may or may not be defined at the time when the researcher first begins the study. Some researchers, however, like to enter the field with a specific research problem already in mind (Stake, 1994). This certainly would be the case for observing environments within the space. Either your client has specific goals that he or she would like to accomplish or you, as the designer of a space, can make recommendations based on your observations.

The qualitative observational researcher must determine what underlying theory or model should document the research. This may mean replicating or building on an earlier study, or it may mean formulating a new model or theory by which to conduct the study. Either way, the theory or model chosen will help the researcher determine how to structure the study (e.g., whether exclusively to study participants in the classroom or to study them outside of the classroom as well, and how and when to use interviews) (Denzin, 1994; Guba, 1985).

Selecting *how* and *when* data will be collected is another essential step in designing qualitative observational research studies. It is extremely important for you to be aware of and sensitive to this. If you make the decision to conduct an observational study of different spaces, proper scheduling and, in most cases, permission and release forms will need to be completed. Questionnaires and student journals can be part of the data-collecting process as well; therefore, it is imperative that the student/researcher be respectful of the participants' time and willingness to help. If questions can be automated online for ease of access and time, this is advantageous. On the other hand, if the researcher would like the participants to fill out information, it should all be organized and completed within a specific time frame.

Internal Review Boards
Many academic institutions will have an **Internal Review Board** (IRB). When students

want to conduct research at these institutions, they must fill out the proper forms and adhere to the guidelines. It is always wise to check with the academic offices at your institution to see if there is an IRB and, if so, what the expectations are. Typically the IRB reviews proposals relate to human and animal subjects, and some departments have their own code of ethics with which one must comply. You are not to begin your research until the IRB committee or board has approved your proposal. This committee does not judge or evaluate your research but rather reviews how your data-collecting and documenting methods will protect the participants and their privacy.

Analyzing Your Data and Writing Your Report

The final two steps to be taken by the qualitative observational researcher are analyzing the data and writing the research report. In **analyzing descriptive data**, the researcher reviews what was witnessed and recorded, and synthesizes it with the observations and words of the participants themselves (Alverman et al., 1996; Huberman, 1994). What researchers choose to include or exclude from the final text can have a tremendous effect on how their results are interpreted by others. Alvermann et al. (1996) proposes that conscientious qualitative researchers might pose the following questions when writing up their findings:

- How much information needs to be included in the text about theories that may have guided the research, disciplinary biases, personal hunches that were followed, etc.?
- Should I include my original research and its changing forms as I conducted my research?
- How much description of myself needs to be included to reveal possible biases or perspectives (gender, ethnicity, age,

academic/social theories adhered to, etc.?
- How can I ensure that the research is interesting without compromising credibility?
- How can I fairly and accurately report my findings within the length limitations of where it will appear (journal, paper presentation, etc.)?
- Are the representations of myself and the studied group fair? Is it clear that there are mere representations or have I presented them as definite factual evidence? (C.S. University, 2002, Writing guide, observation)

They suggest that researchers who take the time to confront these possible problems will produce fairer, clearer reports of their research. Even when the report takes the form of a narrative, researchers must be sure that their "telling of the story" (Denzin, 1994, p. 507) gives readers an accurate and complete picture of the research.

In writing a case study, you're seeking a holistic understanding of an event or situation in question through inductive logic, reasoning from specific to more general terms (Huberman, 1984). Implementing a qualitative case study research project and including observational short- and long-term research techniques can be used to create a case study that demonstrates both reliability and validity.

Qualitative Research Applied to Art and Design

In the area of art and design, case studies and observational research are often referred to as "precedent studies" (Duerk, 1993; Pena, 1987). As noted above, precedent studies compare more than one location or example in a particular area. The majority of precedent studies in the field of design are committed to studying all aspects of the built environment and those who occupy it. It is common to study what has been done in the built environment and learn what has been successful and what has not. The documentation of the findings then becomes the precedent study. In the practice of design, precedent studies are used extensively. Precedent studies in the applied arts typically document the inception of the design process and each phase of design, and then evaluate the success and failures of the space and those who inhabit it (Alexander, 1974; Duerk, 1993; Pena, 1987).

Educational Connoisseurship and Criticism

The art educator Elliott Eisner developed a form of evaluation called "educational connoisseurship and criticism." **Connoisseurship** is the process of being aware of the educational program, and the meaning of it. "Being aware" in this case means observing that educational program's meaning, goals, and objectives. To do this well, the connoisseur "must have expert knowledge of the program being evaluated" (Gall et al., 1996, p. 710). This form of educational criticism focuses on "describing and evaluating that which has been appreciated" (Gall et al., p. 710). The "evaluating" part, of course, is where the criticism comes in. This approach parallels the critique experience that is common in one's academic and professional experiences. The validity of educational connoisseurship and criticism relies heavily on the expertise of the evaluator. Criticism can be approached as the process of helping others to see the qualities of something that they did not see. Unfortunately, when one hears the term "criticism," they often have negative feelings toward the word and experience. Within design, as outlined in Chapter 2, critique and its criticism is an integral part of the process of design. Students are encouraged to seek criticism as a way of improving their design

problems. Eisner (1998) states that "effective criticism functions as the midwife to perception. It helps it come into being, then later refines it and helps it to become more acute" (p. 6).

Many academic examples of qualitative studies within the applied arts are available via the online database resource ProQuest. Many academic institutions also have their own databases of thesis and dissertations available.

APPLYING QUANTITATIVE RESEARCH

Quantitative research methods were originally developed in the natural sciences to study natural phenomena (University, 2002). Quantitative research or positivist research is the inquiry that is grounded in the assumption that features of the social environment constitute an objective reality that is relatively constant across time and settings. The field of design has adopted many of the quantitative research methods for analyzing attitudes toward the built environment.

Survey Research Method

Questionnaires and surveys are quantitative research methods used extensively by designers. Often combined with interviews, both are a very quick and effective way to gather information from the users of a space.

According to Borg and Gall, "The term survey frequently is used to describe research that involves administering questionnaires or interviews. The purpose of a survey is to use questionnaires or interviews to collect data from participants in a sample about their characteristics, experiences, and opinions in order to generalize the findings to a population that the sample is intended to represent" (Borg, Gall, & Borg, 1996 p. 289).

When planning a research survey, Borg and Gall state that the researcher needs to carry out eight steps to ensure thorough documentation. Table 4.2 outlines these eight steps.

The survey method is a research tool that includes questions that are either open-ended or close-ended. You can administer your survey orally, documented in an interview, or as a questionnaire. Your goal in compiling quantitative research in a survey is to "gain specific information about either a specific group or a representative sample of a particular group. Results are typically used to understand the attitudes, beliefs, or knowledge of a particular group" (C.S. University, 2002, Writing guide, Survey research section, ¶ 2).

Compiling Statistical Research

According to Borg and Gall (1996), the last step in both the questionnaire and interview research methods is to compute data into descriptive statistics, or tabulate and analyze the quantitative data. Descriptive statistics describe the data that has been collected, which include descriptive statistics, frequency counts, ranges (high and low scores or values), means, modes, median scores, and standard deviations (C.S. University, 2002, Writing guide, Statistics research section, ¶ 5). The key point in using descriptive statistics is to understand the variables and distributions of the numbers.

Statistics are a set of tools used to organize and analyze data. Data must either be numeric in origin or transformed by researchers into numbers. Employing statistics serves two purposes—descriptions and prediction. Statistics are used to describe the characteristics of groups. These characteristics are referred to as **variables**. Data is gathered and recorded for each variable. Descriptive statistics can then be used to reveal the distribution of the data in each variable (C.S. University, 2002). Predictive statistics can be used to estimate future events with each variable. For example, by knowing the demographics of an area, predictive statistics can be used to determine the type of restaurant that would be the most profitable for a particular location.

Statistics can be used to analyze individual variables, relationships among variables, and differences between groups. For the purpose of employing a survey, questionnaire, or interview research method, analyzing differences between responses could be the means of statistical comparison.

Quantitative Research Methods Applied to Art and Design

Most of what exists in the field of design in advanced research pertains to the physical structure, and very little exists in the area of critical studies of the educational experience of design (AIA, 2007; ASID, 2007; Dutton, 1991). Look to the interior environment and how it is sculpted to study further how space can be enhanced by focused research committed to these areas.

There is a need for future research in applied arts to build a solid foundation of

TABLE 4.2 EIGHT STEPS TO CARRY OUT RESEARCH STUDY USING A QUESTIONNAIRE

STEP	DESCRIPTION
1	Define Research Objective
2	Select a sample
3	Design the questionnaire format
4	Pre-test the questionnaire
5	Pre-contact the sample
6	Write a cover letter and distribute the questionnaire
7	Follow up with non-respondents
8	Analyze questionnaire data

Adapted from *Educational Research: An Introduction*, by Borg, W. J., Gall M. (1996) p. 291.

historical data. Professional organizations have identified the lack of research in the applied arts and have teamed up with industrial partners to help fund further research (AIA, 2007; ASID, 2007; IIDA, 2007). **The American Society of Interior Designers** has spearheaded this effort and collaborated with the University of Minnesota: "They are focusing on some of the following: information on design specialties, needs of small business owners, outreach to educators, new studies on office noise and adaptable design and human behavior and design" (ASID, 2007, Research section ¶2).

InformeDesign has been an instrumental source for obtaining research relating specifically to the interior design profession. InformeDesign is the first searchable database of design and human behavior research on the Internet. The site currently contains "practitioner-friendly" research summaries of findings from research literature transformed into scholarly journals related to design and human behavior. All services on the InformeDesign Web site are available at no cost to visitors.

According to InformeDesign, "Good design, in the end, requires people with different experience, skills, and perspectives drawing on many forms of information in the pursuit of making creative and informed applications of knowledge as they generate and evaluate possible design solutions. Most important of all is a mindset that acknowledges that more information, including that generated through formally structured research processes, has the potential to generate plans and buildings that, as noted earlier, work synergistically on multiple levels" (2008).

APPLYING MIXED METHOD RESEARCH

The combination of qualitative research, including case study, observational short-

term and long-term techniques, and quantitative methods of research, including survey and statistics results in a mixed method approach. This combination of methodology fits into the definition as defined by Creswell (2003): "A mixed method approach: pragmatic knowledge claims collecting of both qualitative and quantitative data sequentially" (p. 12). The possibility of integrating both a qualitative and quantitative approach into one research method such as a questionnaire is an interesting approach (Labuschagne, 2003).

It is important to keep in mind that the purposes and functions of qualitative and quantitative data on questionnaires are different, yet complementary. The statistics from standardized items make summaries, comparisons, and generalizations quite easy and precise. The narrative comments from open-ended questions are typically meant to provide a forum for explanations, meanings, and new ideas (Labuschagune, 2003 ¶15). Integrating both qualitative and quantitative questions in one delivery method to gain insight into statistical and open-ended responses from the same participant is an appealing mixed method approach.

As a mixed method researcher, you need to be familiar with both techniques of research and have an understanding of the rationales for combining both forms of data (Creswell, 1998). Creswell also notes that a mixed method project will take extra time because of the need to collect and analyze both qualitative and quantitative data. Creswell also states that "mixed method research fits a person who enjoys both the structure of quantitative research and the flexibility of qualitative inquiry" (p. 23).

Mixed Method Research Applied to Art and Design

Integrating a mixed method research approach to study art and design amounts to

BOX 4.1 RESOURCES TO HELP INITIATE RESEARCH AND COLLECT INFORMATION

(Also see Appendix D,: "Helpful Resources")

Organizations

American Society of Interior Designers (ASID). ASID is the largest organization of professional interior designers in the world. ASID is a community of people driven by a common love for design and committed to the belief that interior design, as a service to people, is a powerful, multifaceted profession that can positively change people's lives. Through education, knowledge sharing, advocacy, community building, and outreach, the society strives to advance the interior design profession and, in the process, to demonstrate and celebrate the power of design to positively change people's lives. A list of schools with ASID student chapters can be obtained from the national headquarters (www.asid.org).

Building Green. Articles, reviews, and news from Environmental Building News (EBN) are integrated with product listings from the GreenSpec products directory and project case studies from the High-Performance Buildings Database (www.buildinggreen.com).

Council for Interior Design Accreditation. CIDA leads the interior design profession to excellence by setting standards and accrediting academic programs. CIDA sets standards for post-secondary interior design education, evaluates college and university interior design programs, and publishes a list of accredited programs that meet the standard (www.accredit-id.org).

InformeDesign. InformeDesign transforms research into an easy-to-read, easy-to-use format for architects, graphic designers, housing specialists, interior designers, landscape architects, urban designers and planners, and the public. It contains a database of RESEARCH SUMMARIES about design and human behavior research, accessible through either a full-text search or by using the topics listed within the three main categories, "Space," "Issues," or "Occupants." Created by the University of Minnesota (www.informedesign.umn.edu).

International Furnishings and Design Association (IFDA). IFDA is the only all-industry association whose members provide services and products to the furnishings and design industry, and it is the driving force through its programs and services to enhance the professionalism and stature of the industry worldwide (www.ifda.com).

International Interior Design Association (IIDA). IIDA is an internationally recognized organization representing design education and professional interior designers practicing in commercial, education and research, facility planning and design, government, health-care, hospitality, residential, and retail design (www.iida.org).

National Council for Interior Design Qualification (NCIDQ). This organization serves to identify to the public those interior designers who have met the minimum standards for professional practice by passing the NCIDQ examination. The Council endeavors to maintain the most advanced examining procedures, and to update continually the examination to reflect expanding professional knowledge and design development techniques (www.ncidq.org).

United States Access Board ADA Research Reports. A key mission of the Board is developing and maintaining accessibility guidelines and standards under several different laws, including the Americans with Disabilities Act (ADA). This includes design requirements for facilities in the private and public sectors, transportation vehicles, telecommunications equipment, and federal electronic and information technology. Most Board research projects are designed to develop information for its use in writing or updating these design criteria. The Board also funds the development of technical assistance and training materials useful to its audience, including designers, specifiers, and consumers. Such materials offer guidance on accessible design, compliance with Board guidelines, and best practices (www.access-board.gov/research/project-list.htm).

United States Green Building Council (USGBC). This nonprofit organization is committed to expanding sustainable building practices. USGBC is composed of more than 13,500 organizations from across the building industry that are working to advance structures that are environmentally responsible, profitable, and healthy places to live and work. Members include building owners and end users, real estate developers, facility managers, architects, designers, engineers, general contractors, subcontractors, product and building system manufacturers, government agencies, and nonprofits (www.usgbc.org).

Databases

Access to the databases typically is not free. Check with your library as most have institutional memberships.

Applied Science & Technology Index. This index references articles from 1983 to present in journals, magazines and trade publications in engineering, technology, and construction management; a good database for searches on construction topics.

Architectural Index. Online coverage indexing articles from major architectural periodicals are available in this database for 1982 to 1988; print versions of the index are available from 1950 to present.

Art Full Text. This bibliographic database indexes and abstracts articles from art periodicals, yearbooks, and museum bulletins published throughout the world.

Avery Index to Architectural Periodicals. This database offers a comprehensive listing of journal articles on architecture and design, including bibliographic descriptions on subjects such as the history and practice of architecture, landscape architecture, city planning, historic preservation, and interior design and decoration.

DAAI. Design and Applied Arts Index is the leading source of abstracts and bibliographic records for articles, news items, and reviews published in design and applied arts periodicals from 1973 to present. An indispensable tool for students, researchers, and practitioners worldwide, DAAI covers both new designers and the development of design and the applied arts since the mid-nineteenth century, surveying disciplines including ceramics, glass, jewelry, wood, metalsmithing, graphic design, fashion and clothing, textiles, furniture, interior design, architecture, computer-aided design, Web design, computer-generated graphics, animation, product design, industrial design, garden design, and landscape architecture. As of November 2007, DAAI contains more than 177,193 records, with around 1,200 new records added in each monthly update.

Dezignaré Interior Design Collective, Inc. This is a database encompassing over 100 online magazines and resources (www.dezignare.com).

MADCAD. This database provides building codes, knowledge-based design solutions, and guidelines to meet the codes. It also provides cross-referenced collections of building, electrical, mechanical, plumbing, fire, and maintenance codes from BOCA, SBCCI, ICBO, ICC, and NFPA, as well as access to comprehensive state and local codes (www.madcad.com/index.php).

ProQuest. UMI Dissertation Publishing ProQuest has been publishing dissertations and theses since 1938. In that time, they have published more than 1 million graduate works from graduate schools around the world. ProQuest has more than 700 active university publishing partners, and publishes more than 70,000 new graduate works each year (www.proquest.com/products_umi/dissertations/).

Publications

DesignIntelligence. DesignIntelligence is the Design Futures Council's bimonthly report on the future and the repository of timely articles, original research, and industry news. Design leaders rely on DesignIntelligence to deliver insight about emerging trends and management practices, allowing them to make their organization a better-managed, more financially successful enterprise (www.di.net).

The Journal of Interior Design. This is a scholarly, refereed publication dedicated to issues related to the design of the interior environment. (www.journalofinteriordesign.org)

Applications

SimplyMap. An Internet mapping application that lets users create professional-quality thematic maps and reports using United States demographic, business, and marketing data. Data sources include the U.S. Census and Census projections.

a comprehensive study, as it encompasses both qualitative and quantitative techniques. Triangulation will validate findings within a mixed method approach as you implement multiple data collection methods.

In the field of design, most studies are committed to studying all aspects of the built environment (AIA, 2007; ASID, 2008; Dutton, 1991). A mixed method research approach to analyze the built environment will improve programming and schematic design studies. It is another way of helping to eliminate biases opposed to relying exclusively on any one data collection method. Additionally, the analysis of information gathered can help you clarify your approach to the programming task.

SUMMARY

While absolute objectivity is impossible, it is essential that researchers enter the field or study group with an open mind, an awareness of their own biases, and a commitment to detach from those biases as much as possible while observing and representing the group. This will help as you begin to understand and apply the qualitative, quantitative, and mixed method research approaches that have been addressed in this chapter. Most designers are curious by nature and attempt to think outside the box. For the creative thinker, a research process is merely the organization of this instinctive form of exploration.

KEY TERMS

- Action research
- American Society of Interior Design (ASID; www.asid.org)
- Analyzing descriptive data
- Case study research
- Connoisseurship
- Critical instance case studies
- Cumulative case studies
- Ethnography
- Exploratory case studies
- Formal and numerical methods
- Illustrative case studies
- InformeDesign
- Inter-rater or inter-observer reliability
- Internal consistency reliability
- Internal Review Board (IRB)
- Mixed method approach
- Observational research
- Parallel-forms reliability
- Pilot studies
- Precedent study
- Program effects
- Program implementation
- Qualitative research
- Qualitative observational research
- Quantitative research
- Reliability
- Selective coding
- Statistics
- Survey
- Survey methods
- Test-retest reliability
- Thick description
- Thin description
- Validity
- Variable

CHAPTER 5

Historical, Observational, and Interactive Research

CHAPTER OBJECTIVES

After reading this chapter, you should be able to:

- Document historical research.
- Conduct and document observational research.
- Conduct and document interactive research.

What if a client asks you to design a coffee shop? Would you say, "I'm sorry, I've never designed a coffee shop before?"

As a trained designer, you must have the skills to apply good design to a diversity of design applications. You may not have the knowledge of specific technical requirements, but a good designer must have the ability to **research** and analyze the historical aspects of a design. A good designer must be able to assemble a plan to study the requirements and needs of any facility.

The beginning phase of design offers a wonderful opportunity for designers to take time out from everyday tasks and engross themselves in a new topic and in the type of design that new topic requires. In other

words, research gives the designer time to gain insight into programmatic requirements and to learn about the type of design that would best serve those requirements. This chapter introduces skills and training to help you begin thinking like a researcher. Chapter 4, "Research Methods," introduced numerous research methods that you may utilize. This chapter focuses on several types of research most commonly used by interior designers. Chapter 7, "Precedent Studies," should round out your formal research for the programming document.

In business or the classroom, a client or professor assigns the projects. As a student, you may find yourself designing a restaurant or retail space for the first time. It is only natural to have many questions concerning what should go into the space, where the space is located, who will use it, and so on. Intense curiosity is key for the student, programmer, and designer. Asking questions is essential.

It's a good idea to break down this phase of the process into three key areas: historical, observational, and interactive research. Each of these areas will be discussed in this chapter.

BEGINNING THE RESEARCH PROCESS

First, put on your researcher's hat. Try not to have any preconceived notions of the design or solutions—a very hard but crucial concept not only for the designer but for the client as well. Designers are trained to solve problems. But prior to the problem-solving phase, which can encompass both practical and conceptual solutions, designers can learn from the past to redefine and improve applications and solutions, and thereby become even better problem-solvers.

Often a client will contact a designer when they are ready to start a project. They may have a very specific idea in mind about how they envision the end result to look. This is where it is imperative for you as the designer to educate the client about the process of design, as outlined in Chapter 2, "The Process of Design." By including an exploratory research component into your programming phase, you can now also use it as an extra incentive for your client—offering to include them in the process.

Start with an open mind and gather as much information as possible. At this point you are a sponge absorbing as much as you can until you hit your full saturation point.

Let's get to full saturation and learn about historical, observational, and interactive research techniques and how to analyze the data collected.

FIGURE 5.2 **Take time to explore and gather as much information as possible.**

More Than Information Gathering

It is important to note that research is not merely information gathering. "Research is a systematic process of collecting, analyzing, and interpreting information (data) in order to increase our understating of the phenomenon about which we are interested or concerned" (Leedy, 2005, p. 2). This chapter is aimed as a primer for understanding and employing some research methodologies that align in an instinctive application to the programming phase of design. It is not meant to substitute or replace a comprehensive research project, but to identify and provide an overview of such methodologies. It can also serve as an introduction to research and various methodologies.

Historical Research

Starting the historical research aspect of your topic can be exciting and a tad overwhelming. In research terminology it can be compared to starting a **literature review** of the specific topic. The library might sound a bit old-fashioned, but it is the best way to begin the process of collecting historical research. Historical research, as it applies to interior design programming, is directly

FIGURE 5.1 **Researcher, programmer, designer—all three roles fit neatly into your job as interior designer.**

related to collecting information on what is in print and documented. Books, periodicals, newspapers, and journals are some options for collecting historical research. A key factor in your success as a researcher is using the right tools. While starting the process, remember that it is imperative to have patience and not expect to find everything on your first trip to the library or through your first online search.

Reference librarians are a great benefit to using a library. It is helpful to schedule a time to meet with the librarian and discuss your topic of research. Librarians have extensive knowledge as to how to gather information using a multitude of venues, and welcome the opportunity to aide you in your research. Some colleges and universities even have staff designated to work with specific schools and programs. These people have extensive knowledge as it relates to the discipline within the school. If you opt to visit your local library, you will also find that many have research librarians that can assist you.

Judy Harding is a research librarian who has helped students for the past 20 years. She is an important part of their research team. Harding often comes to a class, introduces herself, and shares an overview of how the library and its staff can aide students in their research. She invites the students to call or e-mail her to schedule an individual appointment with her. At these appointments, she discusses the specific design topic that each student has in mind. For example, she has discussed with students the creation of a sustainable design education center in Boston and the renovation and reuse of the Portsmouth naval prison into a Luxury Hotel.

Students begin by doing a literature search that will develop into a literature review. The literature search involves identifying resources such as books, journal articles, dissertations, and previous interior

design theses that relate to the student's selected design topic. This task involves searching specific databases related specifically to the field of interior design.

Once the books and articles are located, the bibliographies of works that are relevant need to be examined to see what the authors are citing. This is a very helpful step because it can help gain further information on the topic. Often Harding helps the students request information through an inter-library loan.

Internet research is the next step. The student needs to understand that not all Internet sites provide authoritative information. Reliable indices, such as the Librarians' Internet Index (http://lii.org), which provides reliable, librarian-selected Web sites, are the way to go. The Librarians' Internet Index, for example, includes a number of excellent resources related to interior design.

The literature search should be as thorough as possible and include recent as well as historical material. Once the literature search is complete, the student needs to write up the literature review. The literature review involves evaluating the information found in the literature search and deciding what sources are relevant to the topic.

In the final step the student creates a **reference or works cited** page to document the research. It is important to document all of your sources as you find them. This will help you in the long run, and save time instead of forcing you to go back and try to locate everything after the fact.

When you are researching your topic, numerous databases can assist in the collection process. These sites should be listed in your literature review.

When documenting historical research, it is important to remain as nonbiased as possible about your topic and findings. Try to identify contradictory evidence, and then strive to locate factual information that helps clarify issues that surface during this exploratory process. Examine historical points of view about the topic that you are designing. Examples follow to help you formulate what, how, and why certain topics are addressed in the historical documentation.

A project by interior design student Liz Carter, for example, demonstrates how you might begin the process. Here, a student chose to design a restaurant that encompasses a winery and brewery located in historic Kittery, Maine. The beginning of her data-collecting process started with a concise historical research of the history and involvement of breweries, wineries, and restaurants:

A watering hole for generation after generation, restaurants and breweries are gathering places for people of all ages because of their atmosphere, food, and beverages. The mix use of a restaurant-brewery-winery introduces a broad history of each subject as well as its concepts. A brief history of brewing will be introduced as well as how malt beverages are made, what types there are, and the comings of micro- breweries. The history of wine-making will follow, with the process of how wine is made. The history of restaurants will be presented followed by the newly found market of brewpubs. To gather further information on all of these operations, observational research will be presented including how these mixed amenities can successfully work together. (Carter, 2007)

Carter's experience also demonstrates how research can turn up unexpected surprises:

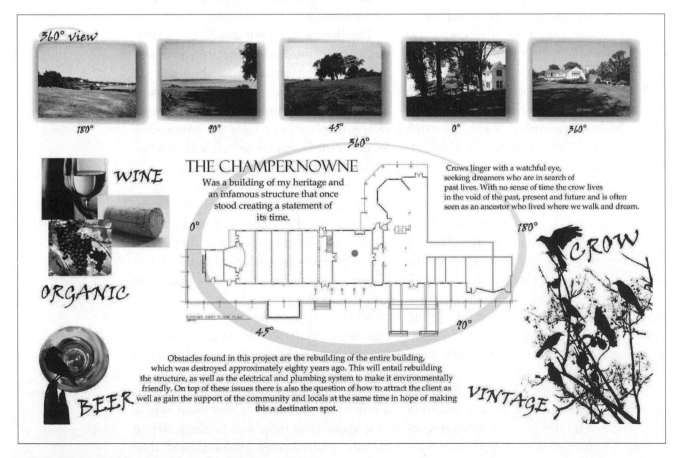

FIGURE 5.3 Introduction to the site and the concept, Liz Carter, 2007.

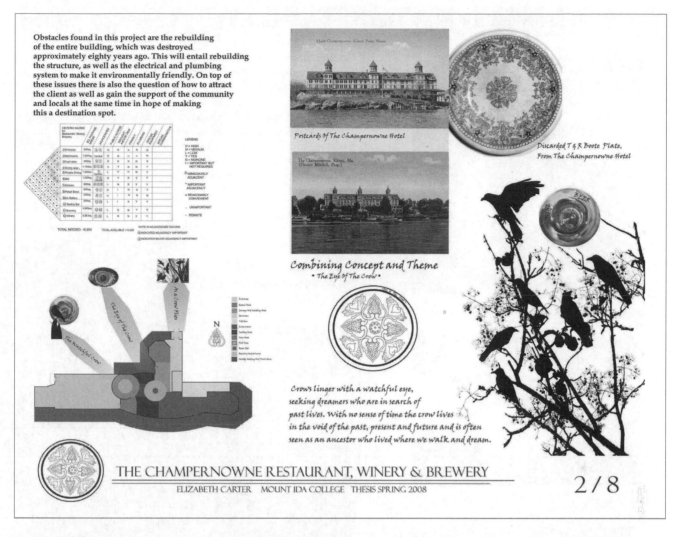

Obstacles found in this project are the rebuilding of the entire building, which was destroyed approximately eighty years ago. This will entail rebuilding the structure, as well as the electrical and plumbing system to make it environmentally friendly. On top of these issues there is also the question of how to attract the client as well as gain the support of the community and locals at the same time in hope of making this a destination spot.

Postcards Of The Champernowne Hotel

Discarded T & R Boote Plate, From The Champernowne Hotel

Combining Concept and Theme
• The Eye Of The Crow •

Crows linger with a watchful eye, seeking dreamers who are in search of past lives. With no sense of time the crow lives in the void of the past, present and future and is often seen as an ancestor who lived where we walk and dream.

THE CHAMPERNOWNE RESTAURANT, WINERY & BREWERY
ELIZABETH CARTER   MOUNT IDA COLLEGE   THESIS SPRING 2008
2/8

FIGURE 5.4 Concept board site with historical and contemporary images.

Part of the historical research exposed me to the beautiful unique sustainable products that are being made from cork. When I located the product, I was able to save it and document it in my sketchbook to implement later in the design process. My design decisions and choices were heavily influenced by sustainability. Finding a product that fused my concept and sustainability with such accuracy was an unexpected and valuable find during the research process.

Another student example explores the design of a sushi restaurant. This was quite a challenge for the student, who does not eat or like sushi. Hence, a key element during the historical research of the topic is to be open to the findings and what will be discovered: "The historical research covered the topic of sushi, sushi bars, and an observational site study to numerous sushi bars in Massachusetts" (Dinsmore, 2007).

The historical research of the selected topic should usually include the following:

- Concise overview of topic
- Application of topic in the built environment
- Timeline identifying at what date you started documenting the topic to current day
- Historical and economic factors that might have influenced topic
- Brief synopsis of topic's application in today's societal and current research

BOX 5.1 STUDENT EXAMPLE: AN UNEXPECTED OUTCOME

BOX FIGURE 5.1A

BOX FIGURE 5.1B

BOX FIGURE 5.1C

Lindsey Dinsmore, an interior design student, found an unexpected outcome in the historical research part of her programming project:

Part of the historical research exposed me to the beautiful colors of Sushi; I not only was fascinated by the vibrancy of the color but by the texture too. This was an unexpected outcome of the research that I documented in my sketchbook and implemented later in the design process, the interior reflected vibrant textural finishes—not unlike the sushi itself.

BOX FIGURE 5.1D Interior finishes for the restaurant are vibrant and textural—not unlike the sushi itself.

- Identification of relevant building codes specific to topic
- Special technological requirements
- Universal design issues relating to topic
- Sustainability issues relating to the topic

Observational Research

Observational research occurs when you take the time to visit locations relating to the type of application that you are studying, within natural settings. As noted in Chapter 4, "Research Methods," observational research techniques are often used within the field of design. The observer's role is to record group interactions and behaviors as objectively as possible in the setting that you are studying. For example, if you are designing a restaurant, visit restaurants that have a similar cliental, location, and the market that you are hoping to achieve and attract. Often the client will share spaces with you he or she might have seen and admire. Or as part of the research, you might go the client's locations and observe that environment.

Observational research techniques solely involve the researchers making observations. There are many positive aspects of the observational research approach. Observations can be flexible or very structured.

How to Conduct Observational Research

Before forming a research question, many researchers choose to conduct observations first in order to help form that question (Social Science, 2008). When conducting an observational visit, keep in mind the following:

- Call ahead and schedule an appointment.
- Ask if you can take photos or a video.
- Bring your sketchbook.

- Remember that you must be able to observe what is relevant to your topic, so plan accordingly.

Many designers don't realize that observational research can be extremely time-consuming. It is very important not only to think through the process but plan for the experience prior to just showing up ready to observe.

Be mindful of your presence as the researcher. Because this form of research involves direct observation, people might see you watching them. This can make them feel and act differently than if you weren't there. Hence, it might be advantageous to visit the site at different times of the day and maybe even week. Randomly observing a space might give the researcher a more realistic idea of how the space is being used.

Recording (e.g., videotape) how people interact in the space is another observation tool. This can prove very interesting in work productivity, specifically in office and health-care design and when observing way-finding paths and the most efficient way the users move and interact in a space. The researcher can then identify different user groups, which helps them clarify needs and program requirements for each group. In some cases, the programmer sets up a video camera to document the way the existing users work in the space. Then, the research analyzes the flow of users (traffic, communication and work flow can all be observed) adjacency, lighting, human factors, ergonomics, and anthropometrics. Any of these areas could warrant further observation and exploration to generate possible programmatic solutions to improve the function of the space.

Behavior Mapping

Behavioral mapping is the process of observing current conditions of an environment. As you observe and study the conditions as they exist, you will gain insight. For example, you could observe how students enter the classroom and based on the layout what seats they might select first.

This is an extremely important tool to employ as you begin to understand a client's organization and the functions of that organization. Dr. Lennie Scott-Webber is an author and professor of interior design. Her research focuses on how the environment impacts behavior, learning, and knowledge sharing. Scott-Webber writes that the "behavioral mapping process is used to better understand people's behavior in an environmental setting. Often what people think they do and what they actually do are two different things" (p. 47).

When conducting an observational study focused on behavioral mapping, consider the following:

- What you need to know about the people using the space.
- The number of people, the users type, the amount of time each user is observed doing different activities, and the exact location of each user within the space. These factors are known as "user type specifications."
- Whether the users' activity is active or passive. Users of a specific space vary in their interaction and participation in that space. For example, the needs of a patient in a hospital are very different in the patient room than those of the doctors and nurses.
- Clues that indicate the physical interaction between user and environment.
- What the setting *tells* the users. Are they welcome to come right in, or are they greeted with visual barriers? (Scott-Webber 1998, Duerk 1993)

Traffic Mapping and Activity Mapping

Duerk identifies two basic types of behavior mapping: traffic and activity. **Traffic**

maps show the paths people take through a space, while **activity maps** show what people are doing when they are stationary (p. 96). Once again, prior preparation on behalf of the researcher is crucial to conduct a behavior mapping study. Both Duerk and Scott-Webber recommend constructing a template first of the space to be studied. A predetermined coding system should also be generated to employ throughout the observation.

Putting Them All Together

Whether you're a professional designer or a student striving to learn more about a space and its functions, observational studies can be extremely valuable. Paired with historical research, observational research is a great way to start gaining insight into an application of design. The third key component is interactive research. If you plan ahead—budgeting enough time for your observational research visit, for example—you'll be able to fit this important area into your research as well.

Interactive Research

While observing a space, you might also conduct some interviews with the users of the space. This activity would fall into the realm of interactive documentation. When the researcher becomes more than just an observer is the point at which interactive research begins. The researcher begins to ask why certain things are done instead of just recording them and theorizing.

If you bring a list of questions with you to the space, then you might be able to elaborate on a bit of observed detail while interviewing a user of the space. When the researcher/programmer seeks input from others, interactive research can encompass a multitude of applications; it is—hence the term—"interactive."

Forging the interaction between two groups does not have to happen in person;

FIGURE 5.5 **Gather the research. Then begin to process all the information.**

with the advancements in technological applications, a growing variety of options include the following:

- Interviewing (over the telephone, computer, etc.).
- Questionnaires.
- Online surveys.
- Electronic mail correspondence.
- Traditional mail correspondence.
- List servers (used to seek information from a focused group of individuals who all have joined a topic based on common interest).
- Web logs. ("Blogs" vary in comment and documentation. Some are personal, while others address newsworthy content.)
- Web conferencing.

Strategize before You Start

It is important to think first about where you want to retrieve information and what are the most efficient means of obtaining it. The instruments listed above should be carefully evaluated prior to administering or committing to any of them. For example, if you decide to conduct a questionnaire, think about the type of questions you will be asking. Will they result in a quantitative (closed) or qualitative (open-ended) response? Consider administering two tools—for example, an interview and a follow-up survey. Also be mindful of how much time you have to implement and retrieve all the information. Think about how much time the respondents will need to complete the task. It is wise to keep the interactive research tool simple, with clear instructions and requiring minimal time from your participants.

DOCUMENTING THE RESEARCH

After you have conducted your historical observational and interactive research, the abundance of material gathered can be overwhelming. You now need to sort through and organize your data so you can represent it through a quantitative or qualitative approach. For example, if you opted to conduct an online survey, the results can be downloaded and can easily be exported into an electronic spreadsheet. Such results are often documented in a quantitative approach. Following are student examples

that employ and document interactive skills. Both students were in the programming phase of their undergraduate thesis and were required to conduct interactive research methods on their proposed thesis topics. As in most cases, this was their first time using a formalized research method to obtain programmatic information.

Student Example: Interactive Research of Restaurants, by Colleen Anderson, 2007

Anderson decided to issue an online questionnaire seeking input from individuals that would be representing the end users perspective of a dining experience.

Restaurant Questionnaire 1

The student example shown in Figure 5.6 involves a survey of eight questions that was created in order to better analyze how customers react to an atmosphere when they are dining out as well as what they prefer in a restaurant. Survey respondents were chosen from a wide variety of age, race, and gender in order to get a well-rounded

FIGURE 5.6 List of questions implementing an online survey.

Restaurant Survey - Senior Thesis Research

Please take a few moments to answer these following questions about restaurants and your personal dining experience. Your answers will be evaluated and used for my senior thesis in the research and the renovation of the Elm Street Fire Station into a restaurant. Thank you for your time!

Q1: What is the average amount of times you will choose to dine out in one month? [1-3 ▲▼]

Q2: How do you choose where you dine? Location, Food, Price, etc.? [_____]

Q3: What is one of your favorite restaurants? Why? [_____]

Q4: Do you prefer to dine out for special occasions? [No ▲▼]

Q5: When dining in a restaurant do you prefer to have a view of the kitchen or have it be hidden out of sight? [Closed View ▲▼]

Q6: Do you prefer a more private intimate atmosphere or a louder and less personal atmosphere? [Quiet and intimate ▲▼]

Q7: What would make it the perfect restaurant for you? [_____]

Q8: When selecting the restaurant which would you prefer: Great Food, or a Great View? [Great Food ▲▼]

[Submit]

response. A total of 21 people responded to the survey.

Interpreting Data from Questionnaire 1

The questionnaire was limited to eight questions requiring both qualitative and quantitative responses. The respondents were coded for confidentiality, as seen in Table 5.1. Each question was designed to help gain insight into restaurant users' preference and why they would select one restaurant over another. Was it food, atmosphere, location, or all of the above? Which one of the prior questions would hold prominence in their decision making? These were a few of the questions by which the student sought re-

sponses, hoping her results would help in programmatic requirements and design decisions later in the process.

Question Eight Asked when dining out, which did they prefer, great food or a great view. Only 4 out of 19 people responded that they would rather have a great view over great food. This was insightful, as diners would choose a restaurant that serves great food over an establishment that offers a great view that the diner can enjoy while eating. This was helpful information, as not always can an establishment offer great food and a great view. Therefore, if a restaurant can satisfy the guests' need for great food and service, the possible extra

TABLE 5.1 SURVEY OF PREFERRED RESTAURANT QUALITIES

QUESTION	RESPONDENT 1	RESPONDENT 2	RESPONDENT 3	RESPONDENT 4	RESPONDENT 5
1	7–10	4–7	1–3	10+	1–3
2	Location	Both Location and Food	Atmosphere	Food, Atmosphere, and Service	Food
3	Nicks Seafood: Great food and very good service	American Joe's: Because of their service, atmosphere, and food. Always something I like to eat.	Montebello's: Sentimental	Chapin's in Dennis, MA: Good food, very friendly, great neighborhood restaurant	Squire: fun atmosphere, really good food, although the prices are a little high
4	Yes	Yes	No	Sometimes; depends on the situation	No
5	Closed view	Closed view	Open view	Open view	It does not matter to my dining experience.
6	Depends on the occasion	Depends on the occasion	Quiet and intimate	Loud and open to the public	Depends on the occasion
7	Good service, good amenities, good food, good alcohol, and good atmosphere	A large menu, a dessert menu with not so much chocolate	Atmosphere and service	Great food, great atmosphere, very clean, great service, great ambiance	Knowing that every meal is good and that I won't be disappointed if I try something new
8	Great Food	Great Food	Great Service	Great Food	Great Food

continued on the next page

continued from the previous page

QUESTION	RESPONDENT 6	RESPONDENT 7	RESPONDENT 8	RESPONDENT 9	RESPONDENT 10
1	1–3	4–7	1–3	4–7	4–7
2	Food, Price	Food	Location	All of the above	Food
3	Scargo Cafe	Mangia Mangia: It's a little Italian restaurant, it's cozy, and it's really good food.	TGI Fridays: Atmosphere.	Lots of different kinds.	Mangia Mangia: It's a little Italian restaurant, it's cozy, and it's really good food.
4	Sometimes; depends on the occasion	Yes	Yes	No	No
5	Closed view	Closed view	Open view	It doesn't matter to my dining experience.	Closed view
6	Depends on the occasion	Depends on the occasion	Depends on the occasion	Depends on the occasion	Depends on the occasion
7	Excellent food, reasonable prices, clean	Attentive, but not annoying servers, great food	Atmosphere.	Funky and hip, great staff.	Attentive but not annoying servers, great food
8	Great Food	Great Food	Great Service	Great Food	Great Food

QUESTION	RESPONDENT 11	RESPONDENT 12	RESPONDENT 13	RESPONDENT 14	RESPONDENT 15
1	1–3	4–7	4–7	4–7	1–3
2	Location	All of the above	Location and food	All of the above	Food
3	TGI Fridays: Atmosphere	Lots of different kinds	Yarmouth House: Good climate and good food	Davide in the North End of Boston: Food is just amazing and the service is very good as well.	Clancy's
4	Yes	No	Yes	Sometimes; depends on the occasion	Sometimes; depends on the occasion
5	Open view	It doesn't matter to my dining experience.	Closed view	Open view	Closed view
6	Depends on the occasion	Depends on the occasion	Depends on the occasion	Depends on the occasion	Quiet and intimate
7	Atmosphere	Funky and hip, great staff	Fast but accurate service, display, taste of food, atmosphere, reasonable price	Great food, great service, great location, and parking would be very nice as well	Price and quality
8	Great Service	Great Food	Great Service	Great Food	Great Food

QUESTION	RESPONDENT 16	RESPONDENT 17	RESPONDENT 18	RESPONDENT 19	RESPONDENT 20
1	1–3	1–3	1–3	1–3	7–10
2	Price, food, and location	Food, word of mouth	Location	Convenience	Reputation and price
3	Scargo Café: Good menu, variety, price, and service	Meritage: "the experience," setting, food, wine, and service	Ocean House: Good food and a great view	Olive Garden: I love pasta.	Impudent Oyster: Consistency
4	Yes	Yes	Yes	Sometimes; depends on the occasion.	Yes.
5	Closed view	Closed view	Open view	Closed view	Closed view
6	Quiet and intimate	Quiet and intimate	Depends on the occasion	Depends on the occasion	Quiet and intimate
7	Good food and good service	Great service	Atmosphere and staff	A perfect mix of great food with a large alcohol selection coupled with a nice, friendly atmosphere	Quality of food, service and atmosphere
8	Great Food	Great Food	Great Food	Great Food	Great Food

QUESTION	RESPONDENT 21	RESPONDENT 22
1	1–3	1–3
2	Food, price, and location	Location and price
3	Old Country Buffet	Bertucci's: Because the rolls and sauce are amazing
4	Sometimes; depends on the occasion	Sometimes; depends on the occasion
5	It doesn't matter to my dining experience.	It doesn't matter to my dining experience.
6	Depends on the occasion	Depends on the occasion
7	Fine food, good price, nice setting	Be given the recipe to the roll sauce
8	Great View	Great Food

Source: Colleen Anderson, 2008

expense of having a great view is not necessary in order for the customers to choose their restaurant over any other.

Question Five When asked if they preferred to have an open view of the kitchen or have it out of sight, only 5 out of the 21 people surveyed replied that they prefer to have an open view of the kitchen. Table 5.1 illustrates the results in the difference of preference. This response is simply a preference that varies with each customer. Some people may enjoy watching the chefs cook and like to see their meal from start to finish. Others may prefer keeping the kitchen out of sight and believe that the overall experience of going out to eat is having someone else cook your meal. Also, one should consider the change in ambiance when a kitchen is introduced into the dining space. Not only does

it create something for the guest to look at while waiting for their food, it also creates a different mood and a louder atmosphere. The chart in Figure 5.7 shows the response when asked what kind of atmosphere one prefers when dining out.

The majority of diners responded that the atmosphere of the restaurant depends on the occasion and why they are dining out to eat. This answer is critical in the design of the proposed thesis topic and location of the Elm Street Fire Station. The intent of the restaurant is to appeal to the masses. The ideal restaurant would cater to both the quiet and intimate settings as well as a louder and less personal atmosphere. This way the diner cannot make a decision on the restaurant based on the occasion if that establishment does not cater to those needs and wants.

Question Five can be compared to the previous one with regard to the choice of atmosphere; the same person who would prefer to have a less personal dining ambiance would also prefer to have an open view of the kitchen. The two are directly correlated with one another; when a restaurant displays their kitchen, it automatically introduces a loud atmosphere. However, the majority of the people who said that they prefer to have a quieter and intimate atmosphere also agreed that they would prefer to have the kitchen out of sight when dining. These findings are helpful to the space planning of the future restaurant on Elm Street, the project featured in the figures. If the restaurant is to serve both intimate and public atmospheres, the kitchen should be closer to the less personal dining experience and kept out of sight for the more intimate settings.

Question Three When asked what their favorite restaurant was and why, one of the respondents chose the restaurant known as Meritage, located in Boston along the harbor. They chose it because of the over-

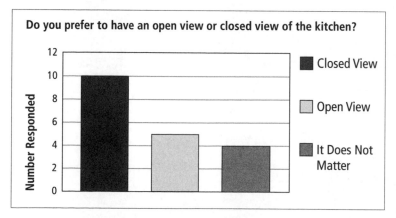

FIGURE 5.7 **Response to the survey question about atmosphere and noise levels.**

all experience they have while dining: the setting, the food and wine selection, and the quality of customer service. Many of the other favorites were chosen because of the food and the atmosphere. For example, Respondent 2 (R2) said that their favorite restaurant was American Joe's "because of their service, atmosphere, and their food." Another respondent chose a restaurant that was their favorite for sentimental reasons. Notice that R3 preferred a great view over great food and also an open view of the kitchen, but preferred a quieter and intimate atmosphere when dining. These responses could be considered contradictions unless the design of the restaurant is constructed especially vigilantly by choosing materials that will absorb the sound coming from the kitchen, and by space planning with foremost attention to detail and the overall feeling.

Another observation made from distilling all of the responses was the repetition of the same words from different responders. Noticing such patterns helps the researcher identify themes. For example, "Food" was the one word repeated most often. "Friendly" was repeated the least. Also, both "Good" and "Atmosphere" were repeated equally. One could conclude that the two are strongly related in the sense that the respondents all wanted to have a "good atmosphere."

Question Seven "What would make a perfect restaurant for you?" This question actually produced similar results from all of the surveyors, and ironically the answers were quite similar to what the respondents liked most about their favorite restaurant. The majority of the responses agreed that their perfect restaurant would consist of great service, with great food, in an inviting atmosphere. These three premises will create a restaurant that all can enjoy and choose to go to over other restaurants.

If you choose a more qualitative format of obtaining your data, your synthesis of the material might be more script intensive. Or if you opted to employ a mixed methodology, the goal is to find a balance in obtaining information and documenting it.

Student Example: Interactive Research: Survey to Rumford Community, by Erin Anthony, 2007

Interior design student Erin Anthony opted to hand-deliver a questionnaire, seeking input from individuals that lived in the community (See Box 5.2).

Questionnaire 2

The student example is based on a questionnaire given to residents of the Rumford Community in Rhode Island. In total, 18 people participated, and respondents varied in age as well as gender.

Interpreting Data from Questionnaire 2

The graph in Figure 5.8 represents three important values gathered from the survey. The first is the number of participants, the second is the number of female to male participants, and the last is the average number of years the participants have lived in the district of Rumford. This graph shows the overall scope of the survey.

Question Two "Do you find the Rumford Chemical Works site to be a convenient location?" This question received overwhelming support from the participants. Figure 5.9 demonstrates that 98 percent of them felt that the location was convenient, while 2 percent did not.

Questions Three and Four Very important aspects of the survey, these questions gave significant insight into how the residents of Rumford feel with regard to their current retail options. Of the 18 participants, only

BOX 5.2 SAMPLE QUESTIONNAIRE

Dear Rumford resident,

My name is Erin Anthony, a Rumford resident, studying interior design at Mount Ida College in Newton, MA. I am currently working on my senior thesis project. This project will entail the design of a retail store located on the Rumford Chemical Works (Rumford Baking Powder) site. As part of my preliminary stages of the design process, I am required to complete an interactive research component. This will help in gathering valuable information to make my project the best it can be! It would be *GREATLY* appreciated if you could take five minutes of your time to answer these quick survey questions. Thank you so much for all your input!

SURVEY QUESTIONS

1. How long have you been a resident of Rumford?
2. Do you find the Rumford Chemical Works site to be a convenient location?
3. Are there any types of stores that are NOT present in Rumford currently?
4. If you answered *yes* to the above question, what kind of stores would you like to see?
5. Are there any special characteristics you expect to see in a store while shopping?
6. Is customer service an important aspect of your shopping experiences?
7. When shopping, do you take time to notice the overall design of the store?
8. If so, what qualities make you recognize the store as one that is well-designed?
9. Would you enjoy seeing the historical elements of the building incorporated within the store design?
10. Would knowing that the design of a store is earth-friendly have an impact on your shopping experience?

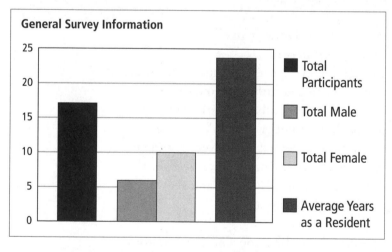

FIGURE 5.8 Graphic chart identifying survey participants.

while shopping?" and "What qualities make you recognize the store as one that is well designed?" The similarities of these two questions require them to be analyzed using a form of qualitative research. A word search was conducted to identify repeating words that were most frequently used by the respondents when they answered the questionnaire, as seen in Table 5.2. This technique of identifying words and how many times they were repeated was employed to see if themes began to emerge from the data collected.

one felt that Rumford already has a diverse mix of retail options. The remaining participants gave a variety of answers to question Four, which was, "What kind of stores would you like to see?" Figure 5.10 graphically depicts the responses as percentages.

Questions Five and Eight In questions five and eight, the participants were asked, "Are there any special characteristics you expect

Drawing Conclusions from Questionnaires 1 and 2

The most influential research gathered within this interactive research came from the surveys (Questionnaires 1 and 2) given to community members of Rumford, Rhode Island. The answers the participants provided shed light on what they expected, needed, and would enjoy seeing in a retail space within their hometown. But most importantly, based on their responses, the de-

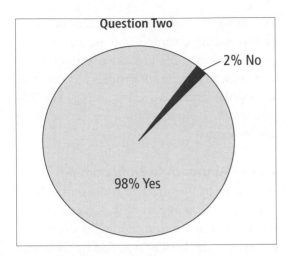

FIGURE 5.9 **Response to Question 2: Do you find the Rumford Chemical Works site to be a convenient location?**

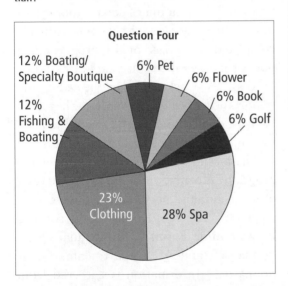

FIGURE 5.10 **Response to Question 4: If you answered yes to the above question (Are there any types of stores that are NOT present in Rumford currently?), what kind of stores would you like to see?**

TABLE 5.2 ANALYSIS OF REPEATED WORDS

In Questions 5 and 8, the participants were asked, "Are there any special characteristics you expect while shopping?" and "What qualities make you recognize the store as one that is well designed?" Table 5.1 shows words that were most frequently used in their answers to these questions. The first part of the survey asked questions that would generate quantitative responses. The second set of questions focused on qualitative responses.

Identifying common themes in the repetition of words is an excellent way to begin to take the research and start to think how it will begin to translate itself into the final design.

WORD	NUMBER OF TIMES USED
Lighting	10
Cleanliness	6
Color	4
Open	3
Space	3
Layout	2
Flow	2
Bright	2
Airy	2
Music	2
Atmosphere	2
Not overcrowded	2
Décor	1
Style	1
Organized	1

Source: Erin Anthony, 2008.

cision to design a spa as the retail space for the proposed thesis project was validated (Anthony, 2007).

The two student examples, Elmwood Street Restaurant and Rumford Chemical Works, employed two different types of questionnaires to the potential users of their spaces to obtain information. Interestingly, they both were looking for indicators to help them design elements, and programmatic requirements of the proposed design projects.

INTERVIEW WITH TSOI/KOBUS & ASSOCIATES

Tsoi/Kobus & Associates was founded in 1983 on the belief in the power of technology and the promise it holds for buildings of all kinds. Since then, they have sought to apply rigor and beauty in equal measure to the design of even the most technologically complex projects for clients in health care, science and technology, college and university, and commercial real estate. This principle has guided their search for design solutions that accommodate intensive technical demands while demonstrating sensitivity to human needs for comfort, dignity, and inspiration.

As architects, planners, and interior designers, they believe that their primary role is to lead their clients to solutions that not only address their building needs but also advance their strategic goals. Their philosophy manifests itself in a design approach that is both innovative and practical, that is rooted in their clients' missions, that relies on intensive collaboration, and that ends with smart architecture rather than celebrating smart designers. They create spaces that support the delivery of compassionate health care that accelerates discovery, that promotes learning, and that enhances the quality of human interaction. Currently, TK&A has a staff of nearly 100 architects, interior designers, planners, and administrative professionals, making it one of the largest design firms in the Boston area.

Associate Principal, Director of Interiors Kate Wendt, IIDA, discussed the programming process in their firm. With nearly 30 years of experience in Boston and Chicago, Kate is a strategic and versatile interior designer who has worked for an array of top-tier health-care, science and technology, college and university, and commercial clients. Kate is especially skilled at leading multidisciplinary teams and overseeing quality assurance. An engaging

FIGURE 5.11 Kate Wendt IIDA, NCIDQ Certificate # 5547

and effective communicator, she is adept at translating clients' needs into attractive and functional designs. Kate's interactive approach to the design process has resulted in sophisticated, award-winning, flexible interior environments for a variety of users and projects.

TK&A's Approach to Programming

According to Wendt, the firm's approach involves the client as part of the team from the outset. A good programming process is progressive in the level of detailed information gathered. Generally, the initial program is a macro-program that identifies basic space types and the amount of square footage required. In many cases, the client has already completed this phase of the program as a part of its overall facility capital planning process. "We acknowledge the value and importance of the information they may have assembled to date and try to incorporate this into our process," says Wendt.

The method of collecting and reporting program information is based on surveys, observation, and personal interviews. (See Appendix A: Tsoi/Kobus & Associates Programming Forms 3, "Individual Questionnaire," and 4, "Departmental Questionnaire.") Information is gathered from different levels within an organization in order to understand the needs of all of the potential users of the space. This top-down and bottom-up survey technique often reveals variations in responses and can point out the need to reach agreement and bring clarity to the information. In addition, it creates an opportunity to communicate with the employees of an organization to discuss anticipated facility changes and the beneficial impact of changes on the corporate goals and objectives of the organization. Wendt states that they have found that this procedure yields the most accurate and appropriate information possible in an expedient time frame.

TK&A's Process Steps

Once the higher-level strategic planning intent has been defined and the goals and objectives are established, the actual programming process can begin. Wendt and her team consider this an opportunity to learn about the client's organization and have "fun" in the process. Their commitment is to make the experience one that is collaborative, without being a burden to the client or their staff. Therefore, they have broken this effort down into a number of clear and concise steps:

• Prior to Kick-Off Meeting—Distribute List of Information Required (See Appendix A: Tsoi/Kobus & Associates Programming Forms 1, "Understanding Your Organization," and 2, "Background Information.")

• Orientation/Kick-Off Meeting
   • Project Introduction and Orientation
   • Organizational Committee Review
   • Project Communications
   • The Future—What Is the Business Plan?
   • Tour of Facilities

• Data Gathering—On-Site Work at Your Facility
   • Personal Interviews
   • Surveys

FIGURE 5.12A
Boston Medical Center Moakley Building.

FIGURE 5.12B Boston Medical Center Moakley Building.

FIGURE 5.12C **Center for Transitional Research, University of Pennsylvania School of Medicine.**

- Observation
- Existing Conditions Documentation

- Program Report Generation
  - Analysis of Information
  - Preliminary Presentation of Results
  - Modeling, Revisions, and Scenarios
  - Final Program Report, Presentation, and Subsequent Information Added

TK&A's Program Document

As discussed in Chapter 3, "Defining Your Topic and Structuring Your Program Document," a program document analyzes and reports information on a number of strategic levels. The reports detail criteria based on information essential to the planning efforts and to the client's decision-making process. The typical structure of the report is as follows:

FIGURE 5.12D **Center for Transitional Research, University of Pennsylvania School of Medicine.**

FIGURE 5.12E Center for Transitional Research, University of Pennsylvania School of Medicine.

- **Executive Summary**
  - Overall Planning Mission Statement
  - Image and Identity
  - Quality of Work Life Goals
  - Schedule and Budget Parameters and Objectives
- **Design Criteria**
  - Recommended Typical Workstation
  - Room Data Sheets
  - Site and Building Design Criteria
  - Technical Building Systems and Engineering Requirements
  - Security and Access Criteria
  - Special Requirements

- **Spatial Requirements**
  - Work Areas
  - Ancillary, Common, Support, and Special-Use Areas
  - Equipment Space Requirements
  - Circulation Requirements

Summary of TK&A Interview

Wendt explains that as a designer it is important to recognize that just as business styles differ, there are different ways to obtain the information needed to design spaces. Using a variety of information-gathering tools can provide a better opportunity for accuracy of the data. In general, Wendt finds personal interviews and observation of existing facilities to be the most beneficial and the use of preprinted survey forms to be the least effective method of gathering the information. Photography, especially video, can be very helpful in situations where the activities occurring within the space are complex or vary with the time of the day.

The programming process and time frame will vary with the level of complexity of the organization and of the space usage.

Programming for health-care projects is often a specialized service performed by those specializing in health-care planning. The technical characteristics of these spaces and the regulatory agencies and guidelines for best practice need to be considered when programming and planning health-care spaces.

Programming for the public spaces within a health-care facility often involves focus group meetings with patients and their families. Precedent studies from other institutions are gathered to help the client validate the space types and space requirements.

Programming for university projects often includes interviews and focus group meetings with student representatives along with the faculty and administration of the university. Sometimes, the decision-making process for a university project may take a little longer than for other projects due to multiple levels of decision making. Additionally, universities tend to take a longer assessment of their facility needs, and there may be several program scenarios developed as a part of a long-term master plan for the university.

In summary, the process and program document outline supplied by TK&A are provided as a guideline and should be modified to meet the specific needs within a market type, project type, and the organization's style and structure of decision making to provide the best information for design planning.

THE VALUE OF GOOD RESEARCH SKILLS

When historical, observational, and interactive research skills are employed and documented, you can begin to build a solid foundation of knowledge regarding a specific type of design. Whether you're observing a residential, commercial, or institutional type of design, the data that you collect becomes of great value as you create your program and move further into the design process.

Information extracted from research can then be employed in a multitude of applications and aid in evidence-based program and design criteria outcomes. With knowledge gleaned from research, you can begin to formulate program requirements and creative ideas. Always keep your sketchbook with you during the research phase because when something triggers, or "clicks," you will want to document it, return to it at a later date, and not lose that idea or thought.

The data obtained from the research should help a client, student, or design professional make intelligent decisions based on quantifiable information. Your observations and research will be compared with that of other similar design types in your precedent studies, as we will discuss in Chapter 7, "Precedent Studies."

KEY TERMS

- Activity map
- Behavioral mapping
- Historical research
- Interactive research
- Literature review
- Reference or works cited
- Research
- Traffic map

CHAPTER 6

Building and Site Analysis

After reading this chapter, you should be able to:

- Document an overview of the state and town where the site is located.
- Document exterior building and site conditions.
- Document interior building and site conditions.
- Identify design constraints and limitations related to the building and site.

Both the building and specific site are vital elements to consider during the programming phase of design. The location can significantly impact decisions when you are evaluating programmatic requirements.

When considering the location, you'll need to address several factors:

- Is there an existing site?
- Is it the best location for the potential use?
- Should more than one site be explored and evaluated?
- How do you locate a site while you are still in school to use as a project?

If the site is specified, you should conduct an extensive site study analysis. If the site is still to be determined, you should explore site analysis. This chapter will help you perform an exploratory site study, which can be a pivotal point for the decision making involved in a specific site location.

WHAT IS A SITE STUDY?

The site is the location where your design project will be located. As a student you might be able to select your own site. Or often your instructor will allocate one for the class.

The Role of the Interior Designer

It is important that an individual who is trained in interior design be included in the process. Typically engineers, developers, architects, and landscape architects are also part of the team that begins to evaluate the proposed site or possible sites. As the interior designer, you must be involved in this process early on as well. Interior designers bring a different set of skills and viewpoints to the table. This chapter addresses the large-scale issues of site evaluation as well as the details; this is also referred to as "a macro-to-micro approach to site analysis."

Explore Community Statistics

Take another careful look at your proposed topic. Compare the design proposal to the current demographics and socioeconomics in the community. When reviewing the proposed site and data, take into consideration growth, economic forecasting, and master planning for the proposed communities. Most of this information can be easily located by conducting an online search of the community's Web site. You should also consider a visit to the local library.

Say your topic is a boutique hotel. Would this fit into all communities? What communities would help make the location successful? The right choice may be a major metropolitan city or a tourist location and maybe not a suburban town with little tourist appeal. This might sound like common sense, but you can use this as a reminder to look at the demographics and average income of the community. It could, for example, help you determine the build-out per square footage cost for the space and help you analyze price points for a restaurateur contemplating a specific location. Looking at the demographics and average income of a community not only helps with design decisions but also provides a realistic "snapshot" for you to give to a client who might be choosing between two or three locations.

Student Example: Sustainability Educational Center, by Monica Mattingly, 2007

An example of community statistics exploration is from interior design student, Monica Mattingly, who was exploring the best possible location for a Sustainability Educational Center. The education sector has had a large impact in the city of Boston. Figure 6.1 demonstrates the location of the colleges currently located in Boston, while Figure 6.2 shows the effect of this large

number of schools on the local economy. The portion of the economic sector is equal to that for business and for natural resources.

In-depth knowledge of proposed locations is extremely important. This can be seen in the student example. According to the student, Monica Mattingly, "The size of Boston was greatly increased throughout the nineteenth century by a series of landfill projects that added a total of 1,071 acres to the original peninsula of only 487 acres ("The History of Landfill in Boston," 2007). The choice of a building site on a landfill will affect the construction and needs to be considered carefully.

As an example of demographics playing a role in the decision-making process, Mattingly states, due to the high percentage of educational facilities, there is a high ratio of young people in the city, as well as a high ratio of educated population (Mattingly, 2007). Projects geared toward this demographic would have a higher probability of success.

The research and statistics in Figures 6.3a and 6.3b help validate the decision to locate the site. They also help in identifying other potential options based on the demographics of the community.

Location Overview

Another reason to look at the site early and on a large scale is to see if the proposed site is adequate in size for the planned use. Is it too large or small? Will it allow for further expansion or reduction if needed? This is especially true when exploring a tenant fit-up facility for a client. Once these decisions have been evaluated, there should be an overview of the location. This can consist of the following:

- State and Country
- Introduction with maps

- Major forms of transportation (e.g., air, train, highway)
- Environmental features

The overview does not have to be extensive, but it should cover a bit about the state and include some maps so that one can visually place the site in a larger context. What is gained from this exercise is extremely valuable as you begin to think and visualize the design from a different vantage point. Is there a water view? Is there any view? Are views important? Where is it in relation to public transportation? Is this important to your design, will it affect the use of the space? Will customers be able to get to your location via public transportation, highways, or plane? What are the parking requirements? The questions are endless.

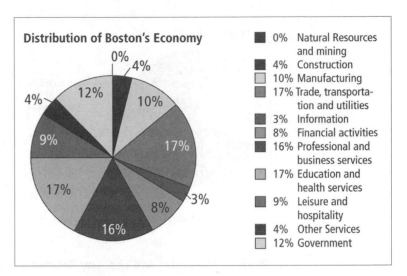

FIGURE 6.1 **Distribution of Boson's economy.**

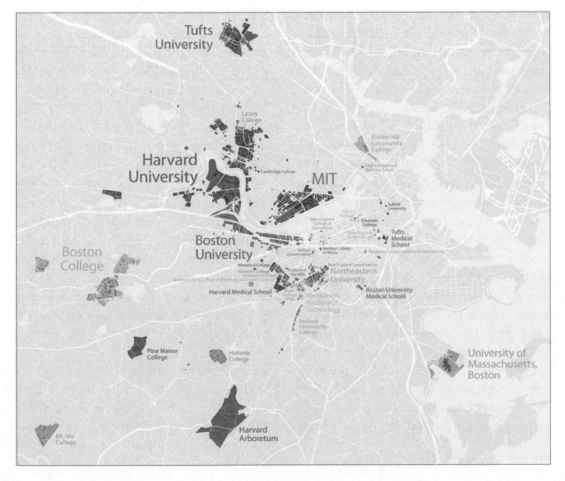

FIGURE 6.2 **Proximity of Boston's colleges and universities to the site.**

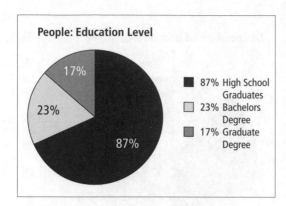

FIGURE 6.3A Education level in the community.

FIGURE 6.3B Age groups within the community.

Student Example: Art Therapy Retreat

Interior design student Nicole Stewart provides an excellent example of a location overview. Stewart wanted to establish an art therapy retreat in an area located in a country atmosphere in Greenwich, New York. With green rolling hills that the local farmers use for their crops, dense woods filled with wild life, and friendly agricultural animals roaming about, the community has a secluded and relaxed environment. As a large city flourishing with residents and business life, Greenwich is an ideal area for an art retreat location.

Stewart anticipates that her choice of geographical location will thrive off of the immediate surroundings of serenity and create a peaceful environment away from one's everyday lifestyle. She hopes that her design for a retreat, where people may experience a serene and peaceful atmosphere, will help individuals improve and become stronger, well-balanced, and composed people (Stewart, 2006). It is important for the project that transportation to the location be easy and convenient. But also the journey to the site could aid in the therapeutic experience. Relaxation can begin as the customer leaves the fast-paced, hectic city for the calm tranquility of the country setting.

Overview of the State

The state of New York is located in the northeastern United States. New York borders with Canada to the north; Vermont, Massachusetts, and Connecticut to the east; New Jersey, Pennsylvania, and a bit of the Atlantic Ocean to the south; and Lake Ontario to the west. Geographically, the state is the center of the Northeast. Because of the dense populations in the southern tip of the state, areas in New York are typically referred to as Downstate and Upstate.

Downstate, including New York City and the immediate suburbs, is densely occupied by commercial and retail spaces and closely knit residential areas. By contrast, the Upstate area is more open and rural; towns are typically separated by green rolling hills and open skies. Commercial businesses are still common and well developed, but there is more of a chance to easily escape the fast-paced life of the city than in the denser region to the south. Greenwich is located in the Upstate region, near Albany, the state capital.

State Transportation

Finding your way in and around New York State can be rather simple at times and a bit challenging at other times. The Upstate area and more specifically the capital region have Albany International Airport for convenient air travel. The major highways of New York seem to branch out from Albany to the extents of the state (see Figure 6.6). The routes travel in different locations, allowing easy accessibility from other surrounding states. Other common forms of transportation within New York State are train and bus (see Figure 6.7; Stewart, 2006).

In most scenarios, analyzing travel to the site can be an insightful exercise. Issues might surface that warrant documentation. In the example above, the experience is a therapeutic one. Conversely, think about traveling by car to a large city; it might have the opposite effect as you begin to deal with a faster pace, traffic, and more noise. You might begin to see very tall buildings. The massive structures reaching to the sky have a monumental feeling about them. Theoretically, this might indicate that they are very important structures with significant activities occurring inside them. This same experience can be applied in numerous ways when you think about traveling to a location by foot. An example could be when one enters a hospital setting and travels by foot through corridors or walkways between buildings to a final destination inside that setting. This experience is referred to within the interior design profession as way-finding. If it is a children's hospital, the travel experience is catered to a child's eye and perspective. Colorful diagrams on the floor may help guide the way. Focus points such as fish tanks may be strategically placed at a child's eye level to engage and relax him or her in this unfamiliar setting. Both interior and exterior travel experiences can affect decision making of programmatic requirements.

Overview of the Town
Documentation of the town where the project is located gives you important, in-depth

FIGURE 6.4 **Scenic view of Greenwich, New York.**

FIGURE 6.5 **Map of New York State.**

details about the town, population, and community. When you are gathering an overview of a town, the following should be addressed:

- A written overview of the town where the project is located.
- Statistical information about the community.
- Places of particular interest (include both text and images)—it is important to keep this focused and not to digress or attempt to document too much. The places of interest that you select should relate to your topic or be of some value. If your topic is a banquet facility that hosts private parties such as weddings, you might consider documenting the

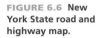

FIGURE 6.6 New York State road and highway map.

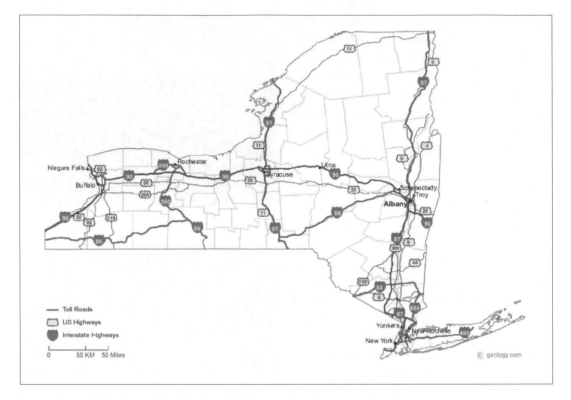

area's religious structures, florists, and scenic locations for photos.

When you document the above, it is important to try and capture the essence of the community in order to deliver a realistic picture of the area and what it encompasses.

WHEN STUDENTS WORK WITH ACTUAL CLIENTS

Often students will work with actual clients for a thesis project and have access to the town and community information via these clients. On occasion, members of the community will seek out students for design services. In many cases this can be a win-win situation for both parties, especially when both parties enter the arrangement with realistic expectations and goals. The student will have immediate access to a client, location, building, and the users of the space. This can create a real-life scenario in which

to experience the programming process. The client can benefit from numerous options being explored, especially if more than one student is working on the project. A client that embraces and participates in academic experience will walk away with many ideas.

Student Example: Pastry Shop

One such experience was a company entitled Dessert Works, currently located in Norwood, Massachusetts. Jen Cilano, an interior design senior contemplating what to do for her thesis, opted to work with Kristen Repa, owner of Dessert Works.

Through interviews, Cilano learned that Repa began her career more than 15 years ago at Konditor Meister, a bakery known for their fine European pastries. Later, she worked as an apprentice pastry chef for the Ritz-Carlton in Boston, and then in 2001 she founded Dessert Works, a shop specializing in unique cakes and pastries (Dessertworks.net, 2006). While working at the

Ritz, she met fellow chef Leonardo Savona, who is now her husband and business partner. She went on to perfect her talents at Gerstner, the world-renowned pastry shop in Vienna, Austria, before opening Dessert Works.

Repa owned and operated Dessert Works in Medfield, Massachusetts, until November 2004, when she relocated to Norwood. In her three and a half years in Medfield, Dessert Works sales increased by 575 percent and quickly grew out of the space (Dessertworks, 2006). The Norwood site currently has a much larger retail space than Medfield, but Dessert Works is quickly growing out of it as well. The current location in Norwood is not easily noticed when passing by. It is in a strip mall that is situated away from vehicle and foot traffic. The goal that Repa expressed to Cilano was to find a new location that will draw in more customers due to foot traffic as well as visibility and accessibility of the main road. She wanted to attract more walk-in customers, promoting the store name and brand.

Cilano could identify that Repa had specific programming needs: the building will be used for multiple purposes, including on-site baking, bakery sales, baking classes, wedding consulting, special-order cakes, and a café-type space. The clientele is typically high-end, which led to the reasoning behind the relocation to Wellesley, Massachusetts, a more affluent community.

After educating herself about her client's needs, Cilano can then turn to the community to see if it is, in fact, the right fit. The best sources to begin obtaining this information would be the town hall, the town's Web site, and the local library.

Wellesley is a town located in Norfolk County, Massachusetts, United States. The population was 26,613 in the 2000 Census. It has the reputation of being one of the most affluent and prestigious suburbs of

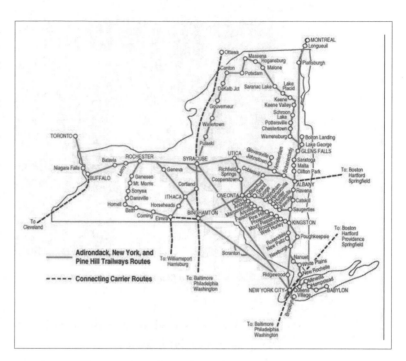

FIGURE 6.7 New York State route map.

Boston. It consistently ranks among the top five wealthiest towns in the state.

Through the foresight of the town fathers who, in 1914, made Wellesley the first town in America to adopt zoning laws, Wellesley grew into a beautiful town by the 1920s. It was then recognized as one of the leading suburbs of Boston. Filene's, the major department store, opened its first branch in Wellesley, where it then became a center for shopping.

The map in Figure 6.9 shows Wellesley's current zoning. Each zoning district is designated by a separate color. Essentially, a **zoning map** acts as a blueprint for a community's future development, showing how the land is divided to accommodate varied development interests. For example, this zoning map shows where Wellesley intends to place houses (i.e., residential) and businesses (i.e., retail, commercial/industrial) and their relationship to each other (Massachusetts EOEA, ¶10).

Washington Street, the potential site on the zoning map, is included in the Indus-

FIGURE 6.8 **Kristen Repa, owner of Dessert Works.**

trial A zone as well as the Lower Falls Village Commercial District.

Another area for Cilano to explore is the demographics of the town. Will the community be able to sustain such a facility?

The median age of Wellesley was 38 years old according to the 2000 census. This indicates that approximately 20 percent of Wellesley's population consists of young professionals. The median income for a household in the town of Wellesley was $113,686, and the median income for a family was $134,769. The average income for males was $100,000, while it was $53,007 for females. Only 3.8 percent of the population in Wellesley was below the poverty line, and that included 4.0 percent who were under the age of 18 and 2.1 percent of those who were 65 years old or older (City-data, ¶2).

The site, image, and statistical documentation demonstrate that the proposed location of the Dessert Works facility in Wellesley appears to be a good fit—it meets the client's needs and goals (Cilano, 2006).

Overview of the Site

Where is north? It may sound simple, but it's one of the most important questions. Do surrounding buildings cast shadows that will affect your interior space? Think about the earth elements and environmental factors. Can you easily implement the use of natural resources? What is the annual precipitation? Is there potential to harvest wind power? A brief introduction to the structure is imperative. It is essential to obtain a clear understanding of existing conditions.

Document the location and street. This can be done very easily online using Internet search tools such as Google Earth or MapQuest. Once you have saved the image, you can then insert the map into Photoshop and add arrows or otherwise highlight specific areas that you might want to reference.

Typically the following should be documented:

- Location and street (text and images)
- Surrounding structures (text and images)
- The exterior of the building (text and images)
- Interior of the building (text and images)

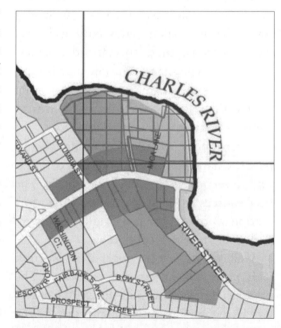

FIGURE 6.9 **This map shows the current zoning of the town of Wellesley, Massachusetts.**

EXTERIOR AND INTERIOR SITE DOCUMENTATION

The observational documentation of the site should start with the exterior. Then documentation should move into the building. When you are documenting the site, it is helpful to have a floor plan to make notations and document the dimensions. Also take a number of photos from various viewpoints. In many cases the space might be occupied, so you need to be efficient and courteous with your presence and that of others in the space.

Student Example: Rumford Chemical Works Site

Interior design student Erin Anthony explored the reuse and renovation of an old warehouse. The entire Rumford Chemical Works property is located at the intersections of North Broadway, and Greenwood and Newman Avenues in Rumford, Rhode Island. The street map and aerial view in Figures 6.10a and b pinpoint the exact location of the site.

Student Example: Waltham Street Site

Kristen Patten, also an interior design student, demonstrates her work in Figure 6.11. Patten's is another example of how to document an overview of a site location on Waltham Street, a few miles from Lexington Center in Massachusetts. The aerial map is shown with color-coded blocking overlaid. The transparency of color is a clever way to help one understand where the building is in relation to surrounding structures.

Site Interior Documentation

When documenting the interior, you should place yourself at specific locations that can then by keyed into the floor plan for future reference. Figures 6.12a to e diagram examples of where you should place yourself. From these locations, document what you see visually, and with your writ-

ten word, capture your experiences when moving through the space. A digital camera is probably the most vital tool to make use of. Some documentation of the site can be taken via video, although for detail and further documentation, digital images truly are the best.

Remember, it is important to be prepared when you go to the site. Call ahead

TABLE 6.1 EDUCATIONAL DEGREES OF WELLESLEY RESIDENTS

In 2000, those at least 25 years old:

High school degree or higher	97.6%
Bachelor's degree or higher	75.9%
Graduate or professional degree	41.2%

Source: Adapted from Department of Housing and Community Development, 2000.

TABLE 6.2 HOUSEHOLD CONFIGURATION OF WELLESLEY RESIDENTS

In the year 2000, there were 8,594 households in Wellesley, out of which had:

Children under the age of 18 living in the household	39.9%
Married couples living together	67.2%
Female householder with no husband present	7.1%
Someone living alone who was 65 years old or older	10.5%

Source: Adapted from Department of Housing and Community Development, 2000.

TABLE 6.3 HOUSEHOLD AGES OF WELLESLEY RESIDENTS

In 2000, the average household size was 2.70 and the average family size was 3.14. The average age of a person living in Wellesley was:

Under age 18	25.1%
18-24 years old	13.9%
25-44 years old	22.9%
45-64 years old	24.2%
65 years old and older	13.9%

Source: Adapted from the Department of Housing and Community Development

to schedule an appointment. Bring all the tools you might need, including camera, graph paper, tape measure, and a friend or two to help.

Student Example: Fire Station Site

Interior design student Colleen Anderson selected a fire station to employ a reuse and renovation of the space. Her project integrates the documentation of both a written analysis and a visual one.

Interior Existing First Floor Conditions

Primarily, the first floor of the building contains the bays for all the trucks. It also houses the kitchen and dispatcher's office. Originally the kitchen was on the second floor; however, the client's needs became too large for this space, and so the kitchen was relocated to the first floor.

Today the second floor consists of the firefighter's barracks, training room, gym,

bathroom, EMT office, chief's office, and miscellaneous storage. The building still has its original wood paneling as well as a tin ceiling, brass fire pole, and many of its original light fixtures. All of this was visually documented with photographs.

When the building was first built in 1899, there were three brass fire poles that were usable. Today, only one still exists and is out of commission due to building and safety hazards. In addition, in the building's original floor plan, there were no sleeping quarters for the firefighters. These were added around the perimeter of the training room. Therefore, no natural light was emitted into that large space that is used for training.

Figure 6.15 shows the existing floor plan and the existing conditions of the second floor. Notice the difference in the height of the original woodwork compared to the added partition along the southwest wall. Detailed photographs were taken of this

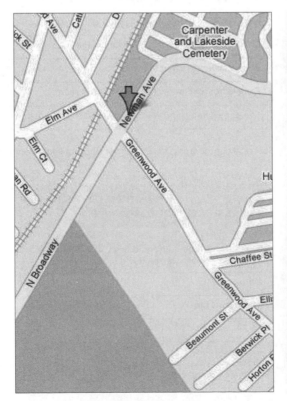

FIGURE 6.10A & B These maps identify the exact street location for the proposed project.

as well. There is also a variation in ceiling height in the main training room in contrast to that of their lounge and EMT office, where through several renovations, the ceiling was dropped from the original tin and typical ceiling tiles were employed. The building has many large windows that have been boxed in with small rooms, causing the majority of natural light to be wasted (Anderson, 2007).

Locating Floor and Site Plans

Locating floor and site plans is an important exercise to explore especially for students selecting a potential building and site for a project. The town hall, in most cases, is where the building department is located, and you can obtain existing site and floor plans for some structures there. Another option is to contact the owner, developer, builder, or architect of the structure directly. If you state that you are using the plans solely for academic purposes, in most cases people will be helpful. Also, many plans for public and historical buildings can be found online by conducting a detailed search. One very clever student found a building that was for sale and contacted the real estate broker, seeking a copy of the plans and requesting a visit to the site. When the student explained he was seeking to explore alternative retail uses for the tenant space, not only did the realtor agree but he also requested a copy of the final project to put on display for potential clients to think about alterative retail options for the space.

Needless to say, it is helpful to think outside the box. Many benefited from the example above. The student gained access to a building, the realtor obtained a unique tool to help lease the space, and the student also gained some exposure from having work on display. If your building has some historical significance, you could call the local town historical society and visit the

FIGURE 6.11 An Internet search via satellite provides a realistic view of a proposed project.

town hall. Most historians are eager to help and share their knowledge.

A COMPLETE SITE ANALYSIS

This chapter aimed to share a variety of approaches to documenting a site analysis. A complete site analysis could encompass the following:

Part 1: Overview of the state
- Introduction (text)
- Maps (images)
- Major forms of transportation (air, train, highway)

Part 2: Overview of the town
- Introduction (text)
- Information about the community (text and images)
- Places of particular interest (text and images)
- Demographics

Part 3: Overview of the site
- Introduction to the structure
- Location and street (text and images)
- Visual Documentation: as diagramed in Figure 6.13.
  - Surrounding structures—noted as 1 in Figure 6.13
  - Exterior of the building—noted as 2 in Figure 6.13

FIGURE 6.12A Front façade of site.

FIGURE 6.12D Rear façade, view 3, of site.

FIGURE 6.12B Rear façade, view 1, of site.

FIGURE 6.12E Satellite view of site.

FIGURE 6.12C Rear façade, view 2, of site.

- Interior of the building—noted as 3 in figure 6.13
- Zoning and building codes

Part 4: Conclusion
- Identify design constraints and limitations related to the site.
- Address both the interior and exterior

The best resources to retrieve this information are found on the Web site of the town where the project site is to be located. You can then review any state-specific codes. You might also defer to International Code Council. Its Web site (www.iccsafe.org/index.html) currently has a map where you can see what state has adopted the ICB. The International Building Code (IBC) is adopted at the state or local level in 50 states plus Washington, D.C. Such codes include the following:

- **International Residential Code** (IRC) is adopted at the state or local level in 46 states plus Washington, D.C.
- **International Fire Code** (IFC) is adopted at the state or local level in 41 states plus Washington, D.C.
- International Plumbing Code (IPC) is adopted at the state or local level in 35 states and Washington, D.C.
- International Mechanical Code (IMC) is adopted at the state or local level in

47 states and Washington, D.C.

- The International Fuel Gas Code (IFGC) is adopted at the state or local level in 46 states and Washington, D.C. (http://www.iccsafe.org/government/adoption.html, 2008).
- ADA codes and guidelines can be retrieved from the Website www.access-board.gov/.

At this stage, try to identify design constraints and limitations that might have surfaced at this point relating to the site. It might be that the existing building has

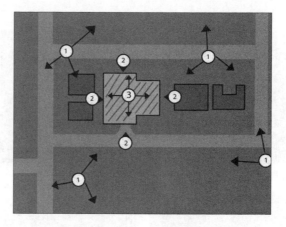

FIGURE 6.13 Digram to help you visually document the site.

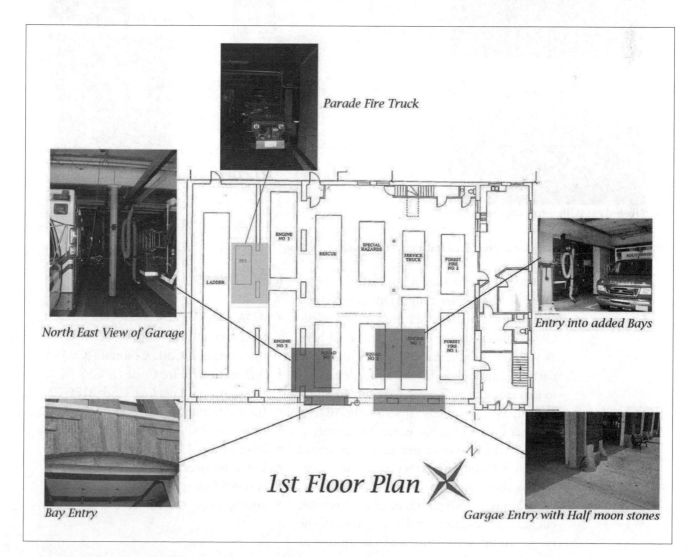

FIGURE 6.14 Floor plan with interior visual documentation of firehouse, first floor.

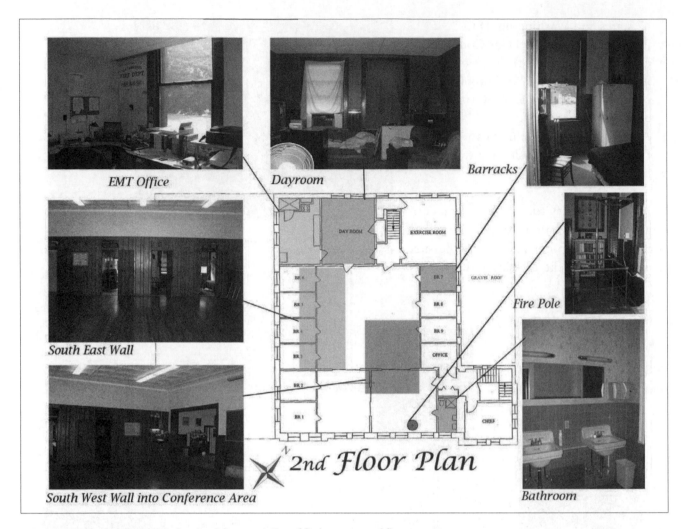

EMT Office
Dayroom
Barracks
South East Wall
Fire Pole
DAY ROOM
EXERCISE ROOM
GRAVEL ROOF
BR 6
BR 7
BR 5
BR 8
BR 4
BR 9
BR 3
OFFICE
BR 2
BR 1
CHIEF
2nd Floor Plan
South West Wall into Conference Area
Bathroom

FIGURE 6.15 Floor plan with interior visual documentation of firehouse, second floor.

limited views, or that it's a historic structure, or that it isn't in ADA compliance and ramps and elevators need to be added. Observations to a site can be included here as well; these might include vehicular flow patterns, and views from interior locations to exterior and vice versa. Daylight analysis encompassing various times of the year is another factor to explore and document.

Your clients might ask you to compare two sites from which they will select one, basing their decision on your analysis. As programmer, your goal is to give the reader, client, and designer a holistic picture of the town, community, site, and conditions at the point you document them.

KEY TERMS

- ADA codes
- International Building Code (IBC)
- International Code Council (ICC)
- International Fire Code (IFC)
- International Fuel Gas Code (IFGC)
- International Mechanical Code (IMC)
- International Plumbing Code (IPC)
- International Residential Code (IRC)
- Location overview
- way-finding
- zoning map

CHAPTER 7

Precedent Studies

After reading this chapter, you should be able to:

- Select appropriate site studies that represent a global perspective.
- Analyze existing examples for a precedent study.
- Document information gleaned from the precedent study to help formulate programmatic requirements.

Imitation may be the highest form of flattery; it's also one of the best ways to learn. We can learn from successes and failures alike, but as designers, our goal is not to imitate success but learn from it and to improve upon it. When a researcher examines successes and failures in something that already exists in order to create something better, it's called a precedent study. Researching examples of what already exists in the realm of one's design topic is a natural process for a designer who's looking to gain insight into a new project.

You would be remiss to approach the design process without taking the time to study what already exists and learn nothing from it. The goal in performing a prec-

edent study of your specific type of design application is to learn from the examples you collect. Thus, analysis of both the strengths and weaknesses of each design are important to document. In order to bolster your project with knowledge gleaned from these previous successes and failures, a precedent study should be performed *before* embarking upon the programming phase of a project.

An example of a precedent study within the built interior environment might be an examination of the various types of color used in educational settings and its potential impact on the users, or circulation patterns in retail design studying the relationship between the consumers path to sales. Numerous studies have been completed on topics that directly relate to virtually every existing aspect of interior design.

Within the design curriculum, it is required that students undertake a precedent study analysis during their education. Your precedent should parallel the type of design that you are employing; hence, you, the researcher, can glean great insight from the study and analysis of different design solutions to the same type of application. The analysis and critique of existing design solutions can take place at many levels throughout your educational experience, and should lay a strong foundation that you can put to work for you throughout your professional design career.

A PRECEDENT STUDY MODEL

The following is a model to use when selecting, documenting, and analyzing precedent studies. As outlined in Chapter 4, "Research Methods," there are many qualitative and quantitative methods that could be applicable in analyzing any given precedent study. Modify this model to meet your needs for any given design project.

- **Step 1: Introduction**—List an overview of each project or site that you have selected to analyze as part of the precedent study. Identify it by name, address, state, and country of its location.
- **Step 2: Description of Each Site**—Write a description for each site. Discuss the same kinds of observations from each site for consistent data comparison, and include a written analysis.
- **Step 3: Qualitative Analysis of Each Site**—Employing a thick or thin description in your analysis, analyze the written content that has been collected from the sites. Identify common and recurring themes that emerge. Examples of a thematic analysis are discussed later in this chapter.
- **Step 4: Quantitative Analysis of Each Site**—Analyze the site's programmatic requirements and create a chart or matrix that outlines the spaces included within each requirement. The matrix-hart could expand to include not only physical requirements but amenities offered as well; examples of this are included in this chapter.
- **Step 5: Summary of Findings**—Document what was gleaned from the above information and analysis.

- **Step 6: Conclusion**—From the precedent study analysis, how and what will impact your design topic and programmatic requirements.

SELECTING YOUR PRECEDENT STUDY

Students should select examples of sites that represent a **global perspective**. As a design student, you should be aware of world views and design considerations that are relevant and can be embraced by all, also noting cultural and regional differences. The precedent study should examine the operations, design layouts, features, amenities, and anything that the researcher feels would help in designing a similar space.

In general, it is advantageous to pick five to eight sites. You will then have accumulated a substantial amount of data that can then be analyzed.

Select examples that are from all over the world. There are numerous ways to obtain this information. You may want to make a site visit to specific locations, where you can employ an observational research method that includes interviews and photos; this might then culminate in a thick description of your site observation. You might obtain further information by generating a questionnaire and sending it out to target groups. You can always gather information from books, journals, and magazines. The Internet is a great resource as well, especially when you are trying to represent a global perspective.

To locate precedent study examples, it is imperative to deeply search all areas of information, from locally accessible library reference books and magazines to reliable online databases. To narrow the search, it is helpful to use descriptive words from your key focus areas. Some locations may have more than one study done, either how the site has changed through time or how the site is considered by different perspectives. For example, City Hall in Boston was built in the Brutalist Modern style during the 1950s to the 1970s. (See Figures 7.1 and 7.2.) It is viewed very differently by designers, who appreciate the style, and by city employees who work in the building and might feel otherwise. The exterior greatly influences the interior. It could be interesting to compare different author's viewpoints of the same site.

When you feel a sufficient amount of data has been collected, it is important to read through each piece, noting key facts or information related to your design focus. Generally, the more noteworthy the resources are, the more likely you are to be able to find the research cited in other works.

FIGURE 7.1 An exterior view of Boston City Hall.

FIGURE 7.2 An interior view of Boston City Hall.

Once you have compiled all of the data to analyze from the sites, make sure that you study the same information from each one. You want to be absolutely sure your analysis plan will be a feasible task. In doing so, be sure to perform the following steps:

- Document the location, size, and interior spaces as well as the exterior.
- Identify what is unique about your example.
- Document your response using a "thick description" technique.
- Use visuals.
- List all the amenities.
- Document unique features.
- If a Web site is available, look to see if it has a mission statement.
- If it is a public space, look to see if customers have written reviews.

Try to consolidate all the information for each site into a template. The template suggested here is very generic, as the applications of design can vary tremendously. When you create your template, be sure that you will be able to retain the same information from each site in order to allow for consistent data comparison.

A MIXED METHOD APPROACH TO PRECEDENT STUDIES

Through each step of the precedent study, always keep in mind that your goal is to gain greater insight into the type of design that you are researching. Also be mindful that the knowledge gained here will be of tremendous value during the next phases of the design process. This cannot be overstated.

It is wise to keep a sketchbook as a way to visually document ideas, or inspirations that might surface, so you can capture the essence of the idea for later use. When analyzing the data collected from the research, you should look at the information using both quantitative and qualitative skills.

Quantitative Analysis to Precedent Studies

At this point in the project, most students are very curious about the existing program requirement for each space. Identifying core requirements is a common approach to analyzing the different precedent examples. Unique spaces might also be identified that could make the difference in a design. Including a simple matrix in your precedent study to analyze the locations seems to work best in this application.

For example, say you have chosen to design a jazz club for your senior thesis. Prior to designing, you should look at other jazz clubs and learn what makes them successful and where areas of improvement can be incorporated. After deciding on the feel of the jazz club, you set out to find locations that combine jazz clubs with a modern-style bar and lounge. You choose these two aspects to research because you wish to combine the feel of jazz and the modern style in the final design. Your precedent studies would be chosen from all over the world so you could get a better idea of the programmatic requirements and design aesthetic that might be included in the design of your jazz club.

After you determine the sites for your precedent study, you gather all the functions of the study—the color palette, furniture style, what seemed to work and what did not, and the lighting of all the studies. After these are determined, you organize your findings by employing various charts. These charts allow you to take a holistic view of the sample that was examined.

You select six sites for your precedent study (PS) to review. Representing a global perspective, these include: Page, Tokyo, Japan (PS-1); Crow Bar, Auckland, New Zealand (PS-2); Mandarin Bar, London,

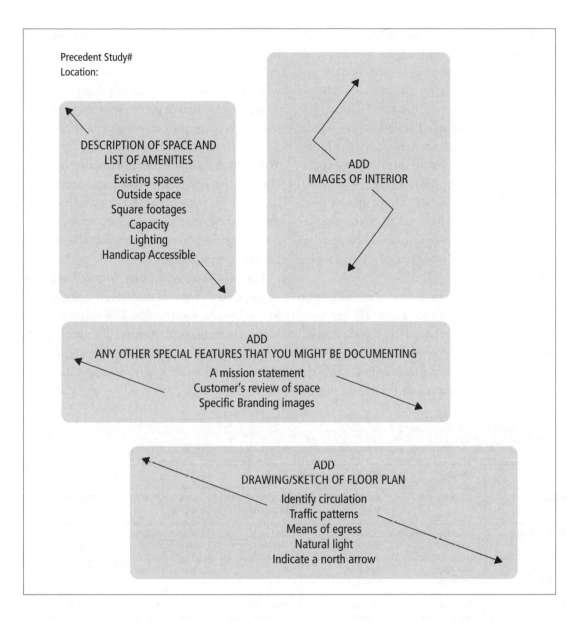

Precedent Study#
Location:

DESCRIPTION OF SPACE AND
LIST OF AMENITIES

Existing spaces
Outside space
Square footages
Capacity
Lighting
Handicap Accessible

ADD
IMAGES OF INTERIOR

ADD
ANY OTHER SPECIAL FEATURES THAT YOU MIGHT BE DOCUMENTING

A mission statement
Customer's review of space
Specific Branding images

ADD
DRAWING/SKETCH OF FLOOR PLAN

Identify circulation
Traffic patterns
Means of egress
Natural light
Indicate a north arrow

FIGURE 7.3 A visual diagram of a precedent study template, created by Rose Mary Botti-Salitsky.

England (PS-3); Buddy Guy's Legends, Chicago, Illinois (PS-4); Iridium Jazz Club, New York, New York (PS-5); and Stampen, Stockholm, Sweden (PS-6) (N. Heerdt, 2007). Once you have collected the data, both quantitative and qualitative, for each site, you document an analysis of them all. After gathering information from each, you then take a closer analysis, looking at location, function, design details, and similarities between them, if any. In doing so, you are integrating both the qualitative and quantitative research as part of your analysis.

Student Example: Jazz Club

Nicole Heerdt is an interior design student exploring a Jazz Club for her senior thesis project. For a first step, Heerdt decided to generate a comparison chart showing the location of each site in her precedent study. In total, they represented a worldwide study. This comparison chart also organized and focused on the design details of each location; these details included lighting, color scheme, and the furniture found throughout each bar.

Comparison charts help organize the design aspects of each site. In this case, the chart demonstrates that some jazz clubs provide an additional source of entertainment for their customers, such as dancing. It also identifies from the selected sample that the most popular color scheme was neutral with accents. The lighting in all the locations featured an array of techniques, all of which focus on an intimate and relaxing atmosphere for customers.

Heerdt's "Amenities" chart differs from the comparison chart in that the former aims to identify programmatic spaces that are included within each of the site (see Table 7.2).

In most cases these sites have common programmatic spaces. They all featured bars, and half of them either had lounges or stages. This comparison proved very useful, as it identified that only two in the sample group had a dance floor, and one included a cigar divan. Such information will be invaluable in developing the programming requirements of the potential space; when looking for typical requirements, the designer can also explore what might be included as a unique feature in the space.

Student Example: Sustainable School

For her senior thesis project, Samantha Roblee, an interior design student, explored primary and secondary school environments that were also sustainable and in LEED compliance.

For this project, Roblee focused on academic structures and employed sustainability to their environments. The selection and focus encompassed two topics that might not always be found simultaneously; hence, the approach was slightly modified. In order to analyze and depict what was success-

TABLE 7.1 COMPARISON CHART: SIX SITE STUDIES

	PS- 1	PS- 2	PS- 3	PS- 4	PS- 5	PS- 6
NAME	**PAGE**	**CROW BAR**	**MANDARIN BAR**	**BUDDY GUY'S LEGEND**	**IRIDIUM JAZZ CLUB**	**STAMPEN**
Location	Tokyo, Japan	Auckland, New Zealand	London, England	Chicago, Illinois	New York City, New York	Stockholm, Sweden
Function	Bar and Lounge	Bar and Lounge	Bar and Lounge	Bar	Bar and Club	Bar
Lighting	Pendants, table lamps, uplighting	Spotlights, wall sconces, candles, pendants	Uplighting, Accent lighting, recessed lighting	Recessed lighting, Track lighting	Pendants, Track lighting	Pendants, Candles, Track lighting
Color Scheme	Neutral: Beige and Black	Accent: Rich Red Neutral: Black	Neutral: Variations of Browns and ochres. Accent: Deep Rich Orange	Black	Pale Rose	Neutral: Taupe
Furniture	Modern Leather Armchairs and Couches	Modern Leather Booths	Art Deco Inspired Bar Chairs and Armchairs	Wooden Dining Style tables and Chairs	Wooden Dining Style table and Chairs	Wooden Bar style stools and tables
Entertainment	None	Dancing	None	Live Music	Live Music	Live Music, Dancing

Source: N. Heerdt, 2007.

TABLE 7.2 AMENITIES CHART FOR PRECEDENT STUDY

AMENITIES	PS- 1	PS-2	PS-3	PS-4	PS-5	PS-6	PERCENTAGE
2 or more floors	No	Yes	No	No	No	Yes	33.33%
Bar	Yes	Yes	Yes	Yes	Yes	Yes	100%
Lounge	Yes	Yes	Yes	No	No	No	50%
Kitchen	Yes	No	No	Yes	Yes	No	50%
-If Yes, kind of food	Appetizers	—	—	Louisiana Style	Tapas	—	—
Dance floor	No	Yes	No	No	No	No	16.67%
Gallery	Yes	No	No	No	No	No	16.67%
Pool Room	No	Yes	No	No	No	No	16.67%

Source: N. Heerdt, 2007.

ful and where improvements were needed, she categorized her precedent study in two equal sections. The academic precedents were strictly limited to renovated school structures, while the sustainable section of the precedent study were to include new and renovated schools that applied sustainable design attributes.

The academic sites (APS) included the Grand View Elementary School in Manhattan Beach, California (APS-1), and the Ben Davis High School in Indianapolis, Indiana (APS-2). Additionally, information was compared and contrasted between the Buffalo, New York-based East Aurora Senior High (APS-3) and the North Warren Central School in Chestertown, New York (APS-4). The sustainable sites for the precedent study (SPS) included Diébédo Francis Kéré's Gando Primary School, Gando Vilage, Burkina Faso, a West African nation (SPS-1); the Newton South High School in Massachusetts (SPS-2); the Bamboo Primary School in Vietnam (SPS-3); and the Druk White Lotus School in India (SPS-4) (Roblee, 2007, p. 57).

The information that Roblee selected to compare in this sample group specifically focused on seeking information on two issues: sustainability and educational K-12 facilities. Roblee chose to focus on this information because it was a key factor that the researcher was aiming to learn more from the precedent study analysis.

The sustainable precedent study matrixes showed that the most substantial contribution to "green" considerations was through use of simplistic systems and local and/or recycled materials. **Passive sustainable systems**, including natural lighting, energy-efficient utilities and fixtures, solar heating and cooling, natural ventilation, and site orientation, were clearly the easiest to adapt to an array of varying environments. However, LEED qualifications would maintain the foundation for further sustainable enhancements (Roblee, 2007, p.73).

Student Example: Spa

As Erin Anthony, an interior design student, began to explore program requirements necessary in designing a spa, her precedent study focused on day spas in the United States and abroad in order to gain a global perspective on the subject. The five sites selected were SenSpa of San Francisco

TABLE 7.3 COMPARISON CHART: FOUR SITE STUDIES

	SITE STUDY #1	SITE STUDY #2	SITE STUDY #3	SITE STUDY #4
	NEWTON SOUTH HIGH SCHOOL	**GANDO PRIMARY SCHOOL**	**L'ÉCOLE SAUVAGE /BAMBOO PRIMARY SCHOOL**	**DRUK WHITE LOTUS SCHOOL**
Site Location	Newton, MA	Gando Village, Burkina Faso, West Africa	Luong Son Village, Nha Trang, Vietnam	Shey, Ladakh, India
SUSTAINABILITY				
Solar Power	*			*
Local Materials	*	*	*	*
Site Orientation		*	*	*
Recycled Materials	*	*	*	*
Carpet Tiles	*			
Low-Zero VOCs	*	*	*	
Natural Ventilation		*	*	*
Natural Lighting	*	*	*	*
Energy Efficient Utilities/Fixtures	*	*	*	*
Rain Water Collection System				*
Low-Flush Toilets	*			
Gardens		*		*
Solar Heating Cooling Insulation		*	*	*
LEED Qualification: Schools Registered Certified Gold Platinum	Registered	N/A	N/A	N/A
Collaborative for High Performance Schools (CHPS)	Best Practices Manual	N/A	N/A	N/A

Source: S. Rooblee, 2007.

(PS-1); Rain Spa of Quebec (PS-2); Villaggio Day Spa of Fishers, Indiana (PS-3); Adamina Spa of London (PS-4); and The Maui Spa and Wellness Center of Boca Raton, Florida (PS-5) .

The first table focuses on the various types of treatment rooms, including the quantity and facilities offered by each spa (see Table 7.5). The second analysis of the five selected sites focused on the types of treatments and services offered to customers by each spa (See Table 7.6). This is an essential part of the research, as it gives an allusion to what needs to be included in the proposed project in order to make it a successful business.

The goal of this precedent study analysis was to gather valuable information by studying projects similar to the one being proposed as a senior thesis project. With data analy-

TABLE 7.4 COMPARISON CHART OF SUSTAINABILITY APPLICATIONS IN THE FOUR SITE STUDIES

SUSTAINABILITY	NUMBER RATIO	TOTAL PERCENTAGE
Solar Power	2:4	50%
Local Materials	4:4	100%
Site Orientation	3:4	75%
Recycled Materials	4:4	100%
Carpet Tiles	1:4	25%
Low-Zero VOCs	3:4	75%
Natural Ventilation	3:4	75%
Natural Lighting	4:4	100%
Energy Efficient Utilities/Fixtures	4:4	100%
Rain Water Collection System	1:4	25%
Low-Flush Toilets	1:4	25%
Gardens	2:4	50%
Solar Heating Cooling Insulation	3:4	75%
LEED Certification:	1:4	25%

Source: S. Roblee, 2007.

sis, valuable information was acquired as to what should be included in the program and design of the proposed spa project. Key indicators identified that the following facilities should included in the program: treatment rooms, relaxation rooms, retail areas, cafés, and exercise areas. Also, it is important to include in the proposed project a wide variety of treatments. These treatments range from massages to herbal medicine. Based on the study, the treatments offered should fall under three basic categories: facial care, body care, and aesthetics.

Additionally, the proposed project should incorporate and focus on themes such as relaxation, rejuvenation, and the body, each of which would be similar to those seen in the precedent study. The design, as well as the business, should be one that evokes relaxation, wellness, rejuvenation, and tranquility within its clients. Overall, the space should consist of soothing qualities and atmospheres to ensure that customers can focus on rejuvenating their body, mind, and spirit (Anthony, 2007 p. 48).

As seen in the preceding precedent studies, when students look at programmatic requirements of existing designs based on what they are aiming to achieve, a quantitative analysis of program spaces is helpful in creating and justifying the program.

Qualitative Analysis to Precedent Studies

Exploring a qualitative analysis to the precedent study exposes many issues that can significantly influence design decision making as well. An example that can be used in analyzing written content that has been collected from the precedent study is the identification of common and recurring themes that emerge. The thematic analysis process starts with the collection of data.

TABLE 7.5 TYPES OF TREATMENT ROOMS AND FACILITIES AT FIVE SPAS					
ANALYSIS OF TREATMENT ROOMS/ FACILITIES	SENSPA SAN FRANCISCO, CA	RAIN SPA QUEBEC, CANADA	VILLAGGIO DAY SPA FISHERS, IN	ADAMINA SPA LONDON, ENGLAND	MAUI SPA AND WELLNESS CENTER BOCA RATON, FL
Treatment Rooms	N/A	N/A	N/A	6	10
Sauna	N/A	N/A	N/A	N/A	1
Steam Room	N/A	N/A	N/A	1	1
Relaxation Rooms	N/A	N/A	2	1	1
Changing Rooms	N/A	N/A	N/A	2	N/A
Retail Space	N/A	1	N/A	1	1
Nail Rooms	N/A	1	1	1	1
Salon	N/A	N/A	1	N/A	1
Check- In/ Reception	1	1	1	1	1
Café	N/A	N/A	N/A	N/A	1

Source: E. Anthony, 2007.

Once the data is organized, "patterns of experiences can be listed [which] can come from direct quotes or paraphrasing common ideas" (Aronson, 1994, ¶4). Once the data is coded, themes serve as a focus derived from patterns (Aronson). Eisner (2002) refers to this as identifying the thematics of the data. This method would be a considered a qualitative approach to analyzing data. Chapter 4 reviews this research method, as well as other qualitative approaches.

Student Example: Vineyard

Liz Carter is an interior design student, exploring the topic of a winery for her senior thesis project. In her precedent study for her winery project, Carter used the Microsoft Word search tool to tally repeating words, phrases, and passages. It is important to make sure that you can obtain similar information from each site that you are analyzing. Repeated words are identified

and can be assigned a color. Carter selected five different sites: Nashoba Valley Winery, Bolton, Massachusetts (PS-1); Wagner Vineyards, Lodi, New York (PS-2); The Round Barn Winery, Baroda Michigan (PS-3); Rio Grande, New Mexico (PS-4); Embudo Station's New Mexico; and Vintara Estate, New Zealand (PS-5). Content was taken from the main Web page of the vineyard corresponding to each site. The description of each winery was then copied and pasted into a Word document. Once the document was formed, a word search was conducted identifying reoccurring words or themes that might have emerged, aiming to characterize common themes throughout the study. As seen in Figure 7.5 and Table 7.8. The most common words found were noted, keyed, and color-coded. They were then categorized and charted by the most prevalent repeated words down to the least repetitive. Also noted were the

TABLE 7.6 TYPES OF SERVICES AT FIVE SPAS

ANALYSIS OF TREATMENTS AND SERVICES	SENSPA, SAN FRANCISCO, CA	RAIN SPA, QUEBEC, CANADA	VILLAGGIO DAY SPA FISHERS, IN	ADAMINA SPA, LONDON, ENGLAND	MAUI SPA AND WELLNESS CENTER, BOCA RATON, FL	PERCENT YES FOR ALL SPAS
Massage	Yes	Yes	Yes	Yes	Yes	100%
Facials	Yes	Yes	Yes	Yes	Yes	100%
Peels	Yes	No	No	Yes	No	40%
Waxing	Yes	Yes	No	Yes	Yes	80%
Hot Stone	Yes	No	Yes	Yes	Yes	80%
Microdermabrasion	Yes	Yes	Yes	Yes	No	80%
Mud Therapy	Yes	No	Yes	No	No	40%
Acupuncture	Yes	No	No	No	Yes	40%
Herbal Medicine	Yes	No	No	No	Yes	40%
Body Scrubs	No	No	Yes	No	Yes	40%
Body Wraps	No	Yes	Yes	Yes	Yes	80%
Hair Removal	No	Yes	No	Yes	No	40%
Manicure/Pedicure	No	Yes	Yes	Yes	Yes	80%
Reflexology	No	Yes	Yes	No	Yes	60%
Gentleman Services	No	No	Yes	Yes	Yes	60%
Couples Services	No	No	Yes	No	Yes	40%
Mom-To-Be Services	Yes	No	Yes	Yes	Yes	80%
Salon Services	No	No	Yes	No	Yes	40%
Meditation	Yes	No	No	No	Yes	40%
Exercise Programs	Yes	No	No	No	Yes	40%
Total Yes	12	8	13	11	16	- - -
Total No	8	12	7	9	4	- - -

Source: E. Anthony, 2007.

number of times the word appeared. This was executed to identify common themes that emerged.

The data identified that the most common theme between the sites were wine; it was used at least 30 times in all the opening statements. Other themes found between these sites were in the words winery, beer, brewery, and restaurants" (L. Carter, 2007, p. 49). These themes could have a significant impact in identifying programmatic requirements, as well as design aesthetic.

Student Example: Loft Space
Ashley Benander, an interior design student, explored the topic of residential loft

FIGURE 7.4 Identi-
fication of common
themes, created by
Ashley Benander,
2007.

Breakdown of Reoccuring Words; in Order of Importance

MOST IMPORTANT
Space is the most popular
and most important when
designing a loft.

MOST IMPORTANT
Light was in the middle
showing an amount
of significance.

LEAST IMPORTANT
Exposed was last,
therefore style of the space
is least important.

Nashoba- Located in the heart of Massachusetts' apple country, Nashoba Valley Winery is a stunning hilltop orchard overlooking the charming town of Bolton. Always growing and ever-beautiful, we are open daily throughout the year, with the exception of The Fourth of July, Thanksgiving Day, Christmas Day and New Year's Day. Since first producing superior fruit wines in 1978, Nashoba Valley Winery has earned wide acclaim as a pioneering winery orchard and a premier destination for visitors seeking excellent wine, exquisitely prepared food, and a gorgeous country setting. The family-owned orchard, winery & restaurant, set on 52 rolling acres, boasts a state-of-the art wine-making and distillation facility, an exceptional wine and gift shoppe, a brewery, and a gourmet restaurant.

With over 100 national and international medals to its credit and accolades from such noteworthy publications as "Boston Magazine", "Wine Enthusiast", "Cooking Light", "Food & Wine", "The Yankee Magazine" 2003 Editors Choice, and "Community Newspaper Company 2004 Readers Choice Award, Nashoba Valley Winery is the ultimate destination for any wine connoisseur. We take the art of winemaking seriously. And with over 20 varieties of wines, a variety of hand crafted beers and distilled spirits, Nashoba Valley is dedicated to quality and is recognized as a premium producer. From its beginning until today, Nashoba Valley remains a family owned winery with our focus on quality and value at the forefront of all we do. Plan a visit to a truly unique American farm and learn why Nashoba Valley was selected as one of the ultimate destination places on the east coast.

Wagner- Wagner offers the most comprehensive tour of any Finger Lakes winery. The tour encompasses all facets of the winemaking operation as well as the viticultural practices important to the production of quality wine grapes. A tasting of a wide selection of our wines and non-alcoholic grape juice follows the tour. Visitors can also take a self-guided brewery tour and taste our craft-brewed beers. **Pub Nights on the Brewdeck** are held every Friday from Memorial Day weekend through Labor Day weekend, with live entertainment, great wine, beer & food on the brewery deck. Visitors can then browse in our retail wine shop where all of our wines and beers are available for sale.

The Round Barn- The Round Barn Winery is a family-owned and operated winery, distillery and brewery and is nestled in the rolling hills of the Southwest Michigan countryside. We specialize in hand-crafted wines, fruit brandies, vodka and microbrews.

Our tasting room is located in a turn of the century post and beam bank barn originally built in 1881 while our still and Banquet/Wedding facilities are housed in our unique Amish-built round barn.

Embudo- At the Embudo Station restaurant you might choose to enjoy our succulent barbequed ribs, charbroiled steaks, grilled chicken, or a variety of authentic New Mexican dishes. People travel for miles to enjoy our unique oak smoked rainbow trout. There are many vegetarian choices, as well as salads, on our menus. Lunches feature choices of sandwiches, including our famous Brisket Sandwich. Along with these choices, try one of our fresh brewed beers or a glass of award winning local wine.

Vintara Estate - Vintara is operated by Lisa and Michael Murtagh. Michael and Lisa were born just down the road (Michael literally married the girl next door) from the Vintara vineyard, having worked in the wine business for over 20 years both in Australia and in many parts of the world, they returned to setup Vintara and reside in the Rutherglen region.

Michael makes the beers and the wines as well as managing the 50 hectares of vineyards, Lisa manages the office and general operations.

Gavin Swalwell, our chef, moved from Melbourne six years ago to run the kitchen at a renowned local restaurant and has never looked back. Gavin's love of traditional flavours, using local products and then presenting them in a contemporary way lifts the food at Vintara to great heights.

Steve Wallace our cellar door and brewery bar manager has over 25 years experience in managing Rutherglen cellar doors and his expertise in our wines and those of the region make him a great guy to talk to about wine and the region, where to stay and what to do.

Alicia Martin is our Restaurant front-of-house and functions manager - give her a call or drop in to see what we have to offer those looking for a unique and pleasurable function experience.

FIGURE 7.5 Analyz-
ing and indentifying
reoccurring words,
created by Liz Carter,
2007.

spaces for her senior thesis project. She employed a qualitative approach in her exploration of lofts. She analyzed five sites for her precedent study, the first three representing a global perspective with the remaining two located within the United States: Oliver's Wharf, London, England (PS-1); The West Shinjuku Lofts, Tokyo, Japan (PS-2); The New River Head Lofts, London, England (PS-3); The O'Malley Residence, Avoca, Pennsylvania (PS-4); The Bay Loft, San Francisco, California (PS-5); and The Pavonia Loft, Jersey City, New Jersey (PS-6).

Table 7.7 lists words that Benander found and the number of times they repeated throughout the six sites. "The first word identified within the table is "Light," which showed up six times. This was not unexpected, as many clients in the precedent study expressed the need for "natural light, a lot of light and a light feel to the environment."

Another reoccurring word was "space"; this word showed up the most out of all identified words from the sample. This is very important when you consider lofts and how one occupies them. "Warehouse" was identified eight times, which displays a uniting factor of historic origins, as many of the spaces have been converted from warehouse industrial use to residential-home use. Another popular word found was "original." This could be reflecting the occupancies' desire to maintain the "original" integrity of the building as a high priority among loft designers/owners (Benander, 2007. p. 41).

The next step was to not only look at words and the amount of times they were repeated but to then try and generate common themes. The chart in Figure 7.4 aims to prioritize the words found and shows visually where these words fall in the realm of importance. "Looking even further into these findings one could conclude

TABLE 7.7 WRITTEN ANALYSIS OF THIN DESCRIPTIONS IDENTIFYING RECURRING WORDS-CONCEPTS IN THE PRECEDENT STUDY

REPEATING WORDS THAT WERE IDENTIFIED	NUMBER OF TIMES USED IN DESCRIPTIVE ANALYSIS OF LOFT
Light	6
Space	14
Warehouse	8
Original	12
Exposed	2
Modern	3
Contemporary	6
Kitchen	6
Steel	5

Source: A. Benander, 2007.

TABLE 7.8 WRITTEN ANALYSIS OF THICK DESCRIPTIONS IDENTIFYING RECURRING WORDS IN THE PRECEDENT STUDY

WORD	# OF TIMES USED
Wine	30
Winery	9
Beer	6
Brewery	5
Restaurant	5
Tour	4
Unique	4
Distill	3
Tasting	2
Variety	2
Gourmet	1
Learn	1

Source: Liz Carter, 2007.

that the actual design of the space, the flow of the rooms and structure are most important. Atmosphere is second to this, such as light and views. And last is the actual style the space is designed in" (Benander, 2007, p.45). Straus and Corbin (1998), who refer to this step as **axial coding**, state that "in axial coding, categories are related to their subcategories to form more precise and complete explanations about phenomena" (p. 124). Chapter 4 explains in more detail this form of research and other approaches. Employing this method of organizing data is very comfortable for designers. As visual thinkers it helps to see things graphically as well.

ANALYZING THE INFORMATION

Once all the data has been sorted and analyzed, it is important to see and document what you have discovered. A synopsis statement should be included as a conclusion to your precedent study. It could reinstate some of the expected outcomes but also identify any unexpected issues that might have surfaced during the precedent study analysis process. It should reflect the five to eight examples that you selected as a sample to study, and document a mixed method approach.

The critique of existing design solutions is common in the design educational experience and within the profession. It is important to train the designer's eye not only in design aesthetic but also in analytical skills that can begin to critique spaces objectively (i.e., to remove personal biases and begin to learn from precedent).

This is a perfect time to predict what you might choose to include in your program of the space you will design based on what you have learned from the precedent study analysis. If you are conducting a precedent study for a client, this is a great tool to analyze existing competitors. The client might aim to emulate some of the programmatic requirements, learning from what exists and planning for future possibilities. This also might be where you include some conceptual and aesthetic findings that surfaced during the study.

KEY TERMS

- Axial coding
- Global perspective
- Passive sustainable systems

CHAPTER 8

Generating the Program

After reading this chapter, you should be able to:

- Generate overall program requirements.
- Generate requirements for each space in your program.
- Calculate square footage and the circulation of a space.

Once the site location and the client's program requirements have been identified, you can compose a list that includes any special features. By program requirements, we mean all the spaces that are needed in order for the site to function. When generating the program for a space, there are a few key aspects to keep in mind. First and foremost are the client's needs and wants, their "must-haves" and their "would-like-to-haves." Second is the data and analysis from the research that you conducted before you began creating this program. These were discussed in previous chapters. Synthesizing both of these factors will help create a program that should meet existing requirements, and anticipate change, such as future growth, or reduction.

The knowledge that you gleaned from the precedent study analysis should be reflected in your program. Your research in the precedent study helped determine necessary spaces to be included in the programmatic requirements. Together, the quantitative and qualitative analyses discussed in the prior chapter should help you create the ideal program for your space.

THE PROPOSED PROGRAM

The program begins to take form as you start to list all the program requirements, determine the circulation, calculate the required square footage, document the existing square footage, and analyze specific needs. Each of these steps are discussed below.

TAKING THE MACRO VIEW

As you may have noticed by now, most programmers find it advantageous to look at everything on a large scale first before delving into the details. After gaining knowledge of the "big picture," programmers only then begin to work their way through the project until every detail has been addressed. This should be an instinctive skill for an interior designer, who is accustomed to observing a space first and then planning for its occupants.

Listing the Program Requirements

The programmer's first task in generating a program is to make a list of program requirements. Most likely at this point in the programming phase, you would have a fairly good idea of what needs to be included from the client's request, interviews, observational studies, and analysis of your precedent study. Remember, by "program requirements," we mean all the spaces that are needed in order for the site to function. When approaching this list, you can look at this task from several vantage points:

- Is there an existing space?
- What is the total square footage of anticipated requirements?
- How much is factored in for circulation?
- How much is factored in for core requirements?
- Do the potential users have projections of growth or downsizing for the next two to three years?
- Are there any special requirements?
- What are the codes that need to be considered?

Document Your Information

To get started, document everything. You need to think of all the individual spaces as well as all necessary support spaces. For example, if you are programming for a retail store, how much space will be allocated for the merchandise? What are the display options? Are the displays freestanding or hanging? What about storage, cash, wrapping, checkout area, circulation, office space, and bathrooms? Sometimes it is easy to overlook details. If, for example, the retail space was specifically set up for apparel, one would

need to add to the program requirements dressing rooms and maybe even a seating area. Document this information in a chart outlining the requirements for your space, including the quantity for each item on this list. The equation in Box 8.1 can help you organize this information and estimate the square footage. Using computer spreadsheet software, like Microsoft Excel, is a great way to organize the material. Design firms typically employ their own standardized templates for organizing this material, as seen in some of the interviews from the design firms throughout the text. Consider Allegro Interior Architecture and Spagnolo/Gisness & Associates, both discussed in Chapter 1; Tsoi/Krobus & Associates in Chapter 5; and MPA | Margulies Perruzzi Architects in Chapter 9. For an academic exercise, however, the template in Figure 8.1 should be sufficient to get you started.

Determining the Circulation

It is important to determine the circulation or space for people to move around that will be allotted. Depending on what percentage is needed for circulation, it can have a significant impact of the size of your other spaces. Typically, circulation should be factored in between 22 to 40 percent. This will vary depending on the type of design project. A low circulation number is often associated with good, efficient space planning. But many factors weigh into this scenario, the most significant being the application for which the space is being designed.

Calculating the Square Footage

Calculating the square footage of your proposed space is important because it gives you a realistic idea for the site and how much room you have to work with. Once you have the program requirements, you can total them. This will give you the total programmatic requirements needed for your site. Then you can figure out how

BOX 8.1 ESTIMATE OF SQUARE FOOTAGE

Space	Quantity	Est. Sq Ft	Total Sq Ft
Add space	How many	Add #	Add total #
Total			#
% of program for Circulation			#
Total Required Square Footage			Add Total #

SCENARIO #1

LEVEL 2

Floor Total SF: 49,226

Departments:

Strategic Partnerships	7444
HR	6744
Finance	6982
DSS	4256

Total Departments: 25426

Common Areas:

NOC	500
Reception	1800
Customer Conf	1000
Training	600
Training Storage	348
Interview	150
Beverage Closet	48
Hotelling	90
Lactation	150
Security	48
Facilities Storage	600
All Staff Meeting	3450
Tel/Data	400

Total Common: 9184

Total Depts & Common: 34610

DELTA: -14,616

LEVEL 3

Floor Total SF: 51,343

Departments:

Tech/Ops	12,618
Manufacturing	3676
Cap Dev	47378

Total Departments: 63672

Common Areas:

Shipping/Receive	250
Man Supply	150
Tel/Data	400

Total Common: 800

Total Depts & Common: 64472

DELTA: 13,129

LEVEL 4

Floor Total SF: 39,667

Departments:

CEO	3,357
Marketing	36,900

Total Departments: 40257

Common Areas:

Tel/Data	400

Total Common: 400

Total Depts & Common: 40657

DELTA: 990

FIGURE 8.1 Generic template for square footage calculations.

much is remaining and determine the circulation or, if there is extra space, decide how it should be allocated.

Most likely, when you conducted the historical, observational, and interactive research, you probably gathered a great deal of relevant information that can help determine the appropriate square footage for each space.

Calculating the square footage of a space can vary based on what formula one opts to employ. It might sound a bit odd that there is not one formula that everyone uses, but there are many factors that come into play, and so formulas must vary to accommodate these differences. For example, if the building is a tenant fit-out and there are common spaces, the landlord would employ a formula that would include a percentage of the "shared spaces" and include this in the square footage cost. If, on the other hand, the building is freestanding and the client owns it, the client will be very aware of every space and how it is going to be used.

Floor Usable Area and Gross Measured Area

It is important to understand what the usable space of a building entails and how to measure the area properly. This calculation can vary based on the type of space you are dealing with and the core components of the space. Following are definitions from the U.S. General Service Administration Facilities:

- **Floor usable area**—Floor usable area is the sum of all office, store, and building common usable areas. Floor usable area is the floor rentable area minus floor common areas that are available primarily for the joint use of tenants on that floor.
- **Gross measured area**—Gross measured area is the total area within the building minus the exterior wall.

Helpful Resources

Resources that can help you find space square-footage standards for specific design applications include the following:

- **American National Standards Institute** (ANSI)—www.ansi.org
- **Building Owners and Managers Association** (BOMA)—www.boma.org
- **The International Facility Managers Association** (IFMA)—www.ifma.org

Documenting the Existing Square Footage

Documenting the existing square footage of the space allows you to see if the program requirements are going to fit into the proposed site. If a few sites are being considered, the total programmatic square footage requirements plus circulation will help you determine what the right space should be. It is helpful to see all the requirements outlined in a list format with the total square footage needed for each space. You can then compare the existing square footage against the proposed square footage; adjustments can then be made where needed.

Student Example: High-Quality, Small-Scale Hotel

Ashley Johnson, an interior design student researched and prepared the programmatic requirements for a high-quality, small-scale hotel. The information that she gathered from the precedent study helped generate programmatic requirements. Table 8.1 shows the areas that are to be included in the proposed hotel. The criteria matrix in Figure 8.2 lends insight into adjacencies and the space-planning phase of design.

Johnson blocked out in concept both the first floor and second floors with the estimated proportion that should be allocated to each space. Also note that she inserted a gray phantom corridor to allocate the circulation. A square footage can then be allocated to it. (See Figure 8.3.)

Analyzing Specific Needs

Once each space and the square footage requirements have been determined on a macro scale, break down each space to analyze the specific needs and document them. For example, within a reception space for an office, you might need to include seating for a certain amount of people, a coat closet, reception desk, task seating, storage, and the like.

Programming for Future Needs

When generating your program, flexibility of design is needed for the optimum use of the total square footage. You might be realistically programming for a longer-range plan that could extend out three to five years.

TABLE 8.1 PROGRAMMIC REQUIREMENTS

MAJOR SPACES	ESTIMATED SQUARE FEET
Check-in/Lobby	870
Lounge/Dining	1,207
Guestrooms (44)	13,860
Kitchen	370
Pool/Hot tub Area	1,045
Employee Office/Lounge	950
Laundry/Storage	1,185
MINOR SPACES	
Public Restroom	41
Fitness Room	508
Gaming/Leisure Room	522
Boiler/Furnace Room	223
Vending/Ice Machine	128
Elevator (1)	64
Stairwells (3)	290

Estimated Square Footage Total: 21,263
Circulation 30%: 6,379
Relevant Codes: Residential Occupancy (R-1), Assembly (A-3), Business (B), Cal. 133, NFPA 701, ADA compliant, ICC/ANSI standard
Source: Ashley Johnson, 2008.

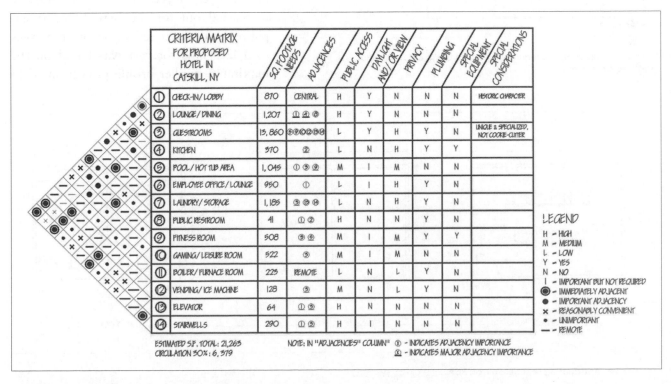

FIGURE 8.2 **Criteria Matrix. Source: Ashley Johnson.**

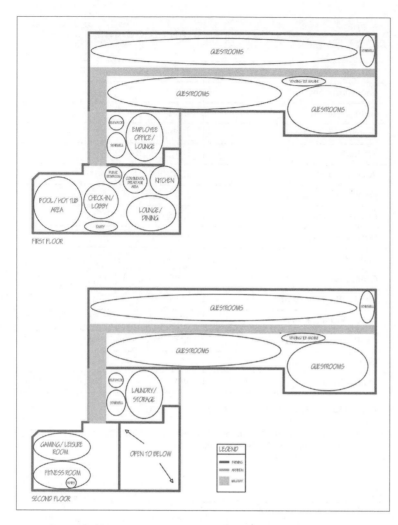

FIGURE 8.3 Blocking out requirements with the phantom corridor indicating circulation.

Space Utilization Studies

Often the programmer is asked to think ahead, planning for the optimum use of space and its utilization. An example of this can be found in the firm profile on Spagnolo/Gisness & Associates in Chapter 1, "What Is Programming?" SG&A analyzes client needs while listing and reflecting on the observational and interactive data that it previously collected. In this case, the client needs a conference room; however, the client's anticipated growth indicates that it will in fact also need more office space within the next few years. Figures 8.4 to 8.7 help the client see how it needs to allocate 300-square-foot spaces for potential future expansion.

Worker Profile Growth and Reduction Analysis

Another example of programming for the future is to analyze the client's projection of worker profile growth and reduction. The chart in Figure 8.8 shows that the firm had 3,742 employees in 1983. The company forecasted out for the year 2000, anticipating a minimal reduction of employees to 3,427. This forecast was based on the maximum worker profile projection of 14

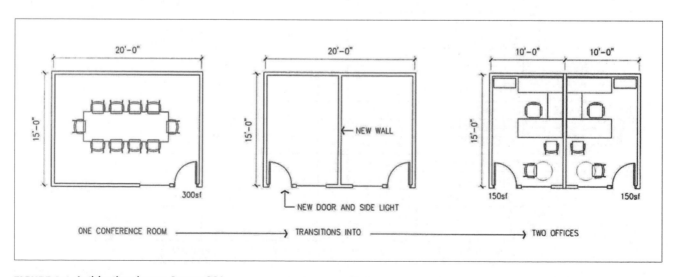

FIGURE 8.4 Anticipating change. Source: SGA.

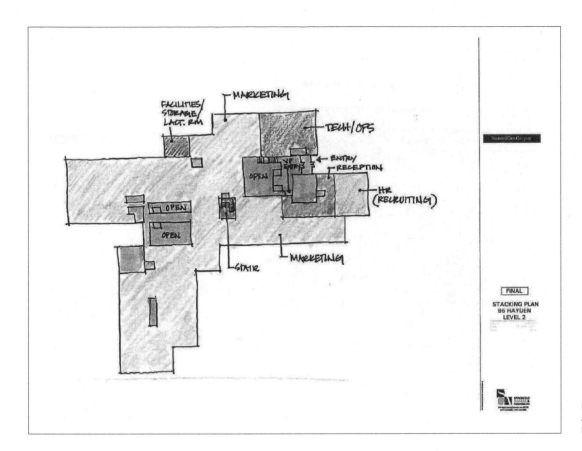

FIGURE 8.5 Example of a freehand blocking diagram 1.

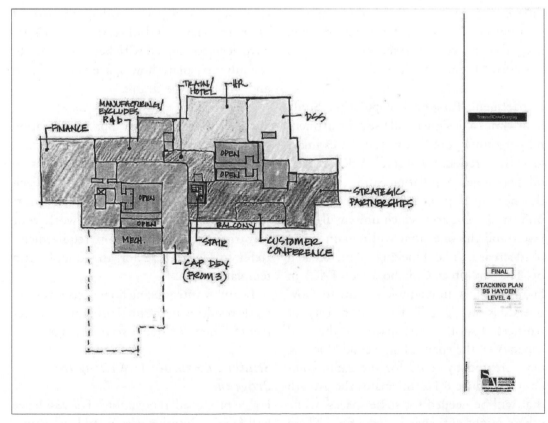

FIGURE 8.6 Example of freehand blocking diagram 2.

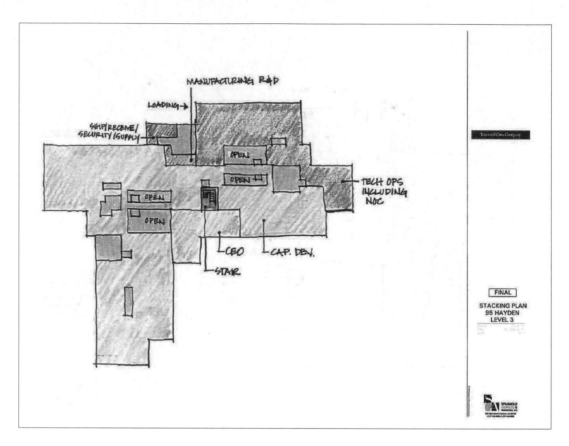

FIGURE 8.7 Example of freehand blocking diagram 3.

different operating units. It's interesting to see that the 1983 forecast was for reduction instead of growth, the trend since the 1990s has been "do more with less."

Department Personnel Population Study
Sometimes a designer will use a departmental personnel population study to estimate growth or reduction in staff. A departmental personnel population study combines the personnel projections with operating units and compares which units will grow faster and the ones that will remain stable or decrease. The blocking plan, created by The Architect Collaborative (TAC) in Figure 8.10, is an example of how to show one division's population and density of workers, visitors to the space and the total capacity of the space. The second blocking plan created by TAC for the same company in Figure 8.11 anticipates the growth that will be needed for some spaces, while others might anticipate a reduction. These

types of blocking plans are diagrammed out after interviews and observational studies have been conducted with key personnel, to visually articulate how space was affected and will be in the future.

Space Utilization Study Space utilization studies often combine written analyzed data that has been gathered with visual concepts. As you begin to document each space with its programmatic requirements, set up a template to help you work your way through each program requirement. Refer to Figure 8.12 for an example of a template to use.

Begin by introducing how decisions were made resulting in the final program requirements. Then document your findings.

Student Example 1: Writing the Program
For a proposed renovation of a residence hall facility, interior design student Jeanna

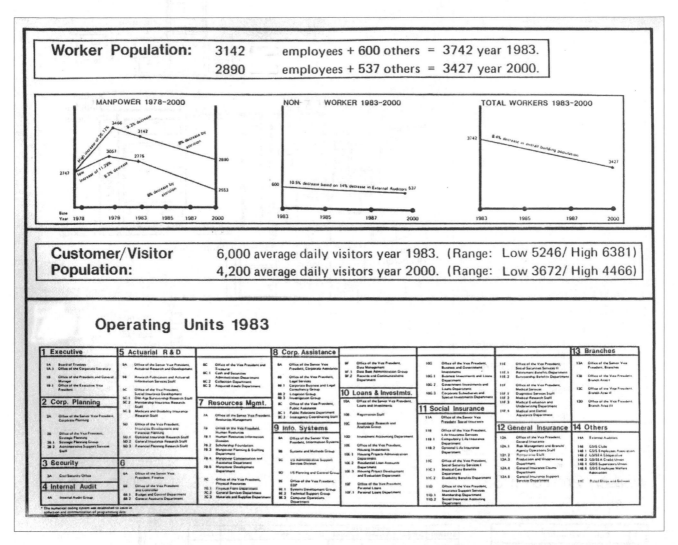

FIGURE 8.8 **Examples of Programming Documentation from The Architects Collaborative's August 17, 1981 Growth Projections.**

Richard first documents that from her precedent study research she was able to outline the amenities and square footages that will be required for students to live comfortably in her proposed residence hall. Table 8.2 is a chart that outlines the proposed space, how many residents it would house, and the total square footage it would require. At the bottom of the chart, the total square footage is documented with the estimated percentage of circulation.

Richard includes a descriptive written introduction as an overview of the program requirements:

The renovation will include suite style rooms, a fitness facility, offices of residence life, a study lounge, kitchens, a laundry facility, entertainment lounges, and apartments for residence life staff. The six residence halls studied in the sample have an average of three hundred and sixty-three square feet of living space available per resident. Currently Residence Hall has one hundred and seventy square feet of living space per student. To create a more comfortable environment and allow for more privacy, the overall resident occupancy will be lowered from three hundred

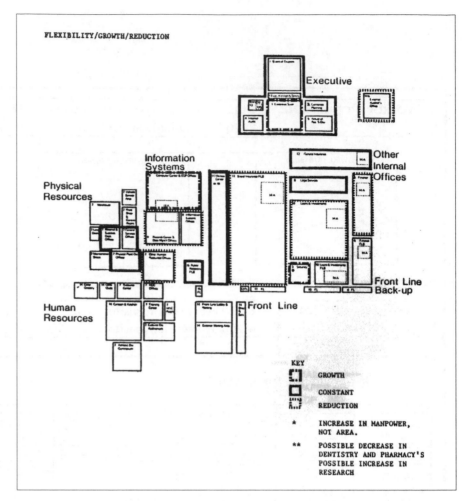

FIGURE 8.9 Examples of Programming Documentation from The Architects Collaborative's August 17, 1981 worker profile projected reduction.

Worker Profile 1983

1983 - 2000

	SOCIAL INSURANCE *	Executive	Colligial	STRUCTURED Managerial	Secretarial	Clerical	Others	TOTAL
11A	Office of the Senior Vice President, Social Insurance	1	1		2	1	1 Utilityman	6
11A.1	Mails and Communications Department	1	1	10	1	34	4 Teletype Operators 2 Post Mach Operators 18 Laborers/Messengers	71
11B	Office of the Vice President, Membership Administration	1	1		1		1 Utilityman	4
11B.1	Membership Department I	1	1	20	1	83	1 Utilityman 6 Terminal Operators 15 DEO	128
11B.2	Membership Department II	1	1	20	1	83	1 Utilityman 6 Terminal Operators 15 DEO	128
11B.3	Membership Department III	1	1	21	1	85	1 Utilityman 6 Terminal Operators 20 DEO 2 URO	138
11B.4	Optional Life Insurance Department	1	6	15	1	58	1 Laborer	82
11B.5	Dividend Processing Division			4		19	2 Laborers	25
11C	Office of the Vice President, Claims Administration	1	1		1		1 Utilityman	4
11C.1	Medicare Claims Benefit Department	1	13	17	1	62	2 Utilityman	96
11C.2	Social Insurance Claims Department I	1	3	12	1	55	1 Utilityman	73
11C.3	Social Insurance Claims Department II	1	3	12	1	55	1 Utilityman	73
11C.4	Social Insurance Claims Department III	1	3	12	1	55	1 Utilityman	73
11C.5	Pension Administration Division			3		14		17
TOTAL								CONT'D

564

1983 1985 1987 2000

Growth Profile:

Reduction in manpower as a result of the developements in information systems and the possibility of phasing out the Houseing Project Developement and evaluation department whose functions will be absorbed by the Houseing Projects Administration Department

*Forecast based on 1983 maximum manpower projection.

* Continued with SOCIAL INSURANCE : MEDICAL GROUP (page 100)

FIGURE 8.10 Example 2, of Programming Documentation from The Architects Collaborative worker profile projected reduction.

Program Elements	Major Program Elements	Program Elements	Gross m²
(blocking diagram)	**Parking** 28,045m²	1 Short Term Service Vehicles 2 Shared Visitor 3 Employee & Executive 4 GSIS Service Vehicles 5 GSIS Vehicles	250 7,735 18,060 250 .1,750
(blocking diagram)	**Front Line & Lobby** 7,092m²	1 Exterior Waiting Area 2 Front Line Lobby/Waiting 3 Social Insurance Center 4 General Insurance Center 5 Loans & Investments Center 6 Finance Center 7 Mails Front-Line Counter 8 Public Relations Center 9 Retail Shops and Services 10 Cooperative Store 11 GSIS Clubs	2,251 1,481 308 67 356 112 96 207 905 741 56A
(blocking diagram)	**Front Line Back-Up** 21,468m²	1 Finance Center Back-up 2 External Auditors (Finance) 3 Loans & Investments Center Back-up 4 External Auditor (Loans & Investments) 5 External Auditor (Social Insurance) 6 Social Insurance Center Back-up 7 Medical Center 8 Monitoring Center and Civil Security Office 9 Mails Counter Back-up 10 Mails Section Offices 11 Public Relations Center Back-Up	2,574 296 1,090 355 489 9,376 3,246 750 296 973 1,223
(blocking diagram)	**MDC Reception** 370m²	1 Manpower Development Center Reception	370
(blocking diagram)	**Human Resources & Other Employee Amenities** 8,164m²	1 Manpower Development Department Offices 2 Resource Center & Publication Services 3 Cultural Division Auditorium 4 Other Human Resources Offices 5 Training Center 6 Canteen/Kitchen	829 1,106 1,109 1,445 703 2,972
(blocking diagram)	**Interior Athletics** 1,613m²	1 Gymnasium 2 Weight Room 3 Equipment Storage 4 Hobby/Craft 5 Meditation Room 6 Clubhouse	889 222 151 122 44 185
(blocking diagram)	**Physical Resources** 6,608m²	1 General Services Dept. Offices 2 Print Shop & Central Reproduction 3 Vehicular Service Area 4 Materials & Supplies Dept. Offices 5 Warehouse & Loading Dock 6 Physical Plant Dept. Offices 7 Maintenance Shops	909 586 296 964 1,733 1,422 696
(blocking diagram)	**Information Systems** 7,771m²	1 Other Information Systems Offices 2 External Auditors (Finance) 3 External Auditors (Records Center) 4 Computer Center & EDP Offices 5 Records Center & Data Management Offices	1,601 343 1,037 3,097 1,693
(blocking diagram)	**Other Internal Offices** 16,916m²	1 Other General Insurance Offices 2 External Auditors (General Insurance) 3 Other Loans and Investment Offices 4 External Auditors (Loans & Investments) 5 Other Finance Offices 6 Other Corporate Assistance Offices	4,214 489 7,449 770 2,244 1,740
(blocking diagram)	**External Auditors** 2,740m²	1 External Auditors Office	2,740
(blocking diagram)	**Management** 6,893m²	1 Board of Trustees Suite 2 Actuarial Research & Development Group 3 Corporate Planning Office 4 Executive Suite 5 Internal Audit Group 6 Branch Offices 7 External Auditors (Branches)	2,103 924 549 1,948 643 578 148

Total Building Program 107,680m²

External Elements

Exterior Athletics	4,120
Developed Outdoor Area	15,927

The New Headquarters Building
Financial Center • Manila - Cavite Coastal Road and Reclamation Project • Pasay City, Metropolitan Manila, Republic of the Philippines

Program Elements

Date : 8-20-79

TAC

FIGURE 8.11 Blocking plan: Analysis of major elements, from The Architects Collaborative.

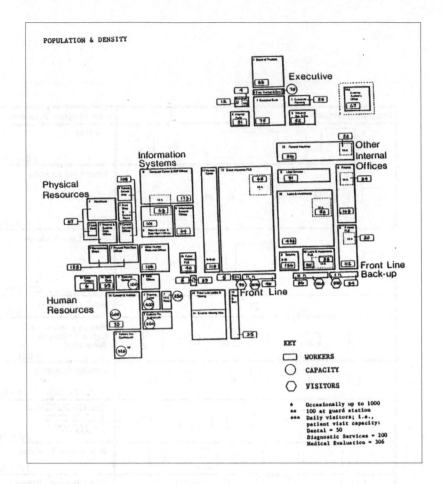

FIGURE 8.12
Programming
Documentation
from The Architects
Collaborative
identifying worker
population and
density study.

TABLE 8.2 FACILITIES AND SPACE REQUIRED FOR MALLOY HALL

AMENITIES REQUIRED	# & LOCATIONS IN BUILDING	TOTAL SQUARE FEET NEEDED
Double-occupancy student rooms	96	225 per room 21,600 total
Restrooms within suite style living spaces 1/suite 24 total	180 per suite 4320 total	
Lounges (within suites)	1 per suite 24 total	300 per suite 7200 total
Lounge for entertainment	3 (one/floor)	450 per floor 1350 total
Lounge for study	1 (ground floor)	400
Staff apartments	3 (one/floor)	350 per apartment 1050 total
Single occupancy suites (Resident assistants)	3 (one/floor)	180 per room 540 total
Kitchen	3 (one/floor)	300 per floor 900 total
Fitness area	1 (ground floor)	350
Offices of Residence Life	1 (ground floor)	400
Lobby/Reception area	1 (ground floor)	300
Laundry facility	1 (ground floor)	250
Building storage and maintenance 3 (1/ floor) 360		
Circulation	+30% of total	12,000

TOTAL SQUARE FEET REQUIRED FOR MALLOY HALL 50,020

TOTAL SQUARE FEET AVAILABLE IN MALLOY HALL 56,000

Source: Jenna Richard, 2006.

and thirty students to approximately two hundred students. The addition of social areas will promote community building within the residence hall, and the use of quality, attractive, durable finishes, materials, and furnishings will allow students to enjoy these spaces for many years to come" (Richard, 2006).

After the written introduction and the program space requirements, as noted in Table 8.2, the chart outlines the proposed space. Adjacencies studies in Figures 8.13 and 8.14 are visual examples of bubble diagramming that take the required space and represent it in the appropriate size and relationship to other spaces. The criteria matrix in Figure 8.15 visually synthesizes the program requirements, space, sizes, and adjacency requirement into one diagram.

Some programmers like to include conceptual images; specific code requirements that might relate to the space, lighting, furniture; and maybe even a written description of how the space should feel. A descriptive statement will help set the tone when the program begins to evolve into the schematic design process. An example might be for a reception area of a spa such as the following:

When one enters the spa the sound of water should be heard, embracing nature to relax and calm customers when they enter. Water in concept is a purifying experience and the spa customers will hear the therapeutic sound then experience it later when in treatment rooms. The seating is to be soft, embracing the customers and absorbing and muffling the outside sounds that might enter through the main entrance. The ceiling can also be lowered over the seating area to help facilitate a sense of intimacy and relaxation while encouraging a peaceful and tranquil experience. A fireplace will be placed in the reception for warmth and visual tranquility.

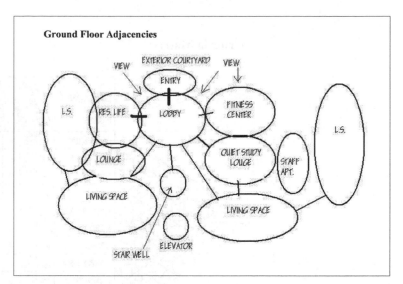

FIGURE 8.13 Ground floor adjacencies 1.

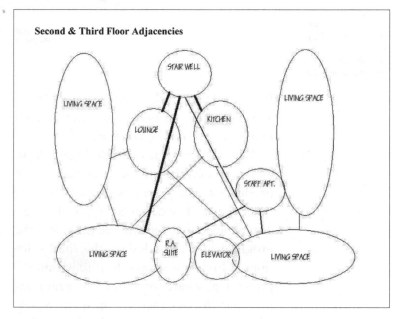

FIGURE 8.14 Second and third floor adjacencies.

Figure 8.16 shows how Richard documents her program for the proposed residence hall. First, she takes the space that she is documenting and places it onto the top of the page. She includes a visual adjacency diagram with the program requirements listed next to it. She also includes some conceptual images with a written description of how the space might feel. Notice how the template of Figure 8.16 is the same at that of

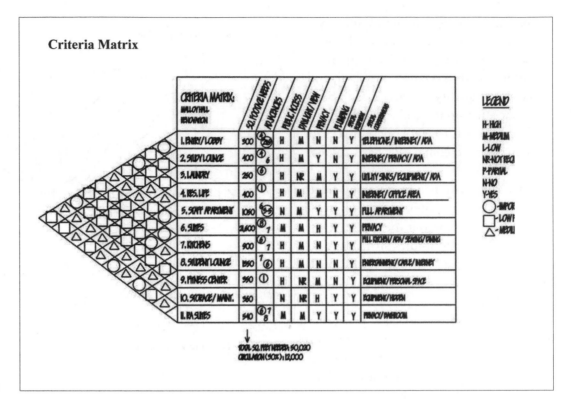

Criteria Matrix

FIGURE 8.15 Student example: Residence Hall matrix requirements, by Jeanna Richard, 2006

Figure 8.17; only the content has changed as Richard inserts each space with its own requirements, needs, and features.

This exercise outlined for Figures 8.16 and 8.17 may be time-consuming, but it produces a comprehensive snapshot of each space that will be designed. Typically, in an academic setting the student generates the program and then designs the final solutions. This is not always the case within the profession, where sometimes the programmer and the designer are different people who may not even work in the same office. Hence, it is imperative to be as detailed and comprehensive in your documentation as possible.

FIRM PROFILE: DESIGN ONE CONSORTIUM

Design One Consortium is a Providence, Rhode Island, design firm, specializing in alternative energy sources and recyclable materials demonstrating that successful business and concern for resources, both

natural and human, can happily coexist. The idea behind the Consortium is to bring together a team of professionals that offers its clients the best possible design solution. The firm's founder, Lynne Bryan Phipps, IIDA LEED AP, believes that every project is a unique and individual endeavor, requiring unique and individual professionals.

Phipps provided this overview of her firm. She trained in interior architecture at the Rhode Island School of Design, where she received a BFA and a BIA. Since 1987, her practice has offered an integrated, holistic approach to design that includes environmental sustainability and reuse, and the psychological effect of the built environment. This expertise can be applied to designing the spaces where people live and work, as well as the tools and furnishings that they use daily. Phipps' clients include corporations, churches, nonprofit organizations, schools, and individuals interested in maximizing their spatial potential from environmental, psychological, and spiritual perspectives.

FIGURE 8.16
Facilities and Space Required for Residence Hall, lobby, and office.

Lobby/Reception Area & Offices of Residence Life

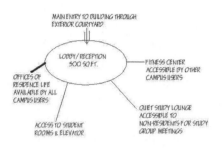

MAIN ENTRY TO BUILDING THROUGH EXTERIOR COURTYARD

LOBBY/RECEPTION 500 SQ.FT.

OFFICES OF RESIDENCE LIFE AVAILABLE BY ALL CAMPUS USERS

FITNESS CENTER ACCESSIBLE BY OTHER CAMPUS USERS

QUIET STUDY LOUNGE ACCESSIBLE TO NON-RESIDENTS FOR STUDY GROUP MEETINGS

ACCESS TO STUDENT ROOMS & ELEVATOR

Lobby Requirements:

- Occasional seating & tables
- Way-finding signage
- Reception/security desk

Conceptual Images:

Image 1

Image 3

Image 2

Image 4

The lobby should feel bright, spacious and accommodating. The main entrance to the building through the exterior courtyard will become the central hub of the building's activity. Offices of Residence Life will remain accessible directly from the outside by all campus users. Seating will be provided for social interaction and waiting areas for the adjacent offices. The atmosphere should be comforting yet reflect upon the busy excitement of collegiate life in Malloy Hall.

FIGURE 8.17
Facilities required for suite-style living area (double occupancy) and private rooms.

Resident Student Suite Style Living Area

Double Occupancy Private Rooms

CORRIDOR

BATHROOM 180 SQ.FT.

D.R. 225 SQ.FT.

D.R. 225 SQ.FT.

DOUBLE ROOM 225 SQ.FT.

LOUNGE 500 SQ.FT.

D.R. 225 SQ.FT.

Student Room Requirements

- Two dressers
- Two desks w/chairs
- Two x-long twin beds
- Two closets
- Built in shelving
- Full-length mirror
- Microfridge
- Wireless connectivity, podcasting, cable television

Conceptual Images:

Image 19

Image 21

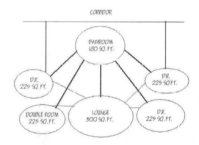

Image 20

Student rooms serve as sleeping rooms, living rooms, and study areas. Residents should be able to make their rooms as personal as possible. Color palettes will remain neutral, durable, and easily cleaned. Ample general and task lighting will be provided to ensure that the space is as functional as possible. Furnishings will be flexible for ease of rearranging. Comfort is of the utmost importance; residence halls are home to students nine months a year and should provide the same sense of relaxation

Phipps states that with architectural design it all begins with space. A core belief of Design One Consortium is that space, or more accurately the perception of space, is a paramount consideration in any design concept. Good design considers space an asset, and whether it is in a corporate or residential environment, the firm works to understand the individuals involved, the organizational structure, and the requirements of each individual client. The firm translates that data into a design that maximizes functionality; maximizes comfort (both psychological and physical); presents the goals, visions, and values of the particular client; and transforms space through a design that will meet its clients' needs better, and endure well into the future.

The business goal of Design One Consortium is to favorably alter traditional thinking about what constitutes good design by delivering alternative solutions to conventional standards.

Design One Consortium's Approach to Programming

The programming phase is a critical component of the design process. Without adequate research and analysis, the design process can be random and directionless. Concepts and approaches for each project grow out of the programming process.

FIGURE 8.18 Lynne Bryan Phipps, IIDA, LEED AP, NCIDQ certificate #023377.

Some of the components of a programming process are as follows:

- **Preliminary research**—Includes systems analysis, comparative analysis, code research, and site research
- **Needs analysis**—Client interview, observational analysis, adjacency matrix, flow diagramming and analysis, bubble diagramming, and analysis

Design One Consortium maintains that the job of a designer is to listen very closely to what people say. Clients will often confuse their wants and needs, and often they will disagree about them. It is the designer's job to discern through interview and observation what actually belongs in the program. Often clients tell the designer that something is a requirement, but through interview and observation, the designer can find a better way to fulfill their needs than that specified "requirement." This work has to be done carefully and respectfully. Solid communication skills are a critical tool for the designer, especially during the development of the program. To get to the heart of the program, Consortium One designers ask a series of questions about the way that the clients live. They ask about personal history, likes and dislikes, and the way that their clients feel about their present space—how it works or does not work for them. It is equally if not more important to understand what doesn't work as it is to ask what one wants. Often when people live/work in a space, they adapt to it so significantly that they don't even notice what works and what doesn't work for them. They don't even realize that they could feel better or function better if something were different.

In this interview process, ask the clients what workdays are like and what their downtime is like. In asking these questions, try to listen carefully for clues about whether or not they are happy, sad, frustrated, or angry about the way things flow. If they have expressed negative feelings, try to identify other questions that need to be asked so that you can discern what could be reworked or done differently to make their lives more comfortable or productive, or help create a more positive experience.

According to Phipps, for residential design a good way to begin is asking the clients to describe a typical day—when they get up, what their morning routine is, what the middle of the day is like, whether or not they cook, what kinds of food they cook/eat/store, and so on. How do they wind down, how do they relax, do they watch TV and when, how does television or computers and other technologies fit into their lives? Questions like these form a mental picture of each space, and help to identify how those spaces relate to one another. If it is discovered through the interview that a client loves to cook but has small children and can't seem to spend time in the kitchen because presently the play space and the cooking space are on two different levels, the designer can identify that as a problem worth trying to solve. How the identified issues fit into the hierarchy of importance will be determined together with the client as the wants and needs are prioritized. (See Appendix C, "Design One Consortium's Residential Program.")

In the context of the corporate world, Phipps says her company maintains that observational analysis is a necessary and often overlooked design tool. Whether it is a camera set up to observe the work patterns of individuals or groups or a designer observing work as it is undertaken and then asking questions about the ease or difficulty by which individuals or groups can accomplish the tasks at hand, observation is often the only way that some work flow difficulties are identified.

Observational analysis is often used in retail design. It is a way of documenting how customers respond to products and space. Just how far will a customer go to get what he or she wants, or will the customer settle for what he or she can reach? If something doesn't sell and it's located on the top shelf where most of the establishment's clientele can't reach, observational analysis may be the way a store discovers the problem.

When Design One Consortium started designing for Meeting Street School, in Providence, Rhode Island, the firm worked to identify a way of signaling a transition that could be understood by students with varying disabilities. How can you signal a change from one wing to the next that can be experienced by someone who can't hear, or someone who can't see, or someone who can't walk? Some concepts were tested and the responses were observed. Could a wheelchair roll over river stones? Is the surface stable enough for someone on crutches to cross over? Can you really feel the transition if you can't see it, and can you really experience it if you can't hear?

Design One Consortium worked with Brown University in the school's office of Religious and Spiritual Life. The staff had a hunch that a common space on their floor was underutilized. Observational analysis was used to document the ways in which students and staff used the common space. The regularity of use was also documented to determine the needs of students and staff, and to program accordingly. These kinds of observational analyses are examples of how, when, and why one might want to make use of this powerful tool.

GENERATING YOUR PROGRAM

After reviewing the various examples, you can now take all the spaces that have been identified as programmatic requirements for your design project and assign the required square footage to each space. Once

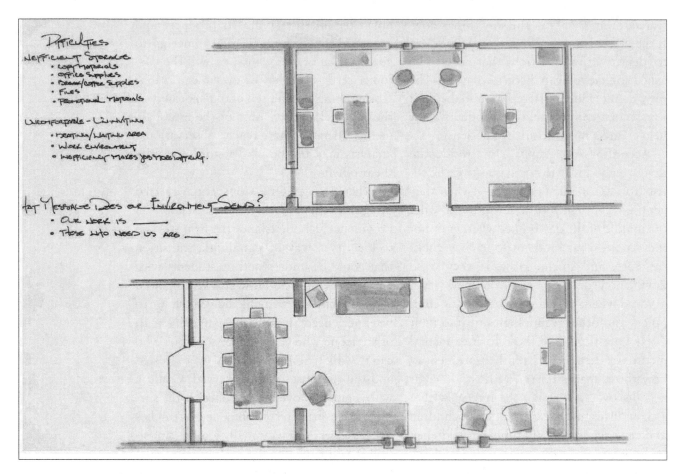

FIGURE 8.19 **Exisiting conditions**

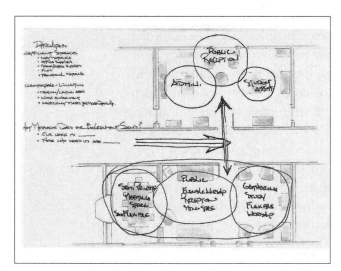

FIGURE 8.20A **Diagramming, flow, and behavioral mapping**

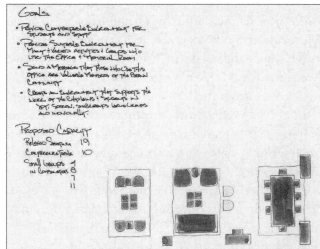

FIGURE 8.20B **Final layout**

FIGURE 8.21 **Photograph of the final design for the Brown University Office of Religious and Spiritual Life.**

TABLE 8.3 ONE-PAGE TEMPLATE FOR EACH SPACE IN YOUR PROGRAM

Name of Space: Add the name of the space that you are programming for

Insert space with visual adjacency requirements.

Insert space with visual adjacency requirements.

Add some conceptual images that you might have found during your historical, observation, or interactive research.

Objects, furniture, words, and poems all can be placed here to help one begin to envision the space at a glance.

Add a brief concept statement about the space. Add Codes to keep in mind that directly apply to this specific space.

the requirements have been documented in a chart with the square footage requirements and circulation needs, you will have a clear picture of how much space will be needed to facilitate the design.

It is important to take the time and document each space, including its own internal requirements, features, and codes. This step is often overlooked during the programming phase perhaps because it's a time-consuming task. But the time invested in documenting and visualizing each space as you implement the template model diagrammed in Table 8.3 will help you and your client begin to visualize the space very early in the process of design. To make changes at this stage in the programming phase is a manageable task. Making changes at this stage should actually be encouraged. Changes in later design phases can be problematic. Say your client requests an extra office space or lounge. Think about when that request could realistically be implemented.

If the client requests this during the design development phase, it could be very problematic to the design, and maybe not even an option at that point. The time invested in developing a comprehensive program is well spent. It gives the client and the design team a complete document to implement, and gives the program requirements good design solutions.

KEY TERMS

- American National Standards Institute (ANSI)—www.ansi.org.
- Building Owners and Managers Association (BOMA) —www.boma.org.
- Department Personnel Population Study
- Floor usable area
- Gross measured area
- International Facility Managers Association (IFMA) —www.ifma.org

CHAPTER 9

Written and Visual Analysis

After reading this chapter, you should be able to:

- Understand the visual language of diagramming.
- Create bubble and blocking plans.
- Create stacking plans.

For this book, many interior designers shared their thoughts as well as the processes they use to solve clients' problems. Much of that data has been synthesized into these pages, and we can see how many of these designers approach programming in a similar manner that varies only slightly. This should not be surprising because the purpose of programming, as we have seen, is to take a look at a given type of design and explore user needs in relation to space. What varies considerably more are the numerous types of spaces that interior designers program as they aim to meet all sorts of needs, codes, requirements, and tastes. In other words, there may be an infinite number of ways to solve design problems, but designers can rely on a relatively straightforward process for arriving at the best solution. Another reoccurring theme in the design firm interviews is that good design solutions come from really understanding the client's needs. Each firm stressed the need to interact with clients through a multitude of interview and data-gathering techniques.

REACHING SOLUTIONS THROUGH IDENTIFICATION AND ANALYSIS

As we have seen from previous chapters, the first important step toward reaching your design solution is to gather as much data as possible. The next phase after generating the programmatic requirements and working with the square footage needs and requirements can be compared to putting together a jigsaw puzzle. Once you have all of the pieces of the puzzle in play, you move them around until they begin to fit together in the best arrangement that suits your client's needs. All the pieces need to fit together properly or the puzzle will not come together. Have you ever tried to fit a piece of the puzzle into a space knowing it was the wrong one but insisting that if you just turn it or flip it, you could make it fit? This frustration can parallel the experience of taking the requirements from the **adjacency matrix** and beginning to translate them into visual blocking or bubble diagrams. If your data is organized and you have documented each space and are working with the appropriate square footage, eventually all the pieces will fit, and your space will come together.

IDENTIFYING YOUR DATA

After you've gathered your data, itself a multi-step process as we've seen in the previous chapters, you can then begin to sort your findings into various categories that meet the needs of each individual project. You may also need to conduct further research in order to identify information critical to finding your solution. Typically, you'll need to identify the following:

- State and local codes
- All of the facets that make up your problem statement, as discussed in Chapter 3, "Defining and Structuring Your Program Document"
- Your precedent study as discussed in Chapter 7, "Precedent Studies"
- The needs of your client

To hone in on information necessary for your particular project, you may also look to **comparative case studies**, interviews, and observation skills. All of this is discussed in the text that follows.

Identifying State and Local Codes

Local and state code requirements need to be researched prior to any programmatic or design decisions. Codes act as boundaries for the design options that can be considered. Therefore, full awareness of all codes is a crucial foundational element to solid design decisions for any client.

At this time, also look for any idiosyncratic, or site-specific information. For example, when you look out the window, are you greeted by a scenic or obstructed view? Research for site-specific information includes studying site plans, plot maps, building restrictions, historical information about the site, and the area around the site that might help with design decisions. Simultaneously, look at site location, longitude and latitude, solar angles, orientation, average wind velocity and direction, and geological information. This information will prove relevant when it comes to alternative energy generation and collection (Phipps, 2008).

Energy Conservation

Energy concepts have been a concern for programmers for many years. The study featured in Figure 9.1, for example, demonstrates the implemented energy concepts for a structure in Manila designed by The Architects Collaborative (TAC) in the early 1980s. TAC was committed to energy-conscious building design, which it characterized by sustained reduced energy concentration levels as compared to that energy performance of buildings predating the worldwide energy crisis. Governmental agencies throughout the world were establishing guidelines to regulate the amount of nonrenewable fuels (i.e., electricity, gas, and oil), which a building may utilize (1981, TAC. p. 54).

The energy conservation goals included in the programming document were as follows:

- **Natural ventilation**—To promote the best use of natural breezes for cooling.
- **Daylighting**—To:
  - Minimize energy consumption of artificial lighting throughout.
  - Maximize use of natural daylight by locating the maximum of office areas within 15 meters of windows, and by locating program elements not requiring daylighting toward the interior.
  - Provide natural daylighting opportu-

nities for natural ventilation, ensuring that office operations can continue during brown- and blackouts without creating undue reliance on emergency power.

- Protect against solar heat gain by:
  - Minimizing east and west exposures
  - Shading of glass areas
  - Insulating walls and roof
  - Rooftop planting
  - Using "active" solar systems where possible for air conditioning of selected areas and heating of domestic hot water
  - Using automated building management systems for maximum efficiency in energy systems operation and lighting control

By using diagrams in the final program document, the environmental aspect of the building is recorded; this helps the design team and the client understand and visualize the programmatic requirements.

United States Green Building Council

When seeking input to include and plan for energy concepts, an excellent place to start is at the **The United States Green Building Council** (USGBC) Web site (www.usgbc.org). This site encompasses an abundance of information. It also lists local chapters where more relevant regional data can be obtained.

Identifying Your Problem Statement

When beginning the process of identifying the problem statement, as addressed in Chapter 3, "Defining and Structuring Your Program Document," it is important to include all the facets that are within the problem. Be mindful that realistically more problems will emerge as you engross yourself in conducting the historical, observa-

tional, and interactive research techniques. These can be introduced as sub-problems. Implementing and/or adapting a research method to help aid in identifying a phenomenon should be part of one's process. Documenting and learning from research benefits not only the designer but also the community at large.

Comparative Case Studies

Most interior design firms conduct comparative case studies, researching other facilities in the client's industry as well as looking outside the box at other industries that might be utilizing innovative technologies or approaches that could be universalized or used in the client's world (Phipps, 2007). This helps the design community look to facts when designing and especially in solving problems that deal with the health, safety, and welfare of the individuals that occupy these spaces.

Identifying Client Requirements

When beginning a particular design problem, the designer should attempt to do everything possible to understand the client requirements. Whether the space is corporate, institutional, or residential, the designer must work to understand how that particular organization functions as an individual system, and in the context of the larger genre. When being asked to design a sustainable residence for a particular family system, for example, first make sure that you understand the family structure in general, and then start to get specific about the family for whom you are designing (Phipps, 2007). The process and approach is not that different for corporate, healthcare, and institutional design.

Professional Example: Siemasko + Verbridge

Jean Verbridge, ASID, IIDA, NCIDQ certificate #005558, maintains that it is impor-

FIGURE 9.1 This redraw is based on TAC energy conservation concepts views and solar issues.

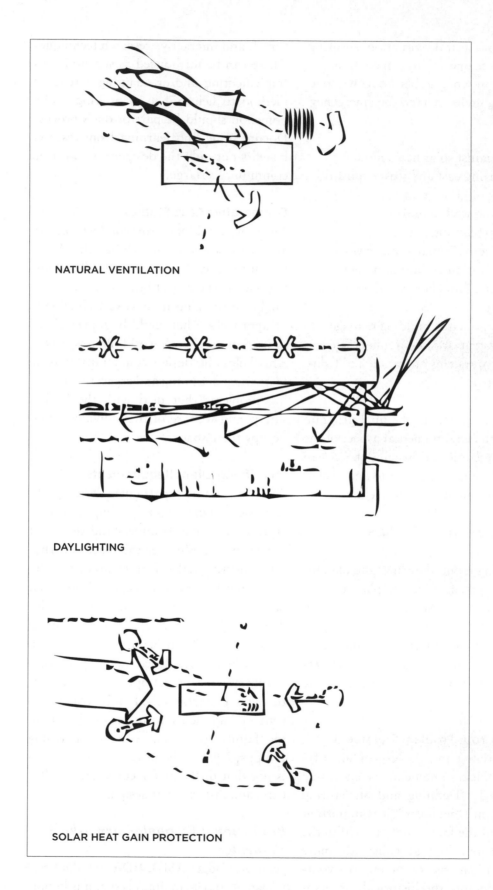

NATURAL VENTILATION

DAYLIGHTING

SOLAR HEAT GAIN PROTECTION

tant to understand the larger context about one's client and their vision. Jean is a principal with Siemasko + Verbridge, a full-service architecture, interior design, landscape architecture, and decorating firm located in Beverly, Massachusetts.

According to Verbridge, the firm's projects encompass residential, corporate, commercial, and institutional design, inclusive of both new construction and renovation work. Its projects reflect what clients would design for themselves, given a designer's training, expertise, and eye. Working in close collaboration with its clients, the firm's design process is a well-researched and thoughtful distillation of client requirements and preferences, with careful consideration of budget. The result is a structure that is appealing and functional, meticulously crafted, and well suited to both the character of the client and the site. The firm has earned a reputation for its commitment to improving the fabric of communities as well as its respect for the environment. The firm's success is confirmed by a strong foundation of repeat clients and referrals (Verbridge, 2007). This level of detail is carefully applied to the programming phase of the projects. Often, Verbridge states, she and her associates approach programming with "big ears, feet, and eyes." In other words, they try to hear everything, go everywhere, and see as much as possible. Then they document everything. The client is an integral part of programming, Verbridge says, and so she and her associates strive to make them aware of this up front.

Professional Example: Studio East Design

Christine Shanahan, ASID, points out the importance of addressing regional connections. Shanahan is principal of Studio East Design, a firm that specializes in hospitality design.

One of the key elements in hospitality design is the regional connection a project will have to its location and culture. According to Shanahan, "We will perform studies on local flavor, spirit, and interest in order to incorporate elements into the guest's experience." The programming for that, she says, may include physical visits to the geographic area, Internet research, interviews with the front desk personnel and concierge on local highlights (if existing), and tours of the competition.

Shanahan finds the market audience of the hotel is a critical component. Programming for this area would include a brand analysis of target audience, interviews with the site (if existing) to determine existing clientele, an interview with ownership to determine desired clientele, financial analysis to formulate the market through rate, and research to determine what are the determining factors for a guest in booking at this location (e.g., a conference center next door or vacation attractions).

Preliminary research is a crucial step in the process and helps to prepare a comprehensive program. Like Shanahan, all of the designers interviewed for this book agreed that without the parameters discovered in the context of preliminary research, they could not come up with solutions that they believe are feasible or even good. Without preliminary research, all agreed that their time and the client's time would be wasted because vital information would either continue to turn up throughout the project, causing them to go back and repeat themselves over and over, or it would be missed altogether. Students conduct their preliminary research in their Historical Observational and Interactive Research outlined in Chapter 5 and the Precedent Study outlined in Chapter 7.

ANALYZING YOUR DATA

After you have gathered your data and identified how it relates to your design problem, you can begin to see how it all fits together and leads to your solution. In analyzing the data, there are several tools you can use. These include interviewing and observation, both of which were discussed in Chapter 5, and will be explored further here; matrix studies; bubble, stacking; and diagramming studies. All of these will be discussed in this section.

Interviewing: Listen More, Talk Less

Interviewing tools for data collection are imperative because they deal with critical questions such as what special needs are required for the space. As discussed in Chapter 2, "The Process of Design," most firms have a standard tool that can be modified for each project. Questionnaires and surveys for corporate and institutional clients are developed more for project-specific tools. For a residential setting, most designers interviewed for this book concurred that they sit down with the individual or couple for whom they are designing, and first and foremost try to build rapport with them (Phipps, 2007). The designer works hard to educate him- or herself about the needs and wants of the client. A diversity of interview templates has been included throughout this text. Encompassing residential, online, and general questionnaires, these interview templates have been included for you to implement and modify for your own programming. (See Appendix B, "MPA | Margulies Perruzzi Architects Design Programming Forms.")

Observation: Watch, Scrutinize, and Study

The art of observing is an intuitive process for individuals within the design fields. Programmers and designers are typically individuals with strong visual orientation—people who plan, create, and envision the sculpted environment. Observational analysis is a design tool that can be applied in numerous applications. It may be a camera set up to observe the work patterns of individuals or groups. It may be a designer observing work as its undertaken and then asking questions about the ease or difficulty that individuals or groups underwent to perform these tasks. But in any case, observational techniques can help identify behavior patterns and the efficiency, or inefficiency, of a design. The example in Figure 9.2 demonstrates the observation and documentation of a typical workday by employee times and activities. The time and activity schedule allows one to look at peeks of high usage of space and under utilized space.

Matrix: Environment, Template, and Space

For some designers, the use of an adjacency matrix is an imperative tool that varies in its application and approach. A simple adjacency matrix can be created to illustrate, confirm, and clarify clients' needs and wants, while in a corporate or institutional setting, there are significant relationships that must be documented and sometimes prove difficult to manage. An adjacency matrix is a helpful tool in the development and analysis of special relationships. In complex situations, it is helpful to be able to refer back to the tool to be sure that the design is accomplishing the documented complex relationships and the goals associated with them. The example in Figure 9.3a demonstrates a student who is studying the adjacency requirements by implementing a simple matrix to study the bubble diagram while illustrating functional relationships for interaction and communication (Gouveia, 2005).

The example in Figure 9.3a is conceptual. The level of detail and complexity

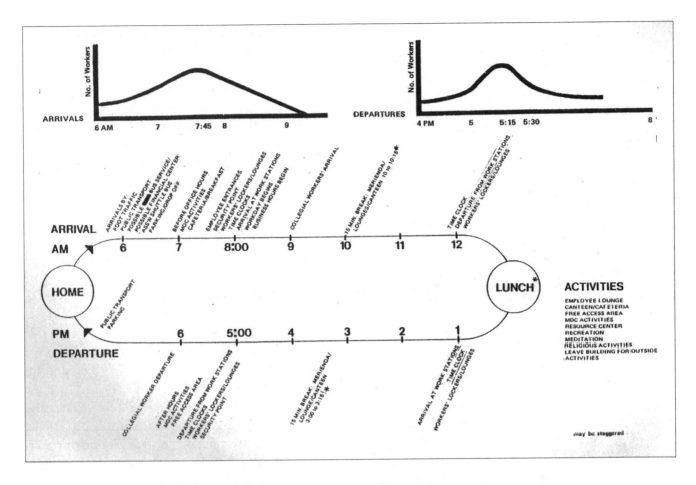

these diagrams can evolve into are endless. The student whose work appears in Figure 9.3a is now working in the profession as an interior designer; she notes that research, programming, and adjacencies are very important to her design process, and something that she thoroughly enjoys. Research allows designers to dig deeper and learn about the project, and it helps them generate ideas. Sometimes an image will help you see or will help create a motif that you normally would not have come up with. Programming allows you to figure out who the users are and what their needs may be so that they will be met throughout the project. Once you know who the users are, adjacencies allow you to utilize bubble diagrams and matrixes to create the layout and refine it. This allows you to create a better project for the client and the end user (Gouveia, 2008).

Professional Example: International Conference Center

Often departmental adjacency and matrix charts are very detailed. The example implemented as a weighing system from very desirable to undesirable is an interpretation of a modified **Likert scale.** Rensis Likert, a sociologist at the University of Michigan from 1946 to 1970, developed the method of scaling and evaluating one's response when asked. This form of response and scaling is commonly referred to as a Likert scaling. Figure 9.4 shows the departmental adjacency matrix that was completed by the various department heads and chart that was subsequently created to summarize that data. This type of summary chart records detailed adjacency requirements between specific areas within the various units. The department that provided the information is identified at the top of the chart, and the

FIGURE 9.2 TAC time and activity schedule.

	STAFF	SUPPORT	HEALTH	RELAXATION	PUBLIC	ACTIVITY	FITNESS
STAFF							
SUPPORT							
HEALTH							
RELAXATION	†		†				
PUBLIC	†	‡		†			
ACTIVITY	‡	†	†	†			
FITNESS	‡	†	†	†			

Adjacency Requirements Matrix indicating proximity with representing critical location to each other, † standing for desirable adjacency, and ‡ meaning as long as it is accessible. By Marcia A Gouveia

FIGURE 9.3A Adjaceny mode.

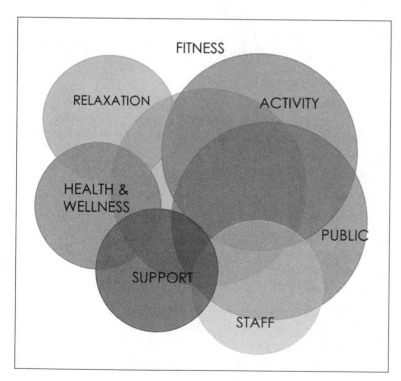

FIGURE 9.3B Conceptual diagram of space.

relationship of each department to the other departments or functions is recorded in the vertical column. This information was used to assist in developing the adjacency for a master plan and was valuable in establishing the interdepartmental relationships for the schematic phase of design. The basic conclusion of this information was that there is a great deal of interaction between units and among the various research departments. A walking relationship between all research departments, technical support functions, and management was necessary to encourage informal exchange of ideas and provide convenient access for collaboration between researchers (TAC, 1981)

Professional Example: Medical Lab
The depth of one's understanding and interpretation of the data collected is often translated to programmatic data charts and flow diagramming charts; these depict how space is utilized. This translation of observation, written, and visual diagramming helps both the designer and the client. Often a **flow diagram** illustrates the path being used as well as the alternatives that could be developed, often with little change. Flow diagrams can illustrate volume of usage, the multiplicity of uses, and conflicts associated with usage. It also can help the programmer understand the function at hand. The example in Figure 9.5 is from a medical lab. Observational studies were conducted, and the documentation resulted in a series of flow diagrams. Some functions were specific to a particular space and task, while others documented the total space.

Blocking: Bubble, Stacking, and Diagramming Studies
Diagramming is a powerful tool. Here, the designer conceptualizes the relationships of spaces discovered in client interviews, adjacency matrices, and flow diagrams, and converts this information to either a bubble

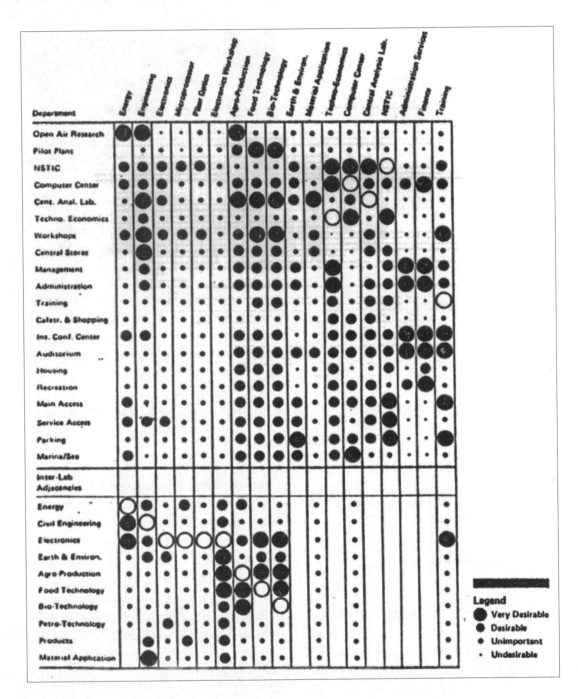

FIGURE 9.4 TAC departmental adjacency model.

or blocking diagram. By using relative bubble or blocking of sizes based upon relative square footage of the space, some idea of size requirements can be seen. But the main purpose of the diagram is the special relationships spaces have to one another. It is imperative at this point to keep the ideas conceptual. Diagramming is a great tool to execute this task; one can move quickly and explore numerous scenarios.

Designer Lynne Phipps shares some of the questions that she thinks about when generating bubble diagrams: How closely are two spaces related? Must they share a common wall? Could they overlap in usage? Could they even share space and usage? Are they totally separate and unrelated? Bubble diagrams are useful to keep the mind open to possibilities.

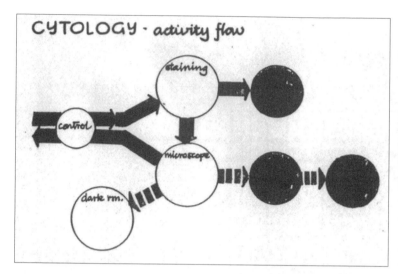

FIGURE 9.6 Cris Cavataio, IDEC, NCIDQ Certificate #9741.

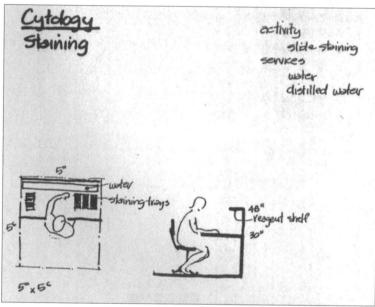

FIGURE 9.5 Laboratory-specific cytology.

Cris Cavataio, IDEC, NCIDQ Certificate #9741, has aided many designers through the study and preparation for their NCIDQ exam. Cavataio adds that color is often used to illustrate data when possible. When using color, a key is implemented to help all understand the data being shown. Would-be interior designers need to be able to take written existing condition statements and client spatial requests and turn these into a layout. A very valuable tool is to be able to diagram the written program information before attempting to plug it into a floor plan. By completing this intermediate step, the NCIDQ exam candidate who is working under a tight time frame will be more likely to succeed in accurately retaining the spatial requirements in the finished layout. For the test taker this can be the difference between passing or failing, as one will be immediately disqualified if any of the space-related programming requirements are omitted.

Diagram-Making Exercise

Cavataio states, "To practice this diagram-making exercise, I have students draw circles to indicate rooms or areas listed in the written program and then symbols to represent the relationship that this space has with other nearby or adjacent spaces. The immediacy of each adjacency can be usually simplified into three levels; high for immediate access, medium for somewhat close, or low for distant rooms or those spaces that don't require easy access to the other areas.

"As students feel comfortable creating these simple diagrams, we move to the next step which is to extract additional information from the written program statement that pertains to other aspects that will likely impact interior design, such as square footage, views, orientation, special equipment, and so forth. The goal is for the designer to be able to use the diagram without need to return to the written statement while moving onto space planning with the given floor plan. This approach seems to work well, saving exam takers precious time, because the underlying assumption is that all designers are visual learners and therefore seem to more quickly see information in diagrams than from reading words" (Cavataio, 2008).

Bubble Diagramming

There are numerous approaches to articulating the concept of bubble diagramming. Many implement color coding as a key to help delineate space and identify specific areas. In making use of these categories, the designer can discover and document when existing spaces and their relationships don't make sense, then conceptualize ways in which spaces and their relationship to one another might make sense in the future. Figures 9.7 to 9.10 are freehand bubble and blocking studies exploring adja-

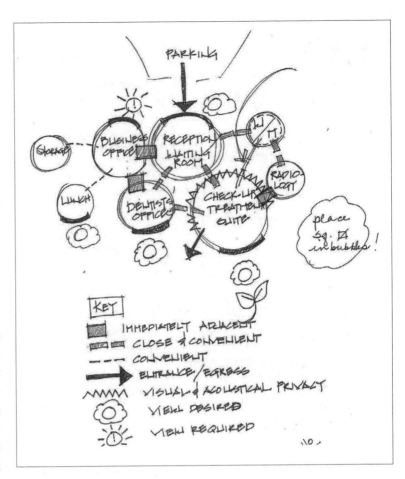

FIGURE 9.7 Color bubble and blocking 1.

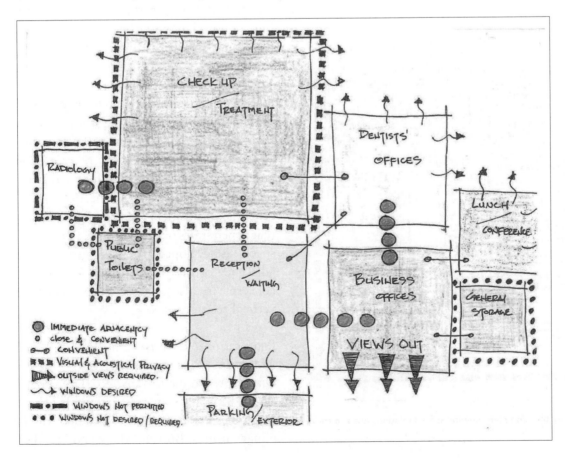

FIGURE 9.8 Color bubble and blocking 2.

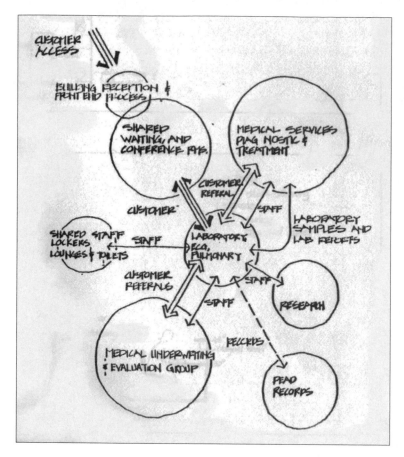

FIGURE 9.9 Laboratory bubble plan showing adjacencies for the cardio-pulmonaty unit.

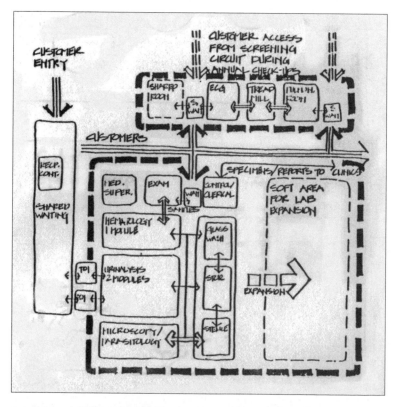

FIGURE 9.10 Laboratory blocking plan showing spatial relationships and traffic flow.

cency and space requirements. These freehand exploratory studies can be generated very quickly, allowing for fast movement and quick discovery of what is working and what is not.

Student Example: Sustainability Center, by Monica Mattingly

The programmatic requirements for the sustainability center were generated and then compiled into a chart format. Box 9.5 contains the written programmatic requirements and an example of the criteria matrix. The written information was then translated into freehand diagrams similar to the examples in Figures 9.5 and 9.6. Then a final diagram for the first floor that blocks out space meeting adjacency and programmatic requirements was created. The final blocking plan is computerized and included the square footage for each space. The last example in Figure 9.11 takes the blocking diagram and demonstrates how it evolves into a floor plan, with the gray indicating a phantom corridor for circulation.

Stacking Plans

Stacking plans are another tool that programmers implement for the study of space both horizontally and vertically. It is important to identify vertical relationships and how they might need to interact. Does there need to be a visual connection? Adjacency takes priority; the visual connection (e.g., open stairs or the creation of two story spaces) is developed after you figure out the adjacency of the vertical stack. Acoustical concerns are also a factor when evaluating vertical relationships.

Professional Example: MPA | Margulies Perruzzi Architects

Dianne A. Dunnell, IIDA, NCIDQ certificate # 015756, is an associate with MPA | Margulies Perruzzi Architects a multidisciplinary firm in Boston, Massachusetts. Per

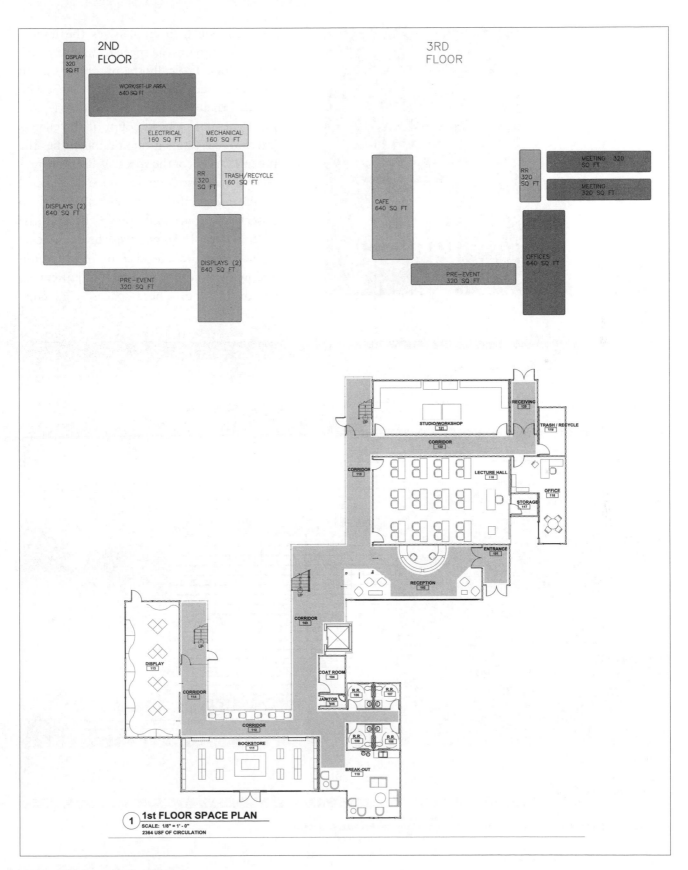

FIGURE 9.11 From Monica Mattingly.

FIGURE 9.12
Dianne A. Dunnell, IIDA, NCIDQ certificate # 015756.

Dunnell, the firm emphasizes the importance of studying the space from many vantage points. Typically the program is given to their project designer from the client who has had their own human resource department calculate a head count or the client's internal real estate group that identifies the potential users of the space. When they first receive the program document, Dunnell states, it is helpful to conduct a site visit to observe the space and double-check all the written data. In some cases the documents include inaccurate head count information, and many times the non-staff requirements are overlooked. These spaces (e.g., copy

Company:						
Date:	6.04.07					

Contact Name:
Department Name
Department Number:
Function:

email:
Location:

The following survey is being conducted to assist in planning for your immediate and long-range real estate needs
Please take a moment to confirm the data below and answer the questions so that we are able to plan for your specific department's needs
Your input and participation are appreciated. Please feel free to add comments or suggestions.

Public Contact?
Security Requirement?
Unusual hours of operation?

Personnel		Jul-06	Dec-07	Dec-08	Dec-09	Dec-10
	Total	0	0	0	0	0
	20 × 15 Office	0	0	0	0	0
	15 × 20 Office	0	0	0	0	0
	12 × 15 Office	0	0	0	0	0
	10 × 15 Office	0	0	0	0	0
	10 × 12 Office	0	0	0	0	0
	8 × 8 Workstation	0	0	0	0	0
	6 × 8 Workstation	0	0	0	0	0

Non-office component

						Comments
12-18 person conference room	(times per week required)	0				
6-10 person conference room	(times per week required)					
Departmental/secure storage	(square feet)					
Common/Secure Filing	(quantity of cabinets)					
Reception/waiting	(square feet)					
Lab	(square feet)					
Workrooms/Team area	(square feet)					

What departments does yours need to be near?

Required:
Preferable:
Desireable but not essential:

Comments

FIGURE 9.13 **Interview template example from MPA | Margulies Perruzzi Architects.**

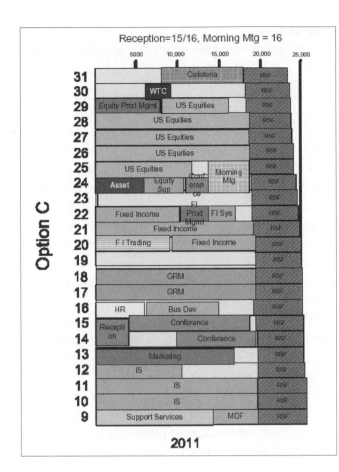

FIGURE 9.14

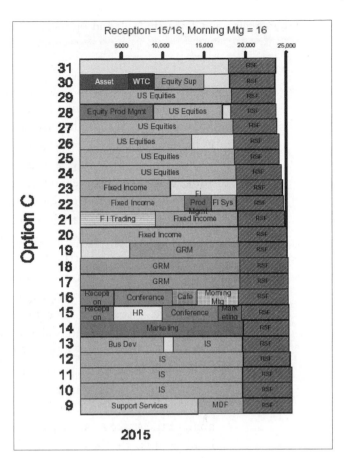

FIGURE 9.15

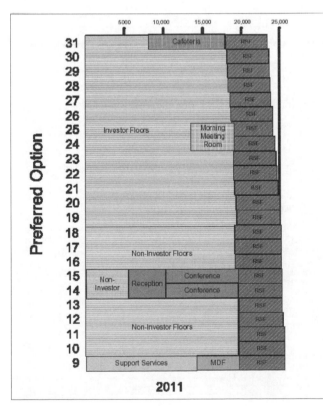

FIGURE 9.16

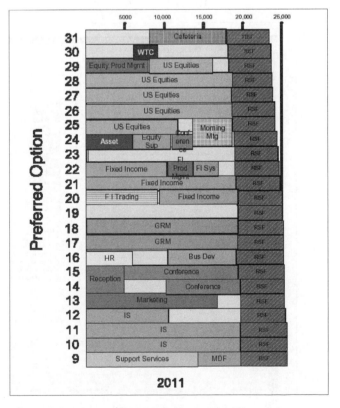

FIGURE 9.17

Examples of stacking diagram options exploring the best location for program requirements. These are typically used for a large projects. The space is represented in a vertical, cross-section to visually see the stacking of requirements on multiple floors. From MPA | Margulies Perruzzi Architects.

room, coffee areas, storage space) need to be identified and planned for because they not only take up space but also are essential in facilitating that daily tasks run smoothly. Often when observing a space, Dunnell adds, she will observe and ask the users who they interact with not only on a daily basis internally within their own group and department but others external to their group, such as departments from other floors or visitors from outside the company. Often she will implement a questionnaire to initiate a program or complement the program data that she has already received (see Figures 9.13). (See Appendix B.)

In most cases, the program document seems to be a moving target of sorts. Dunnell states that as she and her colleagues analyze the space in anticipation of specific head counts, the head counts can change when the company's new quarterly reports are issued from the human resources de-partment. Hence, the program must be up-dated as needed. This is a realistic scenario for a large project aiming to meet an am-bitious move-in date. These are the types of issues that will surface when you have a project that will take approximately three years; the anticipated move-in is 2011, and her firm is programming/designing out for 2013. MPA | Margulies Perruzzi Architects is projecting for three years with antici-pated growth. The programming and sche-matic designs in this scenario are running tandem to each other. Typically, a series of generic test-fit designs will be conducted so they can get the big picture as they await the remaining programming documents. The goal is to understand and know each floor's total staff counts when studying vari-ous percentages of offices per test fit. Figure 9.14 demonstrates an example in test-fit with 61 offices equaling 76 percent of the space being allocated to offices. Figure 9.16

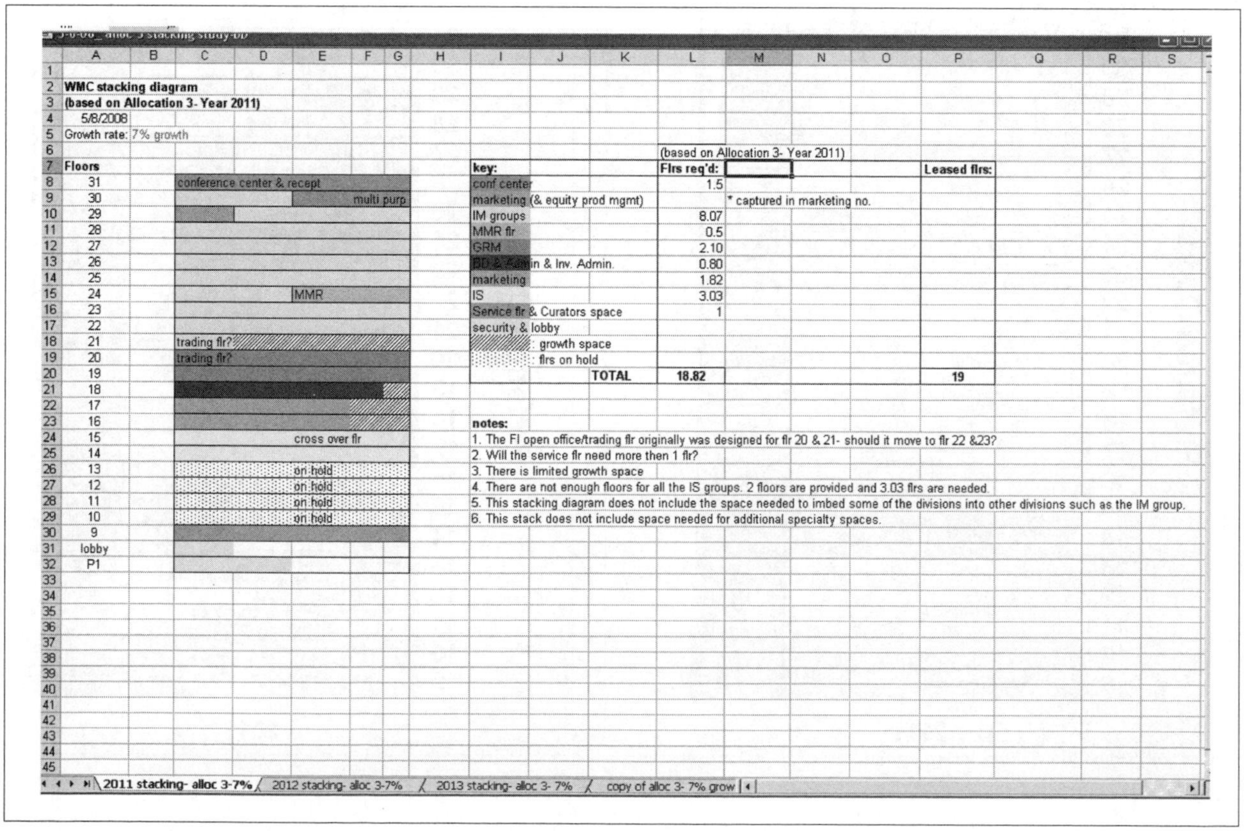

FIGURE 9.18 Stacking plan 1, example from MPA | Margulies Perruzzi Architects, using Microsoft Excel.

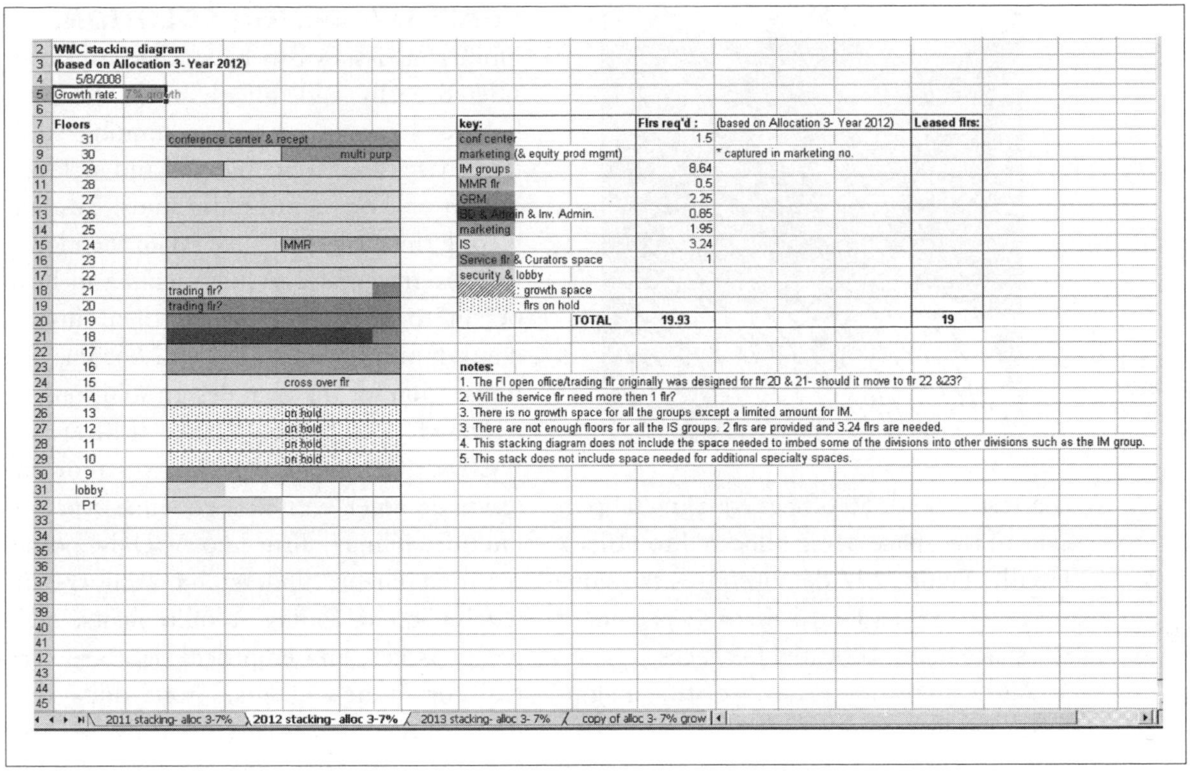

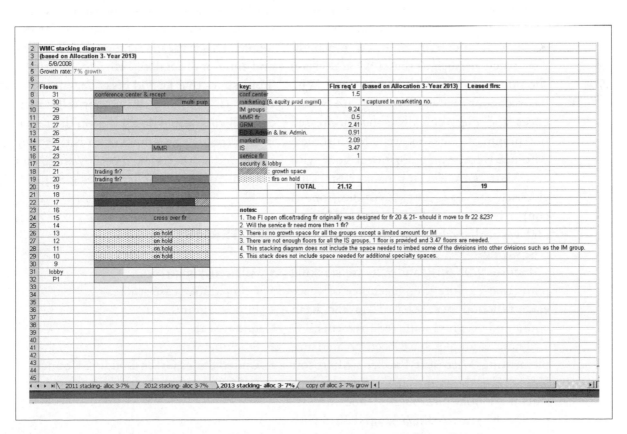

FIGURE 9.19 Stacking plan 2, example from MPA | Margulies Perruzzi Architects, using Microsoft Excel.

FIGURE 9.20 Stacking plan 3, example from MPA | Margulies Perruzzi Architects, using Microsoft Excel .

FIGURE 9.21 David D. Stone, IIDA, LEED AP, NCIDQ Certificate #8043.

is a test-fit with 56 offices equaling 64 percent of the space being allocated to offices. Finally, Figure 9.17 demonstrates the same space test-fitting 47 offices, or 48 percent of the space being allocated to offices.

When analyzing projects of this magnitude, the firm *must study the space vertically*. Stacking studies help visually articulate to the client how many floors and the adjacency relationship to each department. Also other issues need to be addressed regarding the hierarchy of space in a high-rise structure, such as these: What division should be on top with prime view? Who has secondary views? Not only are preferences and hierarchically issues addressed but pragmatic ones as well; for instance, who needs to be on a cross over floor with access to both elevator banks? Stacking electrical spaces is an efficient decision, as copper is expensive and the consolidations and vertical stacking can be a significant cost savings.

Figures 9.18, 9.19, and 9.20 are stacking plans that explore the percentage of space each function needs based on the head count and programmatic requirements.

These examples have been created implementing Microsoft Excel or Microsoft Visio. The diagrams analyze each floor stacking Floors 9 through 31 and forecast out for the years 2011, 2012, and 2013 with a 3 to 7 percent growth rate.

REACHING DESIGN SOLUTIONS

Numerous issues can be studied and considered easily and quickly with blocking, bubble, stacking, and diagramming studies. These can be documented and included as part of the programming study. By completing this task, you have taken the identified programmatic requirements and have begun to visually translate them into a diagramming format that will become the foundation for the final design solutions.

David D. Stone, IIDA, LEED AP, NCIDQ Certificate #8043, a senior interior designer with the Phoenix office of multidisciplinary firm Leo A. Daly, points out that clients understand numbers innately. Square footage requirements, budgetary issues, and empirical data are very real for Stone's clients. Stone adds that the programmer's role is to fully uncover this observed and documented information, transforming it into something that translates the empirical data into a visual language—a diagramming option, for example. This is the magic that programmers and interior designers bring to the table. Stone states that he and his colleagues refer to this as "visioning" when they talk to clients. Clients would do all this on their own if they could. The simple truth is that they can't, and so they seek the knowledge and expertise of you, the interior designer.

KEY TERMS

- Adjacency matrix
- Comparative case studies
- Flow diagram
- Likert scale
- Stacking plan
- United States Green Building Council (USGBC)

CHAPTER 10

Challenging Your Thinking

After reading this chapter, you should be able to:

- Periodically review the process of programming in order to sharpen your skills and knowledge about programming for interior design.
- Review the material that is included in a programming document to assist you in creating one.
- Appreciate the advantages of programming and how it enhances your design decisions.
- Understand how programming fits into your design career.

Remember how you revisit your concept statement after exploring its possibilities in order to sharpen its focus? And recall how you review various parts of your program in light of results for your research, or how you pour through precedent studies of old projects in order to create new designs? You can apply this same approach to your reading of this book to sharpen your understanding of programming and research for interior design.

CHALLENGING YOUR THINKING

This book has given you a holistic overview of programming. The goal is to help you integrate programming and research skills into your work as a student and design professional.

To explore how and why programming is used in the interior design profession, a variety of firms shared how they incorporate programming into their design process. This book brings into the academic setting programming skills that are currently employed in the profession. Chapter by chapter, it has guided you through the process, striving to help you build skills and knowledge and increase your comfort level in developing your own program. Even after you put these skills and knowledge into practice, you can continue to sharpen them by revisiting all that you've learned in light of each new experience in your career.

Think about how we defined programming in Chapter 1. What is the role of programming in the design profession? This will be discussed again at the end of this chapter.

Chapter 2 provided a step-by-step overview of the process of design. How does the process of design in the academic experience differ from that in the professional world?

Chapter 3 showed you how to define a topic and structure your program document, whether you chose your topic or had it assigned to you. Throughout your academic experience and professional life, refer back to the programming document template included in this chapter. Use it as an example to compare against the ones that you are creating now and will create in the future.

Think about the different research methods introduced in Chapter 4. Consider which one(s) would fit right for your project.

Chapter 5 focused on three specific forms of research: historical, observational, and interactive. How can you build a solid foundation of knowledge about a specific type of design using each of these research skills individually and combined?

Chapter 6 focused on conducting a building and site analysis. Why is it important to document such factors as the environment of a design project (e.g., its state and town), exterior building and site conditions, interior building and site conditions, and design constraints and limitations?

How are precedent studies, as discussed in Chapter 7, relevant to programming for interior design? How do you select and analyze them? How do you document the information gleaned from a precedent study to help formulate programmatic requirements?

Finally, consider the written and visual analysis used during the programming phase of design. How do visual diagramming, bubble and blocking, and stacking plans contribute to the unique style of this analysis?

PUTTING TOGETHER YOUR PROGRAMMING DOCUMENT

Programming documents come in many shapes and sizes. For students and professionals alike, variations occur because of the infinite range of potential projects. The reality of client constraints is another major mitigating factor.

The academic experience offers a great opportunity to prepare yourself for the myriad possibilities and challenges that programming will provide for your design career ahead. Introduce yourself to the various aspects of programming in gradual and sequential stages, building your knowledge with each new experience. You might first explore the research component as a group project, with each group sharing all of its data. Taking it one step at a time will help build knowledge, expertise, and confidence to implement the skills on your own. Generating a complete programming document will validate your decision-making abilities in the field of design.

Programming documents, which in some cases might be referred to as a "pre-thesis reports," in many design schools typically include and are devoted to original research. Thus, creating this document is a research- and writing-intensive experience.

Typically, one should follow APA guidelines when generating this document. Make sure that everything is referenced properly, including all of your images. Becoming familiar with the APA guidelines is important. For example, when you enter the profession, programming reports can be essential in obtaining external funding and require a standard of style. For this and many other reasons discussed in this book, good writing skills and attention to detail will serve you well.

A good place to obtain APA guidelines is at your writing center on campus, or directly at the APA Web site. Take full advantage of the writing center on your campus. Have your drafts reviewed and edited. Writing centers offer a great opportunity to work on your writing, clarity of thought, and the organization of your content. Emulate the process of writing a paper for an

English class: numerous revisions and reviews will help you craft a final result that is exponentially better than your first draft. As your thoughts and documentation take form, so will the clarity of your ideas.

In their interviews for this book, many professionals stated that the program document became the primary reference while beginning the design process. Students who have completed a comprehensive programmatic research document enter the schematic design phase with less anxiety and more confidence. Typically the schematic design phase starts with lucid ideas that begin to take form from knowledge gleaned during the programming experience.

Now as an intelligent designer who has completed a full program on the space that you will be designing, you become the "expert." Design options are most likely already floating around in your head, and you are visually able to see numerous solutions!

APPRECIATING THE ADVANTAGES OF PROGRAMMING

By implementing research methods in the programming phase, the results warrant solid documentation of the findings. Conducting historical, observational, and interactive research on your topic emulates the triangulation process as outlined in Chapter 4, "Research Methods." Not only will this help validate your findings by employing a mixed method approach by using multiple data collection methods, but it will also help prevent any biases that might result from relying on one data-collection method (Gall, Borg, & Gall, 1996).

Introduction to research methods and their application to the design process should not be limited to the programming phase of design. As addressed in Chapter 2, "The Process of Design," the whole process encompasses a series of steps to the final solution. Numerous research methods can be employed throughout the phases of design. Programming is a fundamental place to begin. Another very pragmatic time to implement research methods is once the client has occupied the space and you are conducting a post-occupancy evaluation (POE). A POE offers the potential to analyze many research themes; some might be: technologies, health and care of patient environments, effective learning environments, energy in use, lighting, the social and economic aspects of the design, and wayfinding evaluation. This is a small sample of the potential areas that can be studied. By evaluating and documenting the spaces once occupied, the results gleaned from the assessment can be documented and added to the body of knowledge within the interior design profession. Cumulatively this knowledge will benefit future designs and the public as a whole. Your work can then be cited by others in their precedent studies!

Per Dohr and Guerin, "Knowledge of research methods is useful in any business, and the practice of design is ever evolving. Currently, changes seem embedded in our 'information society.' Clients want information in addition to design. They want to know the substance of decisions, the 'why' behind what you designed. While the design community has long held that programming is design research, researchers maintain that design research in its academic interpretation complements not only programming but other stages of the design process as well" (Dohr , Guerin, 2007).

With the research and facts to validate your decision making, the process of design becomes less subjective and more pragmatic. The decision to pursue a career in interior design continues to be a popular educational path. Popular culture and business forecasts illustrate that this trend will continue as more have been exposed to the applied arts as a viable career path. The media interpretation of interior design has caused some public confusion and among students selecting interior design as a career path (Waxman & Clemons, 2007). It is important to emphasize that research and critical thinking is employed to design solutions, not just basing decision making on "I like it, or that's a nice color." Effective programming and research can help the client at the front end of the project to have a realistic idea of budget and timing and to prepare for long-range planning. Also, interior design is a service-driven profession. What better skill to implement than strategies that will meet the needs of the client while understanding their business practices innately? Analyzing and observing their work patterns, behaviors, and habits allows you to generate utilitarian programmatic requirements resulting in an efficient and aesthetic work environment for the users now and in the future.

PURSUING A CAREER IN PROGRAMMING

Typically in all applications of the interior design profession you will be conducting some aspect of programming. Programming is a comprehensive task of identifying all requirements prior to design. In addition, because it is the first phase of design, you will need to retain the data needed to move to the next phase. In an informal sense, we all program in some form or another within the profession. According to White, "Whether we call it programming or not, we all collect and process information for our design decisions. Programming, in this sense does not have to result in a polished report. It can take the form of a conversation with a client, hand scribbled notes, minutes for a meeting or project files. It is helpful to hold an expanded view of what programming is rather than to define it narrowly" (1982, p. 6).

Some large companies have their own in-house facility programmer. It might fall in the realm of a facility manager's task that warrants a full-time position committed to programming. Developers or real estate firms also employ individuals just for programming skills. Some firms interviewed state that they have specific individuals that solely work on the programming requirements for specific clients. This is more prevalent in health care and institutional design. Most design firms offer programming as part of their services to clients.

It is probably inconceivable that one would be working in the profession without implementing programmatic skills in one form or another.

When reviewing the U.S. Office of Personnel Management **series definition** for the profession of interior designer, one can easily see that the large percentage of tasks fall in the realm of programming:

This series includes positions the duties of which are to perform, supervise, or manage work related to the design of interior environments in order to promote employee productivity, health, and welfare, and/or the health and welfare of the public. Typical duties include investigating, identifying, and documenting client needs; analyzing needs, proposing options and, working with the client, developing specific solutions; developing design documents, including contract working drawings and specifications; and, as appropriate, managing design projects performed in-house or by contract. The work requires applying knowledge from a variety of such fields as:

• Interior construction—includes building systems and components, building codes, equipment, materials, and furnishings, working drawings and specification, and codes and standards.

- Contracting—includes cost estimates, bid proposals, negotiations, contract awards, site visits during construction, and pre- and post-occupancy evaluations.
- Facility operation—includes maintenance requirements, traffic patterns, security, and fire protection.
- Aesthetics—includes sense of scale, proportion, and form; color, texture, and finishes; style and visual imagery.
- Psychology—includes privacy and enclosure, and effects of environmental components (e.g., color, texture, space).

- Management—includes design project and resource coordination). (OPM, 1991)

As you transition the knowledge that you have applied in the academic setting to a professional one, it is up to you to educate the client about the benefits of programming and research. Learn from historical, observational, and interactive data not only for the project at hand but for future applications as well. Commit yourself to lifelong learning. Always seek information that will benefit your core body of knowledge, and be intensely curious throughout your career as you implement programming skills to benefit good design for everyone who occupies the spaces you create.

Appendices

The following appendices have been included for your reference. It is helpful to see the tools and approaches to collect and organize pertinent information from clients. Each form should be modified to fit each unique project and to suit your own style.

Tsoi/Kobus & Associates

1. UNDERSTANDING YOUR ORGANIZATION

Figure A.1 is an example of the programming services that Tsoi/Kobus & Associates offers to its clients. Kate Wendt, IIDA, director of interiors, shares this information with the client up front so they are aware of the process and are active participants. For more information on the firm and how it uses these forms, see Chapter 5, "Historical, Observational, and Interactive Research."

Understanding Your Organization

Survey • Interview • Observe • Document

TK&A ⋁ TSOI / KOBUS & ASSOCIATES ARCHITECTS

TK&A ⋁ TSOI / KOBUS & ASSOCIATES
ARCHITECTS

Understanding Your Organization:
Programming and Strategic Facility Planning

Background Information Required From Your Executive Management

	Date Required	Date Received
1. Overall goals and direction for the project		
2. Direction on project-related communication; routing and degree of confidentiality required		
3. Pending organizational changes that will affect the planning process and/or outcome: staffing reductions, reorganizations, computer automation additions, process improvement plans, etc.		
4. Overall budget direction, including any criteria for budget distribution or allocation as well as all items that are a part of the budget (including those that are an owner expense), so that amounts available for construction and furnishings can be determined; also, is cost-center tracking required, and if so, to what degree?		

2. BACKGROUND INFORMATION FORM

Figure A.2 is an example of what Tsoi/ Kobus & Associates issues to its clients prior to the kick-off meeting to gain insight into the client and its organization.

TK&A V TSOI / KOBUS & ASSOCIATES ARCHITECTS

Individual Questionnaire

Part 1 - Background Information (Required)

1. Your current department _____

2. Your job title _____

3. How long have you worked for the company? _____ yrs

4. Which of the following best describes your work setting?
   - Private office
   - Open workstation
   - Team room

5. During a typical week in the office, how much time do you spend in the following locations?

   At your desk

   Somewhere else in the group/team area or nearby

   Elsewhere in the building/in meetings

   At off-site activities (e.g. client, etc.)

   Total (should equal 100%)

6. Do you use alternative work sites? Please list them below.

   _____
   _____
   _____

3. INDIVIDUAL QUESTIONNAIRE

Appendix A.3 is an example of a questionnaire that Tsoi/Kobus & Associates uses to collect pertinent information from individuals and departments.

TK&A V TSOI / KOBUS & ASSOCIATES
ARCHITECTS

Departmental Questionnaire

Your Name: _____ Date: _____

Position: _____ Division: _____

Present Location: _____ Dept.:_____

A. Introduction

Tsoi Kobus & Associates is conducting a planning study of your space needs. We need information about the areas in which you and your coworkers function in order to assure that you will have the space you need to do your job during the upcoming relocation. This is only possible if we have accurate information.

When you are completing the section entitled "General Department Information," please fill in the blanks and check all spaces that apply. To complete "Adjacency Requirements" and the remaining individual sections, please read over the worksheets before filling them out. Complete all spaces pertinent to your department, and leave blank all items that do not apply.

Attach additional sheets of paper if you need to. If you feel that any multiple choice answers do not adequately cover unique situations that may exist in your area, please feel free to write in any comments you may have.

All of your responses will be vital to the success of the study and to you and your department. Please give each question your most careful consideration.

1. What are the strategic objectives of your group? _____

_____

2. What type of physical space will you need to support your business objectives?

_____

4. DEPARTMENTAL QUESTIONNAIRE

Figure A.4 is another example of a ques-tionnaire that Tsoi/Kobus & Associates uses to collect pertinent information from individuals and departments.

TK&A V TSOI / KOBUS & ASSOCIATES
ARCHITECTS

Example Small Projects _____ **Introduction**

The following questionnaire has been developed to determine your department and space planning needs. Please take the time to carefully answer all questions. At least one questionnaire should be complete for each Department. Please photocopy the blank form if more copies are required.

Department: _____ Your Name: _____
Current Location: _____ Title: _____
Phone: _____ Date: _____

This survey has been reviewed and approved by your department manager: _____

General Information

Briefly describe the *function* of this Department. Please attach a current copy of your organization chart.

_____
_____
_____

Indicate the *hours of operation* for your Department. (Check all that apply)

- ☐ Normal Business Hours
- ☐ Evening/Night Shifts
- ☐ Weekend Shifts

- ☐ Weeknight Overtime
- ☐ Weekend Overtime
- ☐ _____

Indicate the level of *security* required for your Department. (Check all that apply)

- ☐ Low – standard building security
- ☐ Medium verification required before outside Visitors are admitted
- ☐ High – area is restricted to company personnel
- ☐ Maximum – area is restricted department personnel

- ☐ Security is required for confidential
- ☐ Security is required for confidential materials/documents
- ☐ Special security devices are required (i.e.: cameras, alarms, mantraps, etc.)

Indicate the types and frequency of *visitors* your Department experiences. (Check all that apply)

- ☐ In-house visitors
- ☐ Outside vendors and/or consultants
- ☐ Customers and clients
- ☐ Messengers and delivery persons

- ☐ Department receives visitors daily
- ☐ Department receives visitors a few times per week
- ☐ Department receives visitors a few times per month
- ☐ Visitors stay within the department for days at a time

Indicate this departments *equipment and environmental systems* requirements. (Check all that apply)

- ☐ Mainframe computer system
- ☐ Local Area Network (LAN) system
- ☐ Wide Area Network (WAN) system

- ☐ Back-up power (UPS, emergency generator)
- ☐ Overtime/24 hour air conditioning
- ☐ _____

What general feeling do you have about our current environment (likes? Dislikes?)?

_____
_____
_____

Page 1

5. EXAMPLE: SMALL PROJECTS

Figure A.5 is an example of a questionnaire that Tsoi/Kobus & Associates uses to collect pertinent information when working on smaller projects.

MPA | Margulies Perruzzi Architects Design Programming Forms

Dianne A. Dunnell, IIDA, NCIDQ certificate #015756, an associate with the firm, implements numerous programming tools when gathering pertinent information from her clients. This appendix contains two examples of the program forms that she uses to organize all the data collected from interviews, questionnaires, and the like (see Figures B-1 and B-2). The forms were created using Microsoft Excel for ease of use, change, and accuracy of information. See Chapter 9, "Written and Visual Analysis," for more information about this firm and how it uses these forms.

CRE MU Programming Form

Design Programming Form - Staffing - 2006

Personnel, Equipment, Centralized Filing for Small Offices, Reference/Supply, Enclosed Areas

Office Name:		Division/Regional Management:	
Office Number: 0001		Approved By:	
Dept Name: LIU		Date:	
Dept Number: Varies			

Form Completed By: B. Spera		Home Office Management:	
Date: November 9, 2006		Approved By:	
		Date:	

PERSONNEL @WS42	Standards Grade Level	Square Feet	Current Staff	2007 Staff	2008 Staff	2009 Staff	2010 Staff	2011 Staff	Design Year *2009	Comments
Vacant	TBD	42	0	1	1	1			42	
Christina Donoghue (reception)	11	42	1	1	1	1			42	
		42							0	
		42							0	
	Total Staff		1	2	2	2	0	0	84	

PERSONNEL @WS84	Standards Grade Level	Square Feet	Current Staff	2007 Staff	2008 Staff	2009 Staff	2010 Staff	2011 Staff	Design Year *2009	Comments
Vacant	TBD	84	0	1	1	1			84	
Haline Magny	15	84	1	1	1	1			84	
		84							0	
	Total Staff		1	2	2	2	0	0	168	

PERSONNEL @PO150/PO120/PO100 (Office Size Varies)	Standards Grade Level	Square Feet	Current Staff	2007 Staff	2008 Staff	2009 Staff	2010 Staff	2011 Staff	Design Year *2009	Comments
Vacant (Chief Risk Officer)	TBD	120	0	1	1	1			120	
Vacant (Finance/HR IT Person)	TBD	120		1	1	1			120	
Ellen Fecteau	21	120	1	1	1	1			120	
Nick Creatura	21	120	1	1	1	1			120	
Kim Briones	19	120	1	1	1	1			120	
Brian Gavini	19	120	1	1	1	1			120	
Karyn Conlon	17	120	1	1	1	1			120	
Steve DerBoghosian	17	120	1	1	1	1			120	
Hoteling	17	120	1	1	1	1			120	
	Total Staff		7	9	9	9	0	0	1,080	

PERSONNEL @PO225 (Office size varies)	Standards Grade Level	Square Feet	Current Staff	2007 Staff	2008 Staff	2009 Staff	2010 Staff	2011 Staff	Design Year *2009	Comments
Danby Forsythe	27	225	1	1	1	1			225	
Vacant (Chief Risk Officer)	TBD	225		1	1	1			225	
Gordon McBurney	23	225	1	1	1	1			225	
Vacant - New for 2007		225		1	1	1			225	
Vacant - New for 2007	23	225	1	1	1	1			225	
	Total Staff		3	5	5	5	0	0	1,125	

EQUIPMENT		Square Feet	Current	2007	2008	2009	2010	2011	Design Year *2009	Comments
Copier		16	0	2	2	2			30	
Printer		4	2	5	5	5			20	1 B&W, 1 Color
Fax		4	1	2	2	2			8	
Shared Computers		8	0	0	0	0			0	
Other Typewriter		15	1	1	1	1			15	
						Total Equipment			73	

STORAGE (if many files req'd-see 'Storage & Filing' form.)		Square Feet	Current	2007	2008	2009	2010	2011	Design Year *2009	File/Shelf Dimensions
36" Lateral Files		5	0	4	4	4			20	
42" Lateral Files		5	2	4	4	4			20	x2 wood 4 drawer, in Reception
Vertical Files - 5 drawer		4	19	22	22	22			88	
Tab Files (include dimensions)		6	0	0	0	0			0	
Shelving units (include dimensions)		5	0	0	0	0			0	
Bookcases (include dimensions)		5	0	0	0	0			0	
Tables		15	1	2	2	2			30	small table i
Storage Cabinets		5	0	2	2	2			10	
Other (explain)		9	0	0	0	0			0	
						Total Storage			168	

ENCLOSED ROOMS		Square Feet	Current	2007	2008	2009	2010	2011	Design Year *2009	Comments
Storage Room		120	0	1	1	1			120	
File Room			0	0	0	0			0	
Tel/data		100	1	2	2	2			200	access in Reception
Lunch Room			0	1	1	1			0	
Reception			1	1	1	1				
Closet		30	1	2	2	2			60	Closet outside of Nick Creatura's office
Conference Room - Large		150	0	1	1	1			150	Conference room: Dedham Rm
Conference Room - Small		300	0	2	2	2			600	
						Total Enclosed Rooms			1,130	

Projected Assigned USF		3,828
Circulation (45%)		1,723
TOTAL PROJECTED DEPARTMENTAL ASSIGNED USF		5,551

*Design Year is the year which the floorplan will be designed for. If another year should be used,

please change the year shown and update the formula in the Design Year Column.

Additional Comments:

BCBS MA Design Programming Form - Staffing - 2007

Personnel, Equipment, Centralized Filing for Offices, Reference/Supply, Enclosed Areas

Office Name: Worcester	
Office Number: [number here]	
Dept Name: [name here]	
Dept Number: [number here]	

Division/Regional Management:	
Approved By:	
Date:	

Form Completed By: [dept head name here]	
Date: [date completed here]	

Home Office Management:	
Approved By:	
Date:	

PERSONNEL @ Vice President level

	Standards Space size	Square Feet	Current Staff	2008 Staff	2009 Staff	2010 Staff	2011 Staff	2012 Staff	Design Year *2010	Comments
[Name A]	12'-0" x 18.75'	180							0	
[Name B]	12'-0" x 18.75'	180							0	
[Name C]	12'-0" x 18.75'	180							0	
[Name D]	12'-0" x 18.75'	180							0	
	Total Staff		0	0	0	0	0	0	0	

PERSONNEL @ Director level

	Standards Space size	Square Feet	Current Staff	2008 Staff	2009 Staff	2010 Staff	2011 Staff	2012 Staff	Design Year *2010	Comments
[Name A]	10'x12'	120							0	
[Name B]	10'x12'	120							0	
[Name C]	10'x12'	120							0	
[Name D]	10'x12'	120							0	
	10'x12'	120							0	
	Total Staff		0	0	0	0	0	0	0	

PERSONNEL @ Manager with direct report & "I" individual contributors

	Standards Space size	Square Feet	Current Staff	2008 Staff	2009 Staff	2010 Staff	2011 Staff	2012 Staff	Design Year *2010	Comments
[Name A]	10'x12'	120							0	
[Name B]	10'x12'	120							0	
[Name C]	10'x12'	120							0	
[Name D]	10'x12'	120							0	
	10'x12'	120							0	
	10'x12'	120							0	
	Total Staff		0	0	0	0	0	0	0	

PERSONNEL @ Manager Cubicle- Manager, Team leaders, Project Manager, Senior Individual contributors

	Standards Space size	Square Feet	Current Staff	2008 Staff	2009 Staff	2010 Staff	2011 Staff	2012 Staff	Design Year *2010	Comments
[Name A]	7'x14'	98							0	
[Name B]	7'x14'	98							0	
[Name C]	7'x14'	98							0	
[Name D]	7'x14'	98							0	
	7'x14'	98							0	
	Total Staff		0	0	0	0	0	0	0	

PERSONNEL @ Administrative Cubicle- Secretary, Receptionist, Project leaders and individual constributors

	Standards Space size	Square Feet	Current Staff	2008 Staff	2009 Staff	2010 Staff	2011 Staff	2012 Staff	Design Year *2010	Comments
[Name A]	7'x14'	98							0	
[Name B]	7'x14'	98							0	
[Name C]	7'x14'	98							0	
[Name D]	7'x14'	98							0	
	7'x14'	98							0	
	Total Staff		0	0	0	0	0	0	0	

PERSONNEL @ Associate Cubicle- Representatives, Processor part time and Contracted associates

	Standards Space size	Square Feet	Current Staff	2008 Staff	2009 Staff	2010 Staff	2011 Staff	2012 Staff	Design Year *2010	Comments
[Name A]	7'x7'	49							0	
[Name B]	7'x7'	49							0	
[Name C]	7'x7'	49							0	
[Name D]	7'x7'	49							0	
[Name E]	7'x7'	49							0	
[Name F]	7'x7'	49							0	
[Name G]	7'x7'	49							0	
[Name H]	7'x7'	49							0	
[Name I]	7'x7'	49							0	
[Name J]	7'x7'	49							0	
	7'x7'	49							0	
	Total Staff		0	0	0	0	0	0	0	

EQUIPMENT

		Square Feet	Current	2008	2009	2010	2011	2012	Design Year *2010	Comments
Copier		15							0	
Printer		4							0	
Fax		4							0	
Shared Computers		8							0	
Pitney Bows machine		8							0	
Shredder		4							0	
Filtered water units- floor models		4							0	
Other (explain)									0	
Other (explain)									0	
						Total Equipment			0	

STORAGE (If many files req'd-see 'Storage & Filing' form.)

		Square Feet	Current	2008	2009	2010	2011	2012	Design Year *2010	File/Shelf Dimensions
36" Lateral Files- 3 drawer		5							0	
36" Lateral Files- 4 drawer		5							0	
42" Lateral Files- 3 drawer		5							0	
42" Lateral Files- 4 drawer		5							0	
Vertical Files - 5 drawer		4							0	
Tab Files (include dimensions)		6							0	
Shelving units- 5 shelves (include dimensions)		5							0	
Shelving units- 4 shelves (include dimensions)		5							0	
Shelving units- 3 shelves (include dimensions)		5							0	
Bookcases- 2 shelf (include dimensions)		5							0	
Bookcases- 4 shelf (include dimensions)		5							0	
Tables (include dimensions)		15							0	
Storage Cabinets- 2 doors (include dimensions)		4							0	
Mail Sorter - (indicate size and type)		8							0	
Mail cart		9							0	
Lge recycle bins		9							0	
Lge trash bins		9							0	
Other (explain)									0	
Other (explain)									0	
						Total Storage			0	

ENCLOSED ROOMS

		Square Feet	Current	2008	2009	2010	2011	2012	Design Year *2010	Comments
Storage Room		120							0	
File Room		120							0	
Tel/data		100							0	
Lunch Room		225							0	
Reception		225							0	
Closet		30							0	
Conference Room - Large		150							0	
Conference Room - Small		300							0	
						Total Enclosed Rooms			0	

Projected Assigned USF	0
Circulation (45%)	0
TOTAL PROJECTED DEPARTMENTAL ASSIGNED USF	0

*Design Year is the year which the floorplan will be designed for. If another year should be used,

Design Consortium's Residential Program

Appendix C is an example of a questionnaire that Lynne Bryan Phipps, principal of Design One Consortium, implements when meeting with a client to collect pertinent information. See Chapter 8, "Generating the Program," for more information about Design One Consortium and how this firms uses this questionnaire.

General

Exterior

FINISH
- ☐ Shingles
- ☐ Clapboard
- ☐ Vertical Siding
- ☐ Brick
- ☐ Stone
- ☐ Other

ROOFING
- ☐ Asphalt Shingles
- ☐ Cedar Shakes
- ☐ Slate
- ☐ Metal
- ☐ Other

FOUNDATION
- ☐ Full Basement
- ☐ Crawl Space
- ☐ Slab on Grade
- ☐ Piers

- ☐ Other

Mechanical

WATER
- ☐ Well
- ☐ Public

Sewage
- ☐ Individual
- ☐ Sand Filter
- ☐ Holding Tank
- ☐ Leaching Field
- ☐ Public

Fuel
- ☐ Oil
- ☐ Gas
- ☐ Propane
- ☐ Electric
- ☐ Geothermal
- ☐ Hydro-electric
- ☐ Wind
- ☐ Solar
- ☐ Other

Heating
- ☐ Forced Hot Water
- ☐ Forced Hot Air
- ☐ Radiant
- ☐ Other

Air Conditioning
- ☐ Central Zoned
- ☐ Master Bedroom
- ☐ Other

Other
- ☐ Central Vacuum System
- ☐ Intercom
- ☐ Music System
- ☐ Security System
- ☐ Cable/Internet
- ☐ Sprinkler System
- ☐ Landscaping
- ☐ Other

Living Room

Furniture

SOFA
- ☐ Love Seat (   )
- ☐ Medium (   )
- ☐ Large (   )
- ☐ Sectional
- ☐ Other

CHAIRS
- ☐ Number (   )

TABLES
- ☐ Size
- ☐ Number (   )
- ☐ Other

OTHER

Built-ins
- ☐ Bookcases
- ☐ Entertainment Center
- ☐ Wet Bar
- ☐ Other

Fuel
- ☐ Wood Burning
- ☐ Gas
- ☐ Electric
- ☐ Zero Clearance
- ☐ Raised Hearth
- ☐ Wood Storage
- ☐ Other

Features
- ☐ Formal
- ☐ Informal
- ☐ Open to Dining
- ☐ Open to Kitchen
- ☐ Access to Outdoors
- ☐ High Ceilings/Vaulted Cathedral
- ☐ Other

Lighting
- ☐ Recessed Light
- ☐ Switch Operated Outlets
- ☐ Floor Lamps (   )
- ☐ Table Lamps (   )
- ☐ Wall Mounted
- ☐ Indirect
- ☐ Track
- ☐ Directional
- ☐ Fans
- ☐ Other

Electrical
- ☐ Telephone Jack
- ☐ TV Outlet
- ☐ Cable
- ☐ High Definition
- ☐ Satellite
- ☐ Internet Outlet
- ☐ Hardwire
- ☐ Wireless System
- ☐ High Speed System
- ☐ Stereo System
- ☐ Entertainment System
- ☐ Built-in Speakers
- ☐ Free Standing
- ☐ Speakers

Dining Room

Furniture
- ☐ Table
- ☐ Size (   )
- ☐ Extra Leaves

CHAIRS
- ☐ Number (   )

BUFFET
- ☐ Size

CHINA CUPBOARD
- ☐ Size

Other

BUILT-INS
- ☐ China Cupboard
- ☐ Linen Storage
- ☐ Other

Features
- ☐ Formal
- ☐ Informal
- ☐ Open to Living Space
- ☐ Open to Kitchen
- ☐ Access to Outdoors
- ☐ High Ceilings/Tray/Vaulted/ Cathedral
- ☐ Other

Lighting
- ☐ Chandelier
- ☐ Recessed Light
- ☐ Directional Light
- ☐ Switch Operated Outlets
- ☐ Wall Mounted
- ☐ Indirect
- ☐ Fans
- ☐ Other

Kitchen

Appliances

SINK
- ☐ Double Bowl
- ☐ Single Bowl
- ☐ Special or Triple
- ☐ Prep Sink
- ☐ Stainless Steel
- ☐ Porcelain
- ☐ In Island
- ☐ Top Mount
- ☐ Bottom Mount
- ☐ Instant Hot Water
- ☐ Other

STOVE
- ☐ Range
- ☐ Cook Top
- ☐ 4-burner
- ☐ 6-burner
- ☐ Dual Fuel
- ☐ Gas
- ☐ Electric
- ☐ Other

OVEN
- ☐ In Range
- ☐ Wall Mounted
- ☐ Double
- ☐ Convection Oven
- ☐ Warming Drawers
- ☐ Other

MICROWAVE
- ☐ Wall Mounted
- ☐ Over Cook Top w/ fan
- ☐ Counter
- ☐ Convection
- ☐ Other

DISHWASHER
- ☐ Yes
- ☐ Dish Drawer
- ☐ Other

REFRIGERATOR
- ☐ Side by Side
- ☐ Freezer Over
- ☐ Freezer Under
- ☐ Counter Depth
- ☐ Ice Maker
- ☐ Bar Fridge
- ☐ Wine Fridge
- ☐ Other

OTHER
- ☐ Garbage Disposal
- ☐ Trash Compactor
- ☐ Recycle Bins (   )
- ☐ Size (   )
- ☐ Other

Other Features

CABINETS
- ☐ Wood
- ☐ Laminate

☐ European Style
☐ Style/Brand
☐ Other

COUNTERTOPS
☐ Laminate
☐ Solid Surface
☐ Concrete
☐ Stone
☐ Tile
☐ Other

EAT-IN AREA
☐ Table & Chairs
☐ Counter & Stools
☐ Breakfast Nook
☐ Other

OTHER
☐ Desk
☐ Island
☐ Pantry
☐ TV Outlet
☐ Internet Outlet
☐ Telephone Jack

Lavet

Fixtures

SINK
☐ Single Bowl
☐ Double Bowl
☐ Makeup Area
☐ Vanity
☐ Pedestal
☐ Other

TOILET
☐ Standard
☐ Elongated
☐ Enclosed
☐ Bidet
☐ Low Vol. Flush
☐ Other

BATHING
☐ Shower
☐ Size (   )
☐ Tile
☐ Prefab
☐ Other

Lighting
☐ Overhead Light
☐ Light
☐ Fan
☐ Heat Lamp
☐ Light over Sink
☐ Fluorescent
☐ Incandescent
☐ Other

Other
☐ Linen Closet
☐ In Bath
☐ Outside Bath
☐ Laundry
☐ Telephone Jack
☐ Window to Outside

Laundry

Fixtures

WASHING MACHINE
☐ Free Standing
☐ Stacked
☐ Front Load
☐ Top Load
☐ Capacity (   )

DRYER
☐ Free Standing
☐ Stacked
☐ Front Load
☐ Top Load
☐ Gas
☐ Electric
☐ Other

OTHER
☐ Folding Counter
☐ Built-in Ironing Board
☐ Utility Sink
☐ Clothes Hamper
☐ Laundry Chute
☐ Sewing Space

Family Room

Furniture

Sofa
- [ ] Love Seat (   )
- [ ] Medium (   )
- [ ] Fullsize (   )
- [ ] Sectional
- [ ] Other

Chairs
- [ ] Number:

Tables
- [ ] Size
- [ ] Number (   )
- [ ] Other

Other

Built-ins
- [ ] Bookcases
- [ ] Entertainment Center
- [ ] Wet Bar
- [ ] Other

Fuel
- [ ] Wood Burning
- [ ] Gas
- [ ] Electric/Remote Start
- [ ] Raised Hearth
- [ ] Wood Storage
- [ ] Zero Clearance
- [ ] Other

Features
- [ ] Formal
- [ ] Informal
- [ ] Open to Dining
- [ ] Open to Kitchen
- [ ] Access to Outdoors
- [ ] High Ceilings/Vault/Cathedral
- [ ] Other

Lighting
- [ ] Recessed Light
- [ ] Switch Operated Outlets
- [ ] Floor Lamps (   )
- [ ] Table Lamps (   )
- [ ] Wall Mounted
- [ ] Indirect
- [ ] Directional
- [ ] Track
- [ ] Fans
- [ ] Other

Electrical
- [ ] Telephone Jack
- [ ] TVOutlet
- [ ] Cable
- [ ] High Definition
- [ ] Satellite
- [ ] Internet Outlet
- [ ] Hardwire
- [ ] Wireless System
- [ ] High Speed System
- [ ] Stereo System
- [ ] Entertainment System
- [ ] Built-in Speakers
- [ ] Free Standing Speakers

Sunroom / Atrium

Purpose
- [ ] Greenhouse
- [ ] Sitting Area
- [ ] Play Space
- [ ] Other

Flooring
- [ ] Concrete
- [ ] Tile
- [ ] Wood
- [ ] Carpet
- [ ] Other

Other
- [ ] Potting Bench
- [ ] Utility Sink
- [ ] Hot Tub
- [ ] Floor Drain
- [ ] Other

Lighting
- ☐ Fluorescent
- ☐ Incandescent
- ☐ Recessed Light
- ☐ Track
- ☐ Directional
- ☐ Special Needs

Electrical
- ☐ Telephone Jack
- ☐ TV Outlet
- ☐ Cable
- ☐ High Definition
- ☐ Satellite
- ☐ Internet Outlet
- ☐ Hardwire
- ☐ Wireless System
- ☐ High Speed System
- ☐ Stereo System
- ☐ Entertainment System
- ☐ Built-in Speakers
- ☐ Floor Speakers

Other
- ☐ Heating
- ☐ Access to Outside
- ☐ Deck
- ☐ Patio
- ☐ Garden
- ☐ Glass Roof
- ☐ Skylights

Master Bedroom

Furniture

BED
- ☐ Double (   )
- ☐ Queen
- ☐ King
- ☐ California King
- ☐ Waterbed
- ☐ Adjustable
- ☐ Other

BUREAU
- ☐ Standard
- ☐ Double
- ☐ Triple
- ☐ High Boy
- ☐ Armoire

NIGHT STANDS
- ☐ One Side
- ☐ Both Sides

OTHER
- ☐ Table (   )
- ☐ Chair (   )
- ☐ Desk (   )
- ☐ Exercise Equipment
- ☐ Other

Features
- ☐ Sitting Area
- ☐ Balcony
- ☐ Attached Bath
- ☐ Access to Outside
- ☐ Fireplace
- ☐ Cathedral Ceilings
- ☐ Desk
- ☐ Built-in Shelves
- ☐ TV Outlet
- ☐ Telephone Jack
- ☐ Stereo System
- ☐ Other

Lighting
- ☐ Recessed Light
- ☐ Directional
- ☐ Switch Operated Outlets
- ☐ Floor Lamps (   )
- ☐ Table Lamps (   )
- ☐ Wall Mounted
- ☐ Indirect
- ☐ Fans
- ☐ Other

Closet
- ☐ Walk-in
- ☐ Standard
- ☐ Other

Master Bath

Fixtures

SINK
- [ ] Single Bowl
- [ ] Double Bowl
- [ ] Makeup Area
- [ ] Separate His/Hers
- [ ] Vanity
- [ ] Pedestal
- [ ] Other

TOILET
- [ ] Standard
- [ ] Elongated
- [ ] Enclosed
- [ ] Bidet
- [ ] Other

BATHING
- [ ] Tub/Shower Unit
- [ ] Stall Shower (   )
- [ ] Claw Footed Tub
- [ ] Hot Tub
- [ ] Whirlpool
- [ ] Other

OTHER
- [ ] Sauna
- [ ] Steam Unit

Master Bath

Fixtures

SINK
- [ ] Single Bowl
- [ ] Double Bowl
- [ ] Makeup Area
- [ ] Separate His/Hers
- [ ] Vanity
- [ ] Pedestal
- [ ] Other

Toilet
- [ ] Standard
- [ ] Elongated
- [ ] Enclosed
- [ ] Bidet
- [ ] Other

Bathing
- [ ] Tub/Shower Unit
- [ ] Stall Shower (   )
- [ ] Claw Footed Tub
- [ ] Hot Tub
- [ ] Whirlpool
- [ ] Other

Other
- [ ] Sauna
- [ ] Steam Unit

Bedroom

Furniture

BED
- [ ] 1 Twin
- [ ] 2 Twin
- [ ] Bunk Beds
- [ ] Double
- [ ] Queen
- [ ] King
- [ ] Waterbed
- [ ] Other

Bureau
- [ ] Standard
- [ ] Double
- [ ] Triple
- [ ] Stacked

Night Stands
- [ ] One Side
- [ ] Both Sides

Features
- [ ] Sitting Area
- [ ] Balcony
- [ ] Access to Outside
- [ ] Desk
- [ ] Built-in Shelves
- [ ] Attached Bath
- [ ] TV Outlet
- [ ] Telephone Jack
- [ ] Internet Jack
- [ ] Cathedral Ceilings

☐ Other

Lighting
- ☐ Recessed Light
- ☐ Directional Light
- ☐ Switch Operated Outlets
- ☐ Floor Lamps (   )
- ☐ Table Lamps (   )
- ☐ Wall Mounted
- ☐ Indirect
- ☐ Fans
- ☐ Other

Closet
- ☐ Walk-in
- ☐ Standard

Other

Bath

Fixtures

SINK
- ☐ Single Bowl
- ☐ Double Bowl
- ☐ Makeup Area
- ☐ Separate His/Hers
- ☐ Vanity
- ☐ Pedestal
- ☐ Other

TOILET
- ☐ Standard
- ☐ Elongated
- ☐ Enclosed
- ☐ Bidet
- ☐ Other

BATHING
- ☐ Tub/Shower Unit
- ☐ Stall Shower (   )
- ☐ Claw Footed Tub
- ☐ Hot Tub
- ☐ Whirlpool
- ☐ Other

OTHER
- ☐ Sauna
- ☐ Steam Unit

Lighting
- ☐ Overhead Light
- ☐ Light
- ☐ Fan
- ☐ Heat Lamp
- ☐ Light over Sink
- ☐ Fluorescent
- ☐ Incandescent
- ☐ Other

Other
- ☐ Linen Closet
- ☐ In Bath
- ☐ Outside Bath
- ☐ Laundry
- ☐ Telephone Jack
- ☐ Access to Outside
- ☐ Balcony
- ☐ Other

Bath

Fixtures

SINK
- ☐ Single Bowl
- ☐ Double Bowl
- ☐ Makeup Area
- ☐ Separate His/Hers
- ☐ Vanity
- ☐ Pedestal
- ☐ Other

TOILET
- ☐ Standard
- ☐ Elongated
- ☐ Enclosed
- ☐ Bidet
- ☐ Other

BATHING
- ☐ Tub/Shower Unit
- ☐ Stall Shower (   )
- ☐ Claw Footed Tub
- ☐ Hot Tub
- ☐ Whirlpool
- ☐ Other

OTHER
- ☐ Sauna

☐ Steam Unit

LIGHTING
☐ Overhead Light
☐ Light
☐ Fan
☐ Heat Lamp
☐ Light over Sink
☐ Fluorescent
☐ Incandescent
☐ Other

OTHER
☐ Linen Closet
☐ In Bath
☐ Outside Bath
☐ Laundry
☐ Telephone Jack
☐ Access to Outside
☐ Balcony
☐ Other

Bath

Fixtures

SINK
☐ Single Bowl
☐ Double Bowl
☐ Makeup Area
☐ Separate His/Hers
☐ Vanity
☐ Pedestal
☐ Other

TOILET
☐ Standard
☐ Elongated
☐ Enclosed
☐ Bidet
☐ Other

BATHING
☐ Tub/Shower Unit
☐ Stall Shower (   )
☐ Claw Footed Tub
☐ Hot Tub
☐ Whirlpool
☐ Other

OTHER
☐ Sauna

☐ Steam Unit

Lighting
☐ Overhead Light
☐ Light
☐ Fan
☐ Heat Lamp
☐ Light over Sink
☐ Fluorescent
☐ Incandescent
☐ Other

Other
☐ Linen Closet
☐ In Bath
☐ Outside Bath
☐ Laundry
☐ Telephone Jack
☐ Access to Outside
☐ Balcony
☐ Other

Workshop

Purpose
☐ Woodworking
☐ Auto Repair
☐ Small Tool Repair
☐ Other

WORKBENCH
☐ No
☐ Yes

Size (   )

Equipment

List major pieces of equipment and their sizes:

Other
☐ Tool Board
☐ Storage Shelves
☐ Utility Sink
☐ Hot Tub
☐ Floor Drain

☐ Other

Lighting
   ☐ Fluorescent
   ☐ Incandescent
   ☐ Special Needs

Electrical
   ☐ Telephone Jack
   ☐ TV Outlet
   ☐ Outlet Strips
   ☐ 220 volt outlet
   ☐ Other

Other
   ☐ Heating
   ☐ Access to Outside
   ☐ Standard Door
   ☐ Double Doors
   ☐ Bulkhead

Garage
   SIZE
   ☐ Single
   ☐ Double
   ☐ Triple
   ☐ Other

Style
   ☐ Attached
   ☐ Breezeway
   ☐ Detached
   ☐ Other

Storage
   ☐ Car Number (   )
   ☐ Boat Size (   )
   ☐ Lawn Mower
   ☐ Workbench

Other

Helpful Resources

- American Association of Retired Persons (AARP) www.aarp.org/families/home_design
- American Disabilities Act (ADA) www.ada.gov
- Adaptive Environments Human Centered Design www.adaptiveenvironments.org/index.php?option=Home
- American Institute of Architects (AIA) www.aia.org/pia/health
- Allsteel Office www.allsteeloffice.com/AllsteelOffice
- AMD3 Foundation www.amd3.org
- American Academy of Healthcare Interior Designers www.aahid.org
- American Educational Research Association www.aera.net/
- American National Standards Institute (ANSI) www.ansi.org
- American Psychological Association (APA) www.apa.org
- The Association of Higher Education Facilities Officers (APPA) www.appa.org
- ArchNewsNow www.archnewsnow.com
- American Society of Interior Design (ASID) www.asid.org
- American Society for Testing and Materials (ASTM) www.astm.org
- Bibme www.bibme.org/bibliography/help
- Building Owners and Managers Association (BOMA) www.boma.org
- Building Green www.buildinggreen.com
- Building Industry Exchange www.building.org
- Buildings Magazine www.buildings.com
- Building Operating Management Magazine www.facilitiesnet.com
- Carmun Connective Wisdom www.carmun.com/easy-bibliography-formatting-APA-MLA.php
- Center for Health Design www.healthdesign.org
- Centers for Disease Control and Prevention www.cdc.gov
- Chain Store Age www.chainstoreage.com
- Council for Interior Design Accreditation (CIDA) www.accredit-id.org
- Colorado State University's online learning environment, the Writing Studio writing.colostate.edu/index.cfm
- Contemporary Long Term Care www.cltcmag.com
- Contract Magazine www.contractmagazine.com

- CorCoreNet www.corenetglobal.org
- Corporate Design Foundation www.cdf.org
- Display and Design Ideas Magazine www.ddimagazine.com
- Design Intelligence www.di.net
- Dezignaré Interior Design Collective, Inc. www.dezignare.com
- Dwell www.dwell.com
- Easy Bib www.easybib.com/
- Elle Décor www.elledecor.com
- EuroFM www.eurofm.org/
- Facility Care www.facilitycare.com
- FM DataComm www.fmdata.com
- FM Link www.fmlink.com
- Frame Magazine www.framemag.com
- Furniture Today www.furnituretoday.com
- Green Guide for Health Care www.gghc.org
- Health Facilities Management Magazine www.hfmmagazine.com
- Hospitality Design (HD) www.hdmag.com/hospitalitydesign/index.jsp
- Hotel Online www.hotel-online.com
- International Building Code (ICB) www.iccsafe.org
- International Federation of Interior Architect/Designer (IFI) www.ifiworld.org
- International Facility Management Association (IFMA) www.ifma.org
- International Furnishings and Design Association (IFDA) www.ifda.com
- International Interior Design Association (IIDA) www.iida.org
- InformeDesign www.informedesign.umn.edu
- InfoTile.com www.infotile.com
- Institute for Family-Centered Care www.familycenteredcare.org
- Interior Design Educators Council www.idec.org
- Interior Design Magazine www.interiordesign.net
- Interiors & Sources Magazine www.isdesignet.com
- International Home Furniture Market www.highpointmarket.org
- The Journal of Interior Design www.journalofinteriordesign.org
- The Librarians' Internet Index lii.org
- Lighting Research Center www.lrc.rpi.edu
- MADCAD www.madcad.com/index.php
- Metropolitan Home www.methome.com
- National Association of Store Fixture Manufacturers www.nasfm.com
- National Kitchen & Bath Association NKBA www.nkba.org
- The National Safety Council www.nsc.org
- National Council for Interior Design Qualification (NCIDQ) www.ncidq.org
- NeoCon World's Trade Fair www.merchandisemart.com/neocon
- ONTHERAIL www.ontherail.com
- ProQuest www.proquest.com/products_umi/dissertations
- Research Design Connections www.researchdesignconnections.com
- Restaurant Business www.restaurant-biz.com
- RetailDesignDiva is the industry's first retail design weblog retaildesigndiva.blogs.com
- Retail Traffic retailtrafficmag.com/
- Shopping Centers Today www.icsc.org
- Social Research Methods www.socialresearchmethods.net
- Society for the Advancement of Gerontological Environments (SAGE) www.sagefederation.org
- Society for the Arts in Healthcare (SAH) www.theSAH.org
- Steelcase www.steelcase.com/na/
- Step Inside Design www.stepinsidedesign.com

- The American Society for Healthcare Engineering www.ashe.org
- The Center for Health Design www.healthdesign.org
- The Council for Interior Design Accreditation www.accredit-id.org
- The Green Roundtable www.greenroundtable.org
- The OWL at Purdue owl.english.purdue.edu/owl/resource/560/01
- U.S. Department of Health and Human Services www.hhs.gov/ohrp/
- U.S. Department of Labor Occupational Safety and Health Administration www.osha.gov/SLTC/
- U.S. Green Building Council, (USGBC) www.usgbc.org
- U.S. General Services Administration www.gsa.gov
- USACE Center of Expertise For Preservation of Historic Buildings & Structures www.nws.usace.army.mil
- VMSD (Visual Merchandising and Store Design) www.visualstore.com

Glossary

action research A focused effort toward finding a solution to improve the quality of the performance of an organization, a group, or an individual in a particular setting. Educators or practitioners who analyze the data to improve the outcomes often perform action research.

activity map A diagram that shows what people are doing when performing a task.

ADA codes The Americans with Disabilities Act's accessibility guidelines for buildings and facilities.

adjacency matrix A visual tool created to illustrate, confirm, and clarify clients' needs and significant relationships between spaces. A helpful tool in the development and analysis of spatial relationships.

aging in place When older individuals choose not to move from their home after retirement.

American Society of Interior Design (ASID) An organization for professional interior designers. A network devoted to keep members updated on the latest products and styles in the industry. Also devoted to

codes and applying them to designs (www.asid.org).

analyzing descriptive data Reviewing and analyzing what a researcher has observed and documented.

anthropometry/anthropometrics The scientific measurement and collection of data regarding a human's physical motion and range of movement.

asset management The use and overseeing of a person's or company's finances.

axial coding An approach to coding where categories are related to their subcategories to form more precise and complete explanations about phenomena.

barrier-free design Design that keeps all pathways free of objects or anything that may block and protrude a means of passage; a design that keeps people safe from injury and harm.

Bauhaus School In 1919, the German architect Walter Gropius founded this school in Weimar, Germany. The school and philosophy promotes individual creative expression and collaboration among the art and design disciplines to create environments.

behavioral mapping The process of observing current conditions of an environment in order to gain insight into that environment. For example, you could observe how students enter a classroom and notice the seats they first select based on the layout of that room.

bubble diagram A visual diagram of spaces' functions depicted in bubble form to give the client an overall idea of where each space will be in relation to the others.

building code requirements Rules and regulations to be followed for the safety in the built environment.

case study research In-depth studies of a particular instance, event, or situation (i.e., a case).

color theory The understanding of color mixing, color combinations, and the visual impact of color.

comparative case studies Research that involves other facilities in the client's industry and other industries that may use innovative technologies or approaches that could be universalized or used in the client's situation.

concept A preliminary idea sought after at the beginning of a project in order to obtain and create a core concept for the design.

concept diagram How the designer begins to organize the physical space in relationship to a conceptual idea.

concept statement The anticipated or desired outcome of a design. When approach-

ing a project, much is unknown because many of the ideas have not been explored yet; therefore, the statement is not definitive but is meant to be challenged by one's own research.

connoisseurship The process of observing the meaning, goals, and objectives of an educational program.

construction documents Official drawings done by a designprofessional that display concise depictions and measurements of everything being constructed.

contract administration The overseeing and administration of the construction phase of a project.

contract documents The final set of documents that are used for construction. Contract documents are considered a legal form of documentation for what will be built.

Council for Interior Design Accreditation (CIDA) A nonprofit organization that promotes high academic standards in interior design schools. CIDA ensures that its guidelines for what should be taught are met by visiting its accredited institutions once every six years (www.accredit-id.org).

critical instance case studies An examination of one or more sites for either the purpose of examining a situation of unique interest with little to no interest in generalization-ability or to call into question or challenge a highly generalized or universal assertion. This method is useful for answering cause-and-effect questions.

critique An act in which someone, usually an expert or a peer, shares his or her personal expertise and/or opinion regarding a presentation of student work.

cumulative case studies Combined information from more than one case study collected at different times.

demographics Human population statistics of a specific location.

department personnel population study A study to estimate growth or reduction in staff. It compares the personnel projections with the operating units to determine which units will grow and which units will remain stable or decrease.

design development The phase that usually follows schematic design and involves the development of the design.

diagrammatic information The transformation of written information into visual information.

École des Beaux Arts School of arts founded in 1648 by Cardinal Mazarin. Disciplines focused on architecture, drawing, painting, sculpture, engraving, modeling, and gem cutting. The school was originally created for the purpose of having artists available to decorate the palaces and paint the royal portraits in France. Now it is a destination for those studying studio arts.

energy efficiency The conservation of the amount of power and cost it may take to run something.

environmental behavior Conduct involving a concern for the environment and an acknowledgment of what may harm it. It also involves developing new ways to improve our surroundings in a healthy, nonharmful manner.

ergonomics The study and design of how people interact efficiently and safely with objects in the built environment.

ethnography The study of making observations in the field with a group in its natural setting. It is important to record as much as possible in the setting in order to document the research.

exploratory case study Condensed, descriptive case studies. Also referred to as pilot studies.

facilities planning The ability to communicate design in terms of financial impact so that corporate leaders can understand and utilize space, design, and knowledge to make complex facilities decisions.

floor usable area The sum of all office, store, and building common usable areas. Floor usable area can be calculated by subtracting by the floor common areas that are available primarily for the joint use of tenants on a floor from the entire floor rentable area.

flow diagram An illustration of a path being used as well as alternatives that could be developed. Flow diagrams can illustrate volume of usage, multiplicity of uses, and conflicts associated with usage. It can also help the programmer understand the function at hand.

formal and numerical methods A test of a specific group using statistical methods to analyze the data.

global perspective Awareness of the world and its diverse cultures. It is important for design students to be aware of world views and design considerations that are relevant and can be embraced by all.

green/sustainable design A movement dedicated to create a cleaner, "greener" lifestyle in our environment through the use of renewable resources and energy. Often accompanied by a refusal to work with materials that harm the earth with harsh chemicals and other unsustainable materials and processes.

gross measured area The total area within the building minus the exterior wall.

hard-line documentation The term used when a design is finalized and ready to go to "hard-lines," which become the final set of construction documents. Can be done by hand or by using CAD software.

health-care design Design specifically for facilities that help improve one's well-being, including places such as hospitals, clinics, cancer centers, dental offices, and hospices.

historic preservation and restoration The preservation of historic structures.

historical research As it applies to interior design programming, the collection of information from printed and otherwise documented material. Books, periodicals, newspapers, and journals are some options for collecting historical research.

human factors A physical or cognitive property of an individual or social behavior that is specific to humans and influences functioning of technological systems as well as human-environment equilibriums.

illustrative case studies Descriptions intended to add in-depth examples.

InformeDesign The first searchable database of design and human behavior research on the Internet. InformeDesign currently contains "practitioner friendly" research summaries of findings from research literature and scholarly journals related to design and human behavior (www.informedesign.umn.edu).

interactive research Research that occurs when the researcher becomes more than just an observer but a participant. Most often includes interviewing users of a specific space.

interior architecture A common term in Europe meaning the same as interior design. Although recently becoming a common term in the United States, interior architecture implies that one has been trained in interior design and has knowledge of structural and load-bearing requirements.

internal consistency reliability Assessment of the consistency of results across items within a test.

Internal Review Board (IRB) The IRB reviews proposals related to human and animal subjects.

International Building Code (IBC) A book filled with safety guidelines for the building industry (www.iccsafe.org).

International Code Council (ICC) A membership association dedicated to building safety and fire prevention. The ICC develops the codes used to construct residential and commercial buildings, including homes and schools. Most U.S. cities, counties, and states that adopt codes choose the international codes developed by the International Code Council (www.iccsafe.org).

International Fire Code (IFC) Requirements relating to fire protection systems, including the most common types of automatic sprinkler systems, alternative automatic extinguishing systems, and standpipe systems. It also involves types of fire alarm and detection and smoke control systems, and addresses additional means to assist or enhance fixed fire protection systems, such as portable fire extinguishers (www.iccsafe.org).

International Fuel Gas Code (IFGC) Requirements that address the design and installation of fuel gas systems and gas-fired appliances through requirements that emphasize performance. This is a comprehensive, excellent reference for code officials, engineers, architects, inspectors, plans examiners, contractors, and anyone who needs a better understanding of these regulations. Prescriptive and performance-based approaches to design are emphasized (www.iccsafe.org).

International Interior Design Association (IIDA) One of the largest professional interior design organizations. (www.iida.org)

International Mechanical Code (IMC) Minimum regulations for mechanical systems using prescriptive and performance-related provisions (www.iccsafe.org).

International Plumbing Code (IPC) Requirement that emphasizes performance for the design and installation of plumbing systems. Provisions are provided for fixtures, piping, fittings, and devices as well as design and installation methods for water supply and sanitary and storm drainage. The code provides comprehensive minimum regulations for plumbing facilities using prescriptive- and performance-related provisions. The objectives of the code provide for the acceptance of new and innovative products, materials, and systems (www.iccsafe.org).

International Residential Code (IRC) A code that establishes minimum regulations for one- and two-family dwellings of three stories or less. It brings together all building, plumbing, mechanical, fuel gas, energy, and electrical provisions for these residences (www.iccsafe.org).

inter-rater or inter-observer reliability Assessment of the degree to which different raters/observers give consistent estimates of the same phenomenon.

laboratory experiments Scientific research into a particular problem or question. Usually employing statistical techniques and sample groups whose selection can vary from specific to random.

LEED AP LEED stands for the Leadership in Energy and Environmental Design, and AP for Accredited Professionals. LEED Professional Accreditation distinguishes building professionals with the knowledge and skills to successfully steward the LEED certification process. A LEED AP has demonstrated a thorough understanding of green building practices and principles and the LEED Rating System (www.usgbc.org).

life cycle cost The amount one pays for the length of useful life of an object.

lighting design The act of producing effective illumination through the use of daylight and artificial illumination.

Likert scale The method of scaling and evaluating responses developed by Rensis Likert, a sociologist at the University of Michigan from 1946 to 1970.

literature review An evaluation of the information found in a literature search and the selection of sources relevant to the topic.

location overview An overall look at a site. It may consist of a study of maps, major forms of transportation, and environmental features. It does not have to be extensive, but it should cover the country and state of the site, and include maps that visually place the site in a larger context.

location productivity How well a residential or business site is efficient in its locality.

macro-to-micro A process that starts on a large scale by taking the big idea and obtaining as much information needed and then moving to the smaller scale, where detailed and precise considerations can then be made.

mediator One who promotes collaboration between two parties.

mixed methods approach A combination of quantitative and qualitative research techniques applied to the same data.

museum and exhibit design Design intended for places that display either historical or artistic material. Objects on display may be captured through the use of special lighting and how they are aesthetically positioned.

National Architectural Accrediting Board (NAAB) The sole agency authorized to accredit professional degree programs in architecture in the United States (www.naab.org).

National Council for Interior Design Qualification (NCIDQ) A national exam that tests minimum competency in the field of interior design (www.ncidq.org).

net-to-gross ratios A measurement of usable floor and unusable space.

observational research Research where a designer photographs or videotapes a specific space over time. Can be similar to a video diary, as it documents users in the space. This form of analysis is extremely helpful, as it provides an outside snapshot peering into the day and life of users and how they interact with their space. It also allows for the documentation of long periods of time, which can show repeating themes.

parallel-forms reliability An assessment of the consistency of the results of two tests constructed in the same way from the same content domain.

physiological human interaction The ways that an individual reacts in a given environment, showing what one's body and mind become accustomed to in any given situation.

pilot studies Small studies typically performed before implementing a large-scale study.

precedent studies Studies that focus on one specific type of design and compare a group of similar examples.

presentation boards A documentation that shows the phases of design emphasizing the concept throughout. Professionals and students use presentation boards to display their work on a project. They can include floor plans, sketches, drawings, material, finishes, and furnishings.

problem statement A clear and concise statement contained within the first chapter of a programmatic research that describes the problem to be solved. Ideally, it should be one sentence, with accompanying sentences that identify a range of sub-problems.

professional practice An understanding of all aspects of being a successful business person.

program effects Effects that use the case study to examine causality and usually involve multi-site, multi-method assessments.

program implementation An investigation of operations, often at several sites and often normatively.

program summary Produced at the end of the interview process, a complete synopsis of all research made before moving on to other design phases. Includes space needs calculated as a sum of the parts, appropriate markups for circulation, rentable factors, and so on.

programming The first predesign step in the design process. Provides a time for designers to research, explore, and investigate numerous facets of a project type in order to gain greater insight into the scope of work.

programming document A comprehensive report that details the programmatic requirements for a project. Addresses an abundance of issues in an attempt to identify and outline the needs for the potential users of the space.

project schedule A specific agenda that includes deadlines of what needs to be done so that a task will be completed in a timely and proficient manner.

qualitative observational research Research in which the observer's role is to record group interactions and behaviors as objectively as possible using various qualitative inquiry tools (e.g., interviews, questionnaires, impressions, and reactions). Consists of many different approaches that often overlap and possess subtle distinctions. The type of approach used depends on the research question and area of discipline.

qualitative research A form of research that relies on discovery, observations of meanings, and interpretations by studying cases intensively in natural settings and by subjecting the resulting data to analytic induction.

quantitative research A form of research that is grounded in the assumption that features of the social environment constitute an objective reality that is relatively constant across time and settings. The dominant methodology is to describe and explain features of this reality by collecting numerical data on observational behaviors of samples and by subjecting these data to statistical analysis (Borg and Gall).

references or works cited A documentation of sources. Documenting sources saves time when returning to the sources. Also used to properly cite material and give credit where it is due.

Registered Architect A person trained in the field of architecture who has passed the National Council of Registration Boards (NCARB) exam demonstrating minimum competency (www.ncarb.org).

research The systematic and careful process of collecting, analyzing, and interpreting information (data) in order to increase awareness and understanding a particular subject.

schedules A means of organization that helps achieve goals on meeting a deadline. Especially necessary to have during the construction documentation phase of design.

schematic design The second step in the design process after programming. It documents some schematic layout options of the design problem. It can also include preliminary ideas of materials, textiles, plumbing, furniture, window, and lighting selections. Everything is done in a schematic fashion, and often more than one design option will be explored at this time.

selective coding Data collected, analyzed, and categorized into main themes. This is a useful tool when analyzing thick or thin descriptions of space or interviews.

sketches Loose drawings used to document preliminary thoughts and ideas. Typically, sketches are hand-drawn.

space-planning adjacencies Approximations of what will be next to each other in the design of any given vicinity.

specifications Documentation of precise details and information of materials, finishes, and furnishings used in order to obtain specific supplies needed to complete a project. Generated for furnishings, equipment, materials, accessories, and lighting. These can be separate from the working drawings or be included within the packet.

square footage A means of calculating the buildings over all floor area.

stacking diagrams Initial studies of vertical relationships between program elements.

stacking plan A tool that programmers implement for the study of space both horizontally and vertically. Helps to visually articulate to the client the number of floors and the adjacency relationship to each department.

statistics A set of tools used to organize and analyze data. Used to describe the characteristics of groups, Statistics can help one analyze individual variables, relationships among variables, and differences between groups. They represent a collection of quantitative data.

strategic planning Planning where an organization looks at its entire structure to determine its goals and how to achieve them for a specific duration. Typically, the organization will then develop a five-year plan.

survey A study that uses questionnaires or interviews to collect data from participants in a sample concerning characteristics, experiences, and opinions in order to generalize the findings about that sample.

survey methods A common method used in business, educational, health-care, and government settings. Surveys are implemented to retain an abundance of information based on the research topic.

test-retest reliability Used to assess the consistency of a measure from one time to another.

thesis statement A statement that summarizes the main point of a paper. The thesis statement contains a clear position of the research or the essay. Often it will be expressed in a sentence or two. It is sometimes limited and does not encompass solving the problem but merely addresses issues and ideas about the problem.

thick description A process used to give an in-depth written account of the study being evaluated.

thin description A process that outlines the facts with no elaboration. May sometimes be formatted in bullet form.

topic The subject, study, or theme that one is planning to research during the programming phase of design.

traffic map A diagram that shows the paths people take through a given space.

United States Green Building Council (USGBC) An environmental agency. When seeking input to include and plan for energy concepts, the USGCB is an excellent place to start. Encompassing an abundance of information, its Web site lists local chapters where more relevant regional data can be obtained (www.usgbc.org).

universal design Design that strives to apply to everyone, including but not limited to those with disabilities. Similar to "barrier-free design" in that its goal is to keep all pathways free of anything that may block and protrude a means of passage.

validity The degree to which a study accurately reflects or assesses a specific concept that a researcher is attempting to measure. When research is valid, it accurately reflects and assesses the specific concept measured.

venture capital Funds that are invested into new start-up companies by professionals and outside investors.

way-finding methods A means of directing and informing people such as signage, landmarks, color, lighting, and maps.

working drawings A complete set of drawings involved in a project. Working drawings consist of a title sheet, an index of the drawings that are included, site plans, floor plans, electrical plans, reflected ceiling plans, elevations, details, cabinetwork, fixtures, moldings, and schedules.

zoning map A map that acts as a blueprint for a community's future development showing how land is divided to accommodate varied development interests.

Resources

AIA. (2007). *AIA, American Institute of Architects*, Retrieved July 6, 2007, from www.aia.org/media/.

Alexander, W. C. (1974). *A pattern language: towns, buildings, construction*. Oxford: Oxford University Press, Incorporated.

Alvermann, D., O'Brian, D., & Dillion, D. (1996). On writing qualitative research. *Reading Research Quarterly, 1*(13), 114–120.

Allen, P., Jones, L., & Stimpson, M. (2004). *Beginnings of interior environments* (9th ed.). Upper Saddle River, NJ: Pearson, Prentice Hall.

Anderson, C. (2007). *Ladder 28 Restaurant & Grille*. Unpublished thesis, Mount Ida College, Newton, MA.

Anthony, E. (2007). *Spa Rumford*. Unpublished thesis, Mount Ida College, Newton, MA.

Anthony, K. (1991). Design juries on trial: The renaissance of the design studio. New York: Van Nostrand Reinhold.

Aronson, J. (1994). A pragmatic view of thematic analysis. *The Qualitative Report*. Retrieved August 19, 2003, from www.nova.edu/ssss/QR /BackIssues/QR2-1/aronson.html.

ASID. (2007). *American Society of Interior Designers*, December 2007, from www.asid.org.

Benander, A. (2007). *Residential Lofts: Cincinnati Ohio*. Unpublished thesis, Mount Ida College, Newton, MA.

Bosworth, F. H., & Jones, R.C. (1932). *A study of architectural schools*. New York: Scribner.

Borg, W. J., Gall M. (1996). *Educational research: An introduction*. White Plains, NY: Longman.

Carter, E. (2007). *The Champernowne*. Unpublished thesis, Mount Ida College, Newton, MA.

Cavataio, C. (2007). Personal communication, May 27, 2007.

Cilano, J (2006). *Dessert Works*. Unpublished thesis, Mount Ida College, Newton, MA.

City-Data. (n.d.). *Boston, Massachusetts*. Retrieved September 15, 2006, from www.city-data.comity/Boston-Massachusetts.html.

Clandinin, J., & Connelly, M. (1994). Personal experience methods. In N. Denzin & Y. S. Lincoln (Ed.), *Handbook of qualitative research* (pp. 413–427). Thousand Oaks, CA: Sage Publications.

Creswell, J. W. (1998). *Qualitative inquiry and research choosing among five traditions.* Thousand Oaks, CA: Sage Publications.

CIDA. (2006a). *CIDA Accreditation Manual.* Grand Rapids, MI. FIDER Inc. www.accredit-id.org/accredmanual.pdf.

CIDA (2008). *Foundation for interior design education research.* Retrieved April 2008, from www.accredit-id.org.

Clark, G. & Thompson, H. (2008). Personal communication, March 2008.

Dinsmore, L. (2007). *RAW Sushi Bar.* Unpublished thesis, Mount Ida College, Newton, MA.

Denzin, N. K., & Lincoln, Y. S. (1994). *Handbook of qualitative research.* Thousand Oaks, CA: Sage publications Inc.

Department of Housing and Community Development Massachusetts. (n.d.). *Wellesley: Norfolk County.* Retrieved August 29, 2006, from www.mass.gov/dhcd/iprofile/324.pdf.

Dessert Works. (2006). Retrieved August 27, 2006, from www.desserworks.net.

Dohr, J. Guerin, D. (2007). Part 1: Research-based practice. InformeDesign. Retrieved March, 2007, from www.informedesign.umn.edu.

Dozois, P. (2001). *Construction through critique: The dialogic form of design studio teaching and learning.* Unpublished master's thesis, University of Manitoba, Canada.

Drucker, P. (1992). *Managing for the future: The 1990's and beyond.* New York: Penguin.

Duderstadt, J., Atkins, D.,& Van Houweling, D. (2002). *Higher education in the digital age: Technologies issues and strategies for American colleges and universities.* Westport, CT: Praeger Publishers.

Duerk, D. P. (1993). *Architectural programming, information management for design.* New York: John Wiley & Sons.

Dutton, T. (1991). The hidden curriculum and the design studio: Toward a critical studio pedagogy. In T. A. Dutton (Ed.), *Voices in architectural education: Culture politics and pedagogy* (pp. 165–194). New York: Bergin & Garvey.

Dunnell, D. (2007). Personal communication, May 27, 2007.

Eisner, E. (1985). *The art of educational evaluation.* New York: Taylor & Francis.

Eisner, E. (1998). *The enlightened eye. Qualitative inquiry and the enhancement of educational practice.* Upper Saddle River, NJ: Merrill, Prentice Hall.

Eisner, E. (2002). *The arts and the creation of mind.* New Haven, CT: Yale University.

Gregg, G. (2003). What are they teaching art students these days? Seventy years after the first degrees in art appeared, schools are wondering how to fit it all in: New technology, theory, marketing savvy, and a growing list of emerging forms. *Art News,* April.

Guba, N. K., & Lincoln, Y.S. (1985). *Naturalistic inquiry.* Beverly Hills, CA: Sage Publications.

Gouveia, M. (2004). *The Fitness Mill: A community athletic and recreational center.* Unpublished thesis, Mount Ida College, Newton, MA.

Gouveia, M. (2008). Personal communication, May 27, 2008.

Harding, J. (2008). Personal communication, March 24, 2008.

Heerdt, N. (2007). *The Waterfront: A jazz bar and lounge.* Unpublished thesis, Mount Ida College, Newton, MA.

Huberman, A. M., Miles, M. B. (1984). *Qualitative data analysis: A source-*

book of new methods. Newbury Park, CA: Sage Publications.

Huberman, A. M., Miles, M. B. (1994). Data management and analysis methods. In N. Denzin, & Y. S. Lincoln (Ed.), *Handbook of qualitative research* (pp. 428–444). Thousand Oaks, CA: Sage Publications.

IDEC. (2007). *Interior Design Educational Council*. Retrieved July 2007, from www.idec.org.

IIDA. (2007). *International Interior Design Association*. Retrieved July 2007, from www.iida.org.

Janesick, V. J. (1994). The dance of qualitative research design: Metaphor, methodolatry, and meaning. In N. Denzin, & Lincoln, Y. S. (Ed.), *Handbook of qualitative research* (pp. 209–219). Thousand Oaks, CA: Sage Publications.

Johnson, A. (2007). *Catskill Hotel NY*. Unpublished thesis, Mount Ida College, Newton, MA.

Kaye, C., & Blcc, T. (Eds.). (1997). *The arts in health care: A palette of possibilities*. King's Lynn, UK: Biddles Ltd.

Koberg, D., & Bagnall, J. (1991). *The universal traveler: A soft-system guide to creativity, problem solving and the process of reaching goals*. Los Altos, CA: Crisp Publications.

Kopacz, J. (2007). Personal communication, February 26, 2007.

Labuschagne, A. (2003). Qualitative research: Airy fairy or fundamental? *The Qualitative Report, 8*(1).

Leedy, P. (2005) Practical research, planning, and design. 8th ed. Upper Saddle River, NJ: Pearson Merrill/Prentice Hall.

Mattingly, M. (2007). Center for Sustainable Design Education, Boston MA. Unpublished thesis, Mount Ida College, Newton, MA.

Mitton, M. (2007). Interior design visual presentation: A guide to graphics, models and presentation techniques (2nd ed.). Hoboken, NJ: John Wiley and Sons, Inc.

NAAB. (2006). *The National Architectural Accrediting Board*, July 2003, from www.naab.org.

National Council for Interior Design Qualification (NCIDQ). (2008). CERTIFICATION & LICENSURE, *Regulatory Agencies, Definition Of Interior Design, Exam Eligibility Requirements*. Retrieved April 2008 from www.ncidq.org.

Neilson, K., & Taylor, D. (2002). *Interiors an introduction*. 3rd ed. New York: McGraw-Hill.

Patten K, (2007). *Wagon Wheel-Market*. Unpublished Thesis, Mount Ida College, Newton, MA.

Pena, W. (1987). *Problem seeking: An architectural programming primer*. 3rd ed. Washington, D.C.: AIA Press.

Phipps L. (2008). Personal communication, May 14, 2008.

Pile, J. (1995). *Interior design*. Englewood Cliffs, NJ: Prentice Hall.

Piotrowski, C. (2004). *Becoming an interior designer*. Hoboken, NJ: John Wiley & Sons.

Richard, J. (2006). *College Residence Hall*. Unpublished thesis, Mount Ida College, Newton, MA.

Roblee, S. (2007). *There's not enough art in our schools: Art department renovation, Schroon Lake Central School*. Unpublished thesis, Mount Ida College, Newton, MA.

Schön, D. A. (1985). *The design studio: An exploration of its traditions and potentials*. London: RIBA Publications Ltd.

Scott-Webber, L. (1998). Programming: A problem solving approach for users of interior spaces. Houston, TX: DAME Publications.

Shanahan, C. (2008). Personal communication, March 12, 2008.

Stake, R. E. (1994). Case studies. In N. Denzin & Y. S. Lincoln (Ed.) *Handbook of qualitative research* (pp. 236–247). Thousand Oaks, CA: Sage Publications.

Social Research Methods. (2008). *Online social research methods.* Retrieved May 14, 2008, from www.socialresearchmethods.net/tutorial/Brown/lauratp.htm.

Stewart, N. (2006). *Healing with art.* Unpublished thesis, Mount Ida College, Newton, MA.

Stone, D. (2007). Personal communication, May 27, 2007.

Strauss, A., & Corbin, J. (1998). *Basics of qualitative, research: Techniques and procedures for developing grounded theory.* (2nd ed.). Thousand Oaks, CA: Sage Publications.

TAC (1981). *The Architects Collaborative: Examples of programming documentation.* Unpublished report, Cambridge, MA.

Tate, A. (1987). *The making of interiors: An introduction.* New York: Harper & Row.

Trochim, William M. *The Research Methods Knowledge Base*, 2nd Ed. Retrieved June 16, 2008, 2007, from www.socialresearchmethods.net/kb/reltypes.php.

United States General Service Administration Facilities standards. (n.d.). *Architectural and Interior Design (P100).* Retrieved May 19, 2007, from www.gsa.gov/.

University, C. S. (2002). *An online resources for teachers and writers.* Retrieved July 31, 2002, from http://writing.colostate.edu

U.S. Census Bureau. *541410 Interior design services.* Retrieved June 4, 2006, from www.census.gov/epcd/ec97/def/541410.HTM.

U.S. Office of Personnel Management (OPM) (1991). Position Classification Flysheet for Interior Design Series, GS-1008 Retrieved June 4, 2006, from www.opm.gov/fedclass/gs1008.pdf.

Verbridge, J (2007). Personal communication, January 14, 2007.

Waxman, L., & Clemons, S. (2007). Student perceptions: Debunking televisions' portrayal of interior design. *Journal of Interior Design, 32*(2), v–xi.

Wendt, K. (2008) Personal communication, February 27, 2008.

White, E. (1982) Project programming: A growing architectural service. Tallahassee, FL: A&M University.

Wikimedia Foundation, Inc. (2006). *New York State.* Retrieved October 30, 2006, from http://en.wikipedia.org/wiki/New_York.

Credits

CHAPTER 1

CHAPTER 2

CHAPTER 3

CHAPTER 4

CHAPTER 5

CHAPTER 6

6.1 Monica Mattingly
6.2 Monica Mattingly
6.3a Monica Mattingly
6.3b Monica Mattingly
6.4 Nicole Stewart, retrieved Nov. 1, 2006 from http://greenwichny. org/tourist/v-tour.cfm
6.5 Nicole Stewart, retrieved Oct. 30, 2006 from http://geology. com/state-map/new-york.shtml
6.6 Nicole Stewart, retrieved Oct. 30, 2006 from http://geology. com/state-map/new-york.shtml
6.7 Nicole Stewart retrieved Oct. 30, 2006 from www.trailwaysny.com
6.8 John Souza Photography
6.10 Student work courtesy of Erin Anthony
6.11 Student work courtesy of K. Patten
6.12 Student work courtesy of Erin Anthony
6.13 Rose Mary Botti-Salitsky
6.14 Colleen Anderson
6.16 Colleen Anderson

CHAPTER 7

7.1 © B.O'Kane/Alamy
7.2 Bill Lebovich/Library of Congress
7.3 Liz Carter, 2007
7.4 Ashley Benander, 2007
7.5 Rose Mary Botti-Salitsky

CHAPTER 8

8.1 SG&A
8.2 Ashley Johnson
8.3 Ashley Johnson
8.4 Ashley Johnson
8.5 SG&A
8.6 SG&A
8.7 SG&A
8.8 The Architects Collaborative
8.9 The Architects Collaborative
8.10 The Architects Collaborative
8.12 Jeana Richard, 2006
8.13 Jeana Richard, 2006
8.14 Jeana Richard, 2006
8.15 Jeana Richard, 2006
8.16 Jeana Richard, 2006
8.17 Jeana Richard, 2006
8-18 Design One Consortium
8.19 Design One Consortium
8.20 Design One Consortium

CHAPTER 9

9.1 The Architects Collaborative
9.2 The Architects Collaborative
9.3 Created by Marcia A Gouveia, 2005
9.4 TAC department adjacency
9.5 Laboratory Specific Cytology
9.6 Cris Cavataio
9.7 Cris Cavataio
9.8 Cris Cavataio
9.9 The Architects Collaborative
9.10 The Architects Collaborative
9.11 Monica Mattingly
9.12 Dianne A. Dunnell, IIDA
9.13 Dianne A. Dunnell, IIDA
9.14 Dianne A. Dunnell, IIDA
9.15 Dianne A. Dunnell, IIDA
9.16 Dianne A. Dunnell, IIDA
9.17 Dianne A. Dunnell, IIDA
9.18 Dianne A. Dunnell, IIDA
9.19 Dianne A. Dunnell, IIDA
9.20 Dianne A. Dunnell, IIDA
9.21 David Stone

APPENDICES

Appendix A.1 TK&A
Appendix A.2 TK&A
Appendix A.3 TK&A
Appendix A.4 TK&A
Appendix A.5 TK&A
Appendix B.1 MARGULIES & ASSOCIATES
Appendix B.2 MARGULIES & ASSOCIATES

Index